D1366611

THE
UNSTOPPABLE
STARTUP

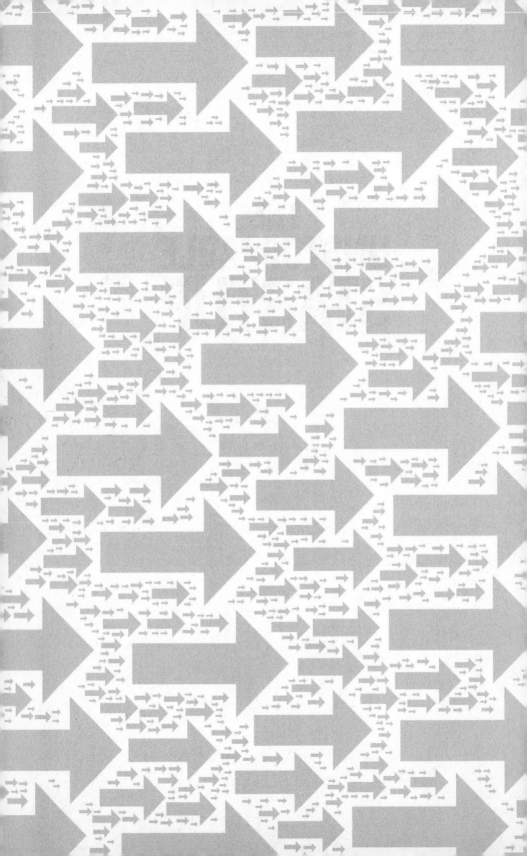

THE UNSTOPPABLE STARTUP

MASTERING ISRAEL'S SECRET RULES

—— *of* ——

CHUTZPAH

URI ADONI

HarperCollins
LEADERSHIP

An Imprint of HarperCollins

Published by HarperCollins Leadership, an imprint of HarperCollins Focus LLC.

Published in association with Kevin Anderson & Associates: https://www.ka-writing.com/.

Book design by Aubrey Khan, Neuwirth & Associates.

ISBN 978-1-4002-1917-9 (eBook)
ISBN 978-1-4002-1916-2 (HC)

Library of Congress Control Number: 2020936717

Printed in the United States of America
20 21 22 23 LSC 10 9 8 7 6 5 4 3 2 1

IN LOVING MEMORY OF MY FATHER, Professor (MD) Amiram Adoni, who taught me by his example to challenge conventional wisdom of every kind, and to never accept the status quo just because someone, no matter how important they might be, says: "This is how things are done." A pioneer, innovator, and early adopter of new technologies, he showed me what creativity truly is.

CONTENTS

FOREWORD

The path to any successful startup venture is fraught with risk, especially in the early stages where scarce resources are needed to maintain a path of growth as the business struggles to prove its viability. The fact is that most technology startups fail in those early stages.

The Unstoppable Startup draws guidelines and provides meaningful insights on how to boldly beat the odds.

In his book, Uri Adoni utilizes his extensive experience in tech, as both an investor and an executive, to guide current and future entrepreneurs, as well as tech investors, highlighting the secret ingredient behind Israel's success story as a global technological leader.

That unique ingredient is ingrained in the Israeli Chutzpah, the bold "can do" attitude and the audacity that enables entrepreneurs to challenge the existing status quo or existing solutions. It is that attitude that makes them believe they can forecast what the world will need in a few years' time, and to pursue their big dream with a deep and strong belief that their venture can and will become a global success.

Throughout this fascinating book, Uri provides his insider's perspective on what makes startups succeed and how to apply these strategies throughout the journey of building a startup. Since the only way to understand Chutzpah is by demonstrating it, this book is full of advice and practical, down-to-earth insights, aiming to provide real-world guidance on how to build and grow a startup the right way. The book also touches on how investors and board members can best assist a startup, and how to implement the rules of Chutzpah when building a new ecosystem.

At Facebook Israel, we work very closely with Israeli startups in their early days, helping them grow and expand, and supporting them in those challenging initial stages. After connecting with hundreds of startups over the years, I see incredible value in having the right guidance and support when building and growing a business while learning from the experience of others in the ecosystem.

The Unstoppable Startup is a wonderful guide for entrepreneurs, investors, and anybody in the startup ecosystem who wants to increase their chances of success by leveraging the experience of others.

Adi Soffer Teeni
General Manager, Facebook Israel

INTRODUCTION

"If there are any questions, I'd be happy to address them," I said as I was wrapping up a presentation at an international tech conference. I paused for a few moments, but the crowd was silent. Then, just as I was about to thank them and take my leave, an energetic man in his twenties called out from the back of the room. "How should I tweet it?" he asked.

"How should you tweet what?" I replied, not fully following his question.

"Well, you just told us all about Israel's high-tech phenomenon—how a small country with a population of just eight million people, constantly threatened by various enemies, has the most venture capital and the highest density of startups per capita of any country in the world. That the only countries that have more companies listed on NASDAQ than Israel are the US and China. But why is that? And how can I tweet your answer in 280 characters?!"

It was actually a great question and I needed to take some time to think about it. "If I had to answer you in one word, it would be Chutzpah," I finally said. "Chutzpah is what makes the difference between Israel's startup ecosystem and other startup ecosystems around the world, and it's what differentiates Israel's entrepreneurs from entrepreneurs from other countries. Chutzpah captures the intellectual and business audacity and charisma that are a must for any startup to succeed, for a new category to be created, and for a tiny region to become a global leader in a specific vertical. *That's* what you should tweet," I concluded. *"That it's all about Chutzpah."*

To tell you the truth, my answer took me by surprise; it both clarified and deepened my thinking. In the months that followed, I approached a number of Israeli high-tech leaders and entrepreneurs and solicited their thoughts. *How do you perceive Chutzpah?* I asked them. *How significant was it for the success of your startup? Is it something that you have to be born with, or can it be taught?*

This book grew out of those conversations and my own experiences in Israeli high tech over the past decade and more. But before I continue, I want to linger for a moment on the word Chutzpah. Chutzpah is often translated from the Hebrew and Yiddish as *audacity*, but depending on the context, it has many meanings. All are delicious and have a way of sparking endless discussions about spunk, insolence, being a visionary, proving your mettle—or just being an incredible jerk. Though Chutzpah can be a valuable trait, grifters and swindlers have it to burn. Israelis are often chastised by their compatriots to refrain from exercising "Israeli Chutzpah" while abroad, so as not to create the perception that Israelis are pushy and rude. On the other hand, Israelis are just as likely to brag about harnessing "Israeli Chutzpah" when it breeds success.

In *The Joys of Yiddish,* Leo Rosten defined Chutzpah as "gall, brazen nerve, effrontery, incredible 'guts,' presumption plus arrogance such as no other word and no other language can do justice to."[1] Guy Kawasaki, a former Apple marketing executive and now a Silicon Valley venture capitalist, believed that Chutzpah was a key element to Apple's success. He describes Chutzpah as "calling up tech support to report a bug on pirated software."[2] It means *nerve* (as in *some nerve*), but perhaps the closest English equivalent is the vulgar *balls* or the Spanish *cojones.*

Dr. Eyal Inbar, a researcher of Israeli Business and International Relations, wrote an academic article analyzing Chutzpah as a unique Israeli cultural trait and its role in encouraging innovation in Israel. He defines Chutzpah as "the challenging and defiance of the prevailing order, traditional thinking, behaviors, and fears, while being ready to take the risk involved."[3] In startups, Chutzpah means a total denial of the long odds that the business will even survive, never mind revolutionize whole markets, with no fear of failure. Entrepreneurs with Chutzpah behave as if their companies are changing the world before they've earned a single dollar. This unshakable self-confidence, in defiance of all reality, is essential to their success.

Chutzpah is much more than a word: it's a whole mindset, both a way of thinking and an operational approach. It is almost a philosophy. Many of the Israeli entrepreneurs I talked to about it were unaware that it could be applied to them, but when they reverse-engineered their successes, they realized what an important role it played.

So, what is an "unstoppable" startup, and why are unstoppableness and Chutzpah so closely related?

Building a new technology venture is never an easy thing. There are so many potential hurdles along the way, and in most cases more than one of them emerge as real challenges. Their causes may be related to the team running the startup, the technology, the product itself, or its marketing, branding, and positioning, its distribution channels and pricing, its customers' behavior, the moves that a competitor makes, changes in the market, and so much else. So, almost by definition, a startup that is not totally committed to its mission, meaning it is not fully determined to persevere and succeed, will most likely fail.

Any startup needs to be unstoppable! No hurdle should be too high and no challenge should be impossible for it to deal with. As Marvin Gaye and Tammi Terrell sang, "Ain't no mountain high enough, ain't no valley low enough, ain't no river wide enough to keep me from getting to you."[4] It is not a smooth ride, it is more of a roller coaster, but successful startups stay on the tracks and keep moving forward. Chutzpah is a big part of what enables entrepreneurs to push on.

As I will explain later, Chutzpah is not something people are born with; it is an acquired mindset. Understanding it and implementing it can assist any entrepreneur in running their venture, and I believe, significantly increase its chances for success.

Chutzpah has certainly played an enormous role at Jerusalem Venture Partners, where I was a partner in the JVP Media Labs Incubator for twelve years. Founded in 1993 by Dr. Erel Margalit, JVP was one of the first venture capital firms in Israel.[5] In recent years it has garnered a host of honors. Preqin recognized it as one of the Most Consistent Performing Venture Capital Fund[s] in 2018; the IVC named it the Most Active VC Fund in 2014; and in 2016, Geektime chose it as its Fund of the Year.[6] To date, it has raised over $1.4 billion and invested in more than 140 companies.[7] Twelve of them have been listed on the NASDAQ, and many more have been sold to the likes of Cisco, Walmart, Redhat, Microsoft, EMC, PayPal, Sony, Sales-Force, Broadcom, CA, Hitachi, Alcatel, and many others, generating a total transactional value of over $20 billion.[8] A hands-on investor, JVP's practice is to work closely with companies from their inception, while maintaining a strong focus on its key technology investment themes, such as cybersecurity, big data, analytics, computer vision, artificial intelligence, enterprise software and storage, mobile technologies, internet of things (IoT), and disrupting global markets such as financial services, retail, wellness, media, commerce, and industry, to name but a few. Naturally, the interpretations and comments on JVP throughout the book, including on the period before I joined the fund, are all mine.

Because of the high interest in the Israeli high-tech phenomena, as a partner with the JVP Media Labs I had the pleasure of hosting hundreds of delegations, from literally all over the world (the United States, Argentina, Brazil, Colombia, France, Germany, UK, Italy, Switzerland, Netherlands, Belgium, Spain, Finland, Romania, Latvia, Russia, Ukraine, China, South Korea, Japan, Singapore, Taiwan, India, Africa, and Australia, to name a few). I have also had the privilege to be invited to speak at international conferences, like the one where I had my Chutzpah epiphany.

As an investor, one strives to incubate Chutzpah in the portfolio of companies (though most of them have a healthy dose of it from day one); as an author, I want to spark Chutzpah in the hearts of entrepreneurs, early stage investors, accelerators, and incubators, no matter where they live. So rather than rhapsodizing about Chutzpah, this book will break it down, analyze it, and then suggest a system or pattern that enables its positive effects to take hold.

In Part I of this book, I draw on my impressions as a partner in recent years with JVP Media Labs, as well as observations as an investor, to try to explain the unique workings of Israel's "Chutzpah Inside" component (to borrow a phrase from Intel).[9] Because the only way to get Chutzpah across is by giving examples of it, this book is full of insider stories that I gleaned from my interviews with Israeli tech leaders: about the pursuit of unknown unknowns in cyber security; how Waze managed to scale and be purchased by Google for $1.15 billion; the technological breakthroughs that undergird the Iron Dome; and much more.

In Part II, I describe how Israeli startups manage to build, test, validate, scale, and cater to markets that are half a globe away. In this respect, the book is a how-to for any startup and for any would-be international company. I describe the phases of startup growth, what it means to build oneself as a multinational from day one, and how your company's approach must challenge existing technological solutions. In Part III, I elucidate the workings of incubators and other early stage investment vehicles, and show how startups can get the most out of them. In Part IV, I write about the importance of high-tech ecosystems and show how they can be built from the ground up in the unlikeliest of places. I describe how JVP under the leadership of its founder and chairman, Dr. Erel Margalit, created high-tech communities in Jerusalem and in Be'er Sheva, before branching out farther to the north of Israel and to New York City. In the epilogue, I talk about the various vectors that drive building a new startup and investing in one.

One of the main messages of the book is that, unlike charisma, an inborn quality that is probably impossible to teach, Chutzpah *can* be learned, exported to anywhere in the world, and implemented by existing and would-be entrepreneurs.

This book also imparts a unique view of some of the key cultural and behavioral aspects of building and running a startup, especially if it is launched far away from Silicon Valley. Chutzpah is a common thread in many of them—the Chutzpah to challenge existing solutions in the market, the Chutzpah to think that the startup can become a global category leader, the Chutzpah to address large multinationals as potential clients at a very early stage of development, and the Chutzpah to think one can forecast what the market will need in a few years' time. I also explain the importance of a sense of urgency, what a "mission completion" culture is, how and when to challenge authority, and how to deal with and learn from failure.

In the chapters that follow, I will:

- Further define Chutzpah and break it down into a set of rules for entrepreneurs and startups
- Elucidate the characteristics of a successful entrepreneurial culture
- Lay out a proven three-phase process for making startups fundable
- Explain how startups can partner with large corporations that are looking for innovation
- Delve into the nuts and bolts of building and operating an early stage technology incubator
- Provide a model for building and developing a successful high-tech ecosystem

A practical guide for early- and mid-stage startups, *The Unstoppable Startup* is for anyone who is trying to launch or fund a startup, who works in high-tech as an entrepreneur or an investor, or who is trying to build a better ecosystem. Just as there is no standard manual on how to build a successful startup, there is no tried-and-true formula for bottling and using Chutzpah. But I believe that the stories and the insights that I share will give you the tools and inspiration that you need to get started or to improve what you already have underway.

THE
UNSTOPPABLE
STARTUP

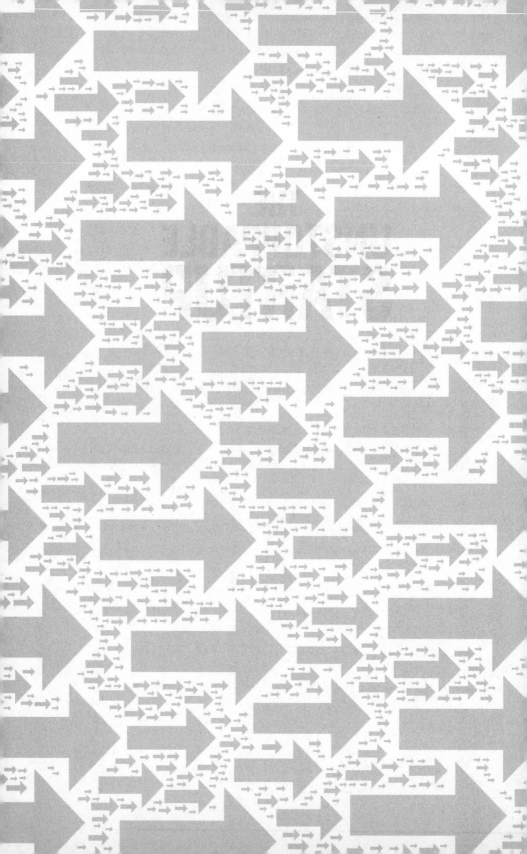

PART I
THE SIX RULES OF CHUTZPAH

1

WHAT IS CHUTZPAH? AND WHAT IS A STARTUP?

Nothing important was ever accomplished without chutzpah. —ALAN ALDA

Israel's startup nation has many drivers: creative individuals, well-structured government support, mandatory army service with a focus on technology innovation, leading academic institutions, and established technology clusters. A number of cultural drivers are also at play. One of the more interesting ones is Chutzpah, a behavioral quality that is both good and bad and that is deeply engrained in the Israeli character. But Chutzpah isn't limited to Israel—for better or for worse, it is the secret behind most exceptional technology companies and entrepreneurs. Just look at Steve Jobs's famous "reality distortion field," or Elon Musk's audacious goals, like journeying to Mars.[1]

Though many Israelis are born with it, Chutzpah is an attitude that can be cultivated and taught. As it applies to entrepreneurship and technology startups, we believe that it should be. But before we get into that, let's take a closer look at what Chutzpah actually is in practice.

SOMETIMES, CHUTZPAH MEANS flying in the face of reality or probability. Liran Tancman is a redheaded twenty-nine-year-old who sold his less-than-two-year-old company, CyActive, to PayPal in early 2015 for a sum reported to be between $60 and $80 million. His is a story of Chutzpah in both the technological and the deal-making sense. Listening to Tancman, one senses that Chutzpah means, among other things, telling a story that people can't help but be skeptical about.

"I've learned that when you start pitching your startup to someone, you should closely follow how they react to you," he says. "You will notice their ears prick up all of a sudden if they realize that money can be made. But at the same time, you can also tell when a person is skeptical about your idea but curious to see whether it can actually play out. I think that if the person isn't skeptical at all, it means the idea isn't good enough—it's too easy to believe. At CyActive, the skepticism was about everything, not just about the technology and product but how the company would go to market, since going to market in our case wasn't at all trivial. The issue here wasn't just the Chutzpah behind the technological claims we were making; there were doubts about a great many other things we were planning."[2]

The technological audacity behind CyActive, the company Tancman cofounded with Shlomi Boutnaru to foil cybersecurity attacks, is that it didn't set its sights on preventing attacks by known, existing malware. Instead, like a clairvoyant, it claimed to be able to protect companies from computer viruses and worms that hackers hadn't thought of yet. It claimed to do that through the application of algorithms that were derived from the processes of biological evolution. That's part of what made Tancman's listeners so skeptical and at the same time so intrigued. CyActive was challenging the whole antivirus market as it had existed up until then, defining a bold paradigm shift in how it attacked its problem. CyActive's Chutzpah-laden premise was that malware behaves like a real, biological virus: it mutates as it spreads, adapting to outmaneuver the security measures that are put in its way.

"Hackers stand on the shoulders of giants, i.e., other hackers," Tancman explains. "Each malware attack is an adaptation of a past malware attack that worked. That's why malware attacks are so cheap to launch—you make an adaptation to the code and try the malware again, just like a virus mutates. You don't have to rewrite the whole thing. If hackers had to write all the code from scratch for each malware attack, they would lose much of their power, because they would be priced out of the market.

"There is an investment asymmetry between hackers/attackers and defenders," he continues. "Hackers can create malware very easily, cheaply, and quickly. There is also a financial asymmetry, because for every dollar invested by hackers, companies spend many thousands of dollars to defend against the new malware. But 98 percent of malwares are variants of known versions. In an entire attack chain, you will not find even one element that isn't the result of the recycling of another component."

What CyActive does is fast-forward through the future of malware evolution. Its technology predicts the hundreds and thousands of ways in which hackers could try to evade security measures. It then uses machine learning to create an algorithm that can detect future versions of the malware.

One example is the Poison Ivy Trojan malware that first appeared in 2006—even today, its permutations are potent and malicious. To prove that its evolutionary algorithms worked, CyActive took a Poison Ivy sample from 2008 and put it into its engine. Fast-forwarding through five years of malware evolution, CyActive correctly predicted several "wild" Poison Ivy variants that had actually appeared between 2012 and 2013.

"We had to think about the problem beyond just permuting the code," Tancman says, using a startling metaphor. "If the hacker is the god of the evolution of malware, what is the hacker optimizing for? We figured he is optimizing for two things: the malicious functionality of the malware, and its stealth. So we generated five hundred viruses and chose the ones that were the most malicious and stealthiest. And then we merged them with others, and so on. Instead of looking for each unique signature of each unique virus, which is what reactive cyberprotection was about, we created a mathematical model that reflects what's common to this cloud of viruses we've prepared and that can defend against it, although it doesn't exist yet."

The brilliance of the CyActive approach—its technological Chutzpah—was taking a biological idea—evolutionary algorithms—and applying it to the world of cyberattacks. When CyActive began, Tancman, a veteran of the Intelligence Corps at the Israeli Defense Forces (IDF), was a biology and cognitive sciences student at the Hebrew University. He did many other things too: he advised Israel's security chiefs about creating a department that could protect Israel from cyberattacks, and he worked as a strategy consultant. He also studied at a Yeshiva once a week. While fundraising for a nonprofit at the university, he met Sara, who was fundraising for another nonprofit. They married soon afterward. By then, Tancman was working as a research assistant at a university lab, studying biological evolutionary algorithms. His plan, he told Sara, was to first study for a doctorate and then found a startup. Sara thought it would be better if he did the startup first.

"Actually, the initial idea for the startup was Sara's," Tancman admits. "I came home from the lab and talked about the evolutionary algorithms I was working on and she asked me why I wasn't using them to predict new computer viruses."

Evolutionary algorithms have been around for years, but no one had ever thought of applying them to computer viruses. CyActive was the first to have the Chutzpah to do so.

FIRST AND FOREMOST, Chutzpah is about daring. It's not about daring to be cruelly honest, or to act without regard to others. It is the daring that leads someone to pursue an impossible goal—a great quality for an entrepreneur—and to do so boldly and with laser focus.

"Israel's high-tech success is the subject of a lot of curiosity—people from all over the world want to know what the secret is," says Dr. Eyal Inbar. "In my research, I've looked at the cultural dimensions by Geert

Hofstede, who ranked Israel low on power distance, which in my view is a key for understanding Israel's so-called secret—Chutzpah."[3]

Power distance, according to Hoftstede's theory, is the degree of acceptance of power, namely the degree to which lower-power people accept the fact that they have less power.[4] In high-power distance cultures, lower-power people exhibit high degrees of acquiescence and deferral to higher-level people, perceiving it as the natural order.

In low-power-distance cultures like Israel's, there is a relatively small emotional distance between people with varying degrees of power; relations are more democratic and consultative. Add a healthy dose of Chutzpah and the result is a constant challenging of authority and a constant passion to do things better, regardless of what your boss thinks about it. Stories about technology multinationals entering Israel and being amazed that low-level employees challenge their managers abound. Even more shocking to those multinationals is the fact that those challenges aren't perceived as out of line.

Kobi Rozengarten, formerly President and COO of Saifun Semiconductors, a world-leading provider of IP solutions for the nonvolatile memory market that went public on NASDAQ, recollects, "Before Saifun, I was an operations manager in an Israeli company. We had an operations plan, as we should, but operations didn't run according to plan. You always had to supervise the actual implementation of the plan since in Israel employees keep challenging its logic, and many things are open for debate, by anyone. There is no real management pyramid."[5] Indeed, lower-power-distance cultures tend to have a flatter management structure or disregard for hierarchy.[6]

When Rozengarten moved to the US, things were suddenly different, radically so. "When you come to the US as a manager, you discover that you are listened to, and that 90 percent of the people just do as they are told, following the operational plan with no debate. Surprise!—Work as planned! Your plans and decisions aren't challenged. In Israel, conversely, you present your plan and someone says it isn't a good plan and that person is the least important person in the manufacturing line. The thing is that sometimes this person has a good point. As a manager, you have two options; you can feel threatened by the challenger and try to silence them, or, you can listen to what they have to say."[7]

"Historically, Chutzpah has been about taking a contrarian position," says Dr. Eyal Inbar. "In the Talmud [a central text of Rabbinic Judaism] the root of the word Chutzpah is mentioned as a way of being insolent, contrarian. In many ways, I believe this is the core of Chutzpah today—standing up to something, challenging the existing order, defying it. It really is a matter of national culture. According to some interpretationas, even the name *Israel* means "struggled with God."[8] Abraham bargained with God in order to try to save Sodom and Gomorrah from being punished, and Moses argued with God against punishing his people in the desert on several occasions, to name just few examples. The Israelis rebelled against the great Greek and Roman Empires, and managed to remain intact as a people for two thousand years in the diaspora. The establishment of the State of Israel is Chutzpah too—in a very hostile environment, almost against all odds. Other well-known examples are the establishment of Israel's nuclear research complex in 1959 under the radar of the Superpowers, the escape of Israeli Navy ships from France in 1969 despite the French embargo on Israel, the development of Israel's military industry with very limited resources, and the rescue of hostages in Entebbe (Uganda) in 1976.

"I am frequently asked," says Inbar, "whether Chutzpah can be taught. On the one hand, this is a part of Israel's DNA. Whoever grows up in Israel's culture is imbued with Chutzpah, so it seems contained in the culture, in the country. But Chutzpah is a way of thinking and behaving; thus you can definitely teach it and train people to use it."[9]

Israel hosts many delegations from countries seeking to create startup cultures and ecosystems like Israel's. "The Chinese asked us how to increase creativity, what KPIs [key performance indicators] signify that creativity exists," says Kobi Rozengarten.[10] "So we told them three things. The first is that people should break the rules. Israelis are good at that. Some of it is thinking outside of the box, some isn't always nice, but that's how you cook this dish. This leads to the second thing: don't fear social sanction. Israelis aren't offended when they're thrown out the door or told that they are wrong; they keep trying. The third is that you can't accept things as they are. The need to always ask questions positively impacts creativity.

"Chutzpah can also result from an inability to understand the environment you are working in," Rozengarten adds. "The entrepreneur genuinely doesn't understand why things are as they are. So they ask around, take on challenges that are too complex to meet, or take them on when they don't have the right amount of infrastructure and resources. This is an inability to understand what can and can't happen. In this regard, Chutzpah is essentially the tool of the weak. And I have to admit that some of the success stories we see in our startup nation are a direct result of this inability."

TEACHING CHUTZPAH

Liran Tancman says he learned Chutzpah during his military service. "When I was drafted into the army, I joined the Intelligence Corps. At the time, Israel's geopolitical situation was radically changing and many of the plans we had in the Intelligence Corps were becoming obsolete. I became part of a 'subversive' group of intelligence officers—which included people ranked from brigadier general to young intelligence officers, like myself—who created an alternative plan. No one asked us to do it and it certainly defied the current order. At some point, we wanted to make the plan known beyond our small group—but we didn't want to go through the ordinary chain of command and send it up to the head of the Intelligence Corps and then to the IDF's commander-in-chief. Instead, we decided to bring it directly to the defense minister and the prime minister. The way we did this was by writing a memo that we were certain the prime minister would read. I don't think other intelligence organizations in other countries allow this kind of behavior."[11]

Yet the plan worked—the prime minister read it and the plan was adopted throughout the entire military.[12]

"Another thing I learned in the army is that Chutzpah is how a group of people develops a radical idea," adds Tancman. "I believe thinking is by definition a group effort, since we stand on the shoulders of our predecessors. I learned so much in the Intelligence Corps. How to bring together a team of high-quality thinkers. How to go and pitch an idea and get people invested in it. The taste of this is exhilarating. Top people listen to what you have to say, and tens of thousands of people end up reorganizing according to a plan that you had a part in devising, as part of a self-selected group that acted on the sidelines. In the IDF the things we had planned came to fruition within three years. In CyActive it took eighteen months and then we got sold to PayPal."[13]

THE THREE PARTS OF CHUTZPAH

For the purposes of this book, Chutzpah can be construed as three things:

1. A way of thinking
2. A way of doing business
3. A way of interacting with people

Most people focus on how Chutzpah affects interpersonal interactions, such as telling captains of industry that your company has a better solution than theirs, or announcing that your startup is about to change the world. Yet, Chutzpah is, first and foremost, an intellectually audacious way of thinking about the world and of acting upon the results. This is why some argue that Chutzpah has become the new charisma.

Charisma is all about surfaces—how a person conveys themself and their message to the world. It is never about the power of the idea behind the charismatic person; indeed, at its worst charisma can be a charming façade behind which little else resides, the attitude of a used-car salesperson, or worse, a cult leader or demagogue.

Chutzpah, in contrast, is about a set of beliefs and a way of thinking that challenges reality as we know it and carries the seeds of radical change. This is why Chutzpah is a must-have for startups and technology disruption, and why charisma, as the rise of nerd culture demonstrates, is not. Entrepreneurs with Chutzpah are followed just as avidly as the charismatic leaders of the past were.

There are six rules of Chutzpah, which will be covered in the next chapters. Yet one can fit all of them in a nutshell, as *the drive to think boldly and creatively and to act accordingly.*

WHAT CHUTZPAH ISN'T

In Hebrew, Chutzpah is also used to signify when someone has overstepped the boundaries of acceptable social behavior. Explaining Chutzpah, a Chasidic website (an Orthodox Jewish sect) aphorizes: "You need two opposites: A sense of shame that prevents you from acting with Chutzpah to do the wrong thing, and a sense of Chutzpah that prevents you from being ashamed to do the right thing."[14]

Don't ever be arrogant! If you behave arrogantly, chances are that you will not achieve your goals, and will waste opportunities along the way. But when done right and with conviction, Chutzpah works. It generates an energy that can't be ignored.

Chutzpah should always be grounded in a nucleus of truth and decorum. Use it to connect with the right people, to tell them about your vision, and to earn their trust. Your company's way of thinking, its strategy, products, partnerships, and goals should all be thick with Chutzpah. But the recommendation to possess some Chutzpah is in no way a license to be rude.

Asked about his views on Chutzpah, Kobi Rozengarten begins with a warning, reminding us that it isn't a be-all and end-all solution to the question of startup success: "Chutzpah is like a fertilizer—it is an essential component that makes a tree grow and flourish, but if it's too concentrated, it may be harmful. You should have Chutzpah in just the right balance."[15]

Chutzpah should be a source of internal energy and drive but it should never manifest itself in an ugly way. Chutzpah needs to be turned off and on. Turn it on when you're doing business—don't be ashamed of thinking big, of approaching large organizations at an early stage, of challenging existing solutions. But when it's time to turn it off, turn it off.

BEFORE WE DELVE into why Chutzpah is so crucial for startups, and even more so for early stage ones, let's examine what being a startup actually means.

WHAT IS A STARTUP?

A technology startup is much more than the dictionary definition of "a new business venture."[16] One crucial point to make up front is related to the "technology" part of "technology startup." In many cases, when investors select a startup to invest in, they don't necessarily look for hard-core technology innovation. They do, however, require a technology edge or technology-driven go-to-market that enables them to do new things or do something in a new and better or cheaper way. In many cases, technology is what enables the disruption of an existing nontechnological market: a new way of ordering a cab or take-out food, comparing prices of products, accessing talent to recruit, highly targeting advertising, and so on.

Unlike a restaurant, or a bakery selling artisanal bread, a technology-driven startup has a business model that allows it to grow extremely rapidly and cover markets that are global or at least very large. A startup can scale exponentially at nonexponential costs. Restaurants and bakeries are always tied to their buildings, and to their food and labor costs. In most cases, technology can't help them escape from the cost-plus straitjacket.

This is also where Chutzpah comes into play, since many startups' business models reverse the existing logic of common business models. In some cases, they even defy what is considered possible scientifically, as we'll see in the case of Tipa, a compostable packaging startup, or Secret Double Octopus (what a name!), which defied the common wisdom in information security and cryptology.

ANOTHER IMPORTANT ELEMENT to discuss before we delve further into defining startups is the concept of the "exit"—which is investor jargon for going public (getting listed on a stock exchange) or being merged into another company or acquired by it. The term "exit" refers to the fact that investors will be able to sell—"exit"—their holdings and recoup their investment, preferably with an upside. Exits are important since startups typically don't distribute dividends or pay management fees. The value of the potential exit is therefore an important determinant in any investment decision.

Startup founders surveyed by *Forbes* used these definitions of a startup: "a business idea that has minimal traction" (Daniel Roubi-chaud, founder of PasswordBox), "a group of people working toward a common goal, generally with limited time" (Iqram Magdon-Ismail, cofounder of Venmo), "a company looking to solve a problem where the solution isn't obvious and success is not guaranteed" (Neil Blumenthal, cofounder and co-CEO of Warby Parker), and "a small high growth company based on a big idea" (Ariel Garten, cofounder and CEO of InteraXon).[17]

Alex Wilhelm proposes a rule he dubs "50-100-500" to help determine what's a startup and what isn't: if your company has a $50 million revenue run rate (forward twelve months); one hundred or more employees; or is worth more than $500 million, on paper or otherwise, you are not a startup anymore.[18]

Steve Blank, a serial entrepreneur, defines a startup as "a temporary organization designed to search for a repeatable and scalable business model."[19] In many ways, he's right. Startups are small teams of people who are focused on a product and market (a "business model") that is repeatable (i.e., sales are not a one-off occurrence or to only one customer, but continuous and to many customers) and scalable (i.e., it can grow rapidly and efficiently, released from the "cost plus" model). Many people believe that the core challenge of the startup is developing the product, but in many cases, finding a scalable and repeatable business model is even more difficult. Many startups fail not because they are unsuccessful in developing a technology or a product, but because they can't get market traction or develop a viable business model for their proposition.

Blank argues that startups are "temporary" organizations in the sense that startups eventually stop being startups and evolve into big companies, which are a different type of beast. Startups, one should always remember, can also shut down—and dealing with failure is one of the other things you must have the Chutzpah to deal with.

Eric Ries, the entrepreneur, blogger, and author of *The Lean Startup,* argues that a startup isn't just any two exceptional people working in a garage. For him, "a startup is a human institution designed to deliver a new product or service under conditions of extreme uncertainty."[20] There's actually a lot to unpack in that brief definition:

- *Human*: We mustn't lose sight of the fact that a startup isn't a product or technology alone; its value lies in its people, their passion, and their interactions.
- *Institution*: Startups engage in institution-building—hiring creative employees, coordinating their activities, and creating a company culture that delivers results. These activities are crucial to its success.
- *New*: The organization is looking to find or create a new source of value for its customers or users; it wants to make them better off. Innovation doesn't necessarily require new technology. It can also mean "repurposing an existing technology for a new use, devising a new business model that unlocks value that was previously hidden, or even simply bringing a product or service to a new location or set of customers previously underserved. In all of these cases, innovation is at the heart of the company's success."[21]

- *Extreme uncertainty*: This is the context of innovation—and where most "ordinary" businesses do not fit the mold. When an ordinary business is founded, its underlying model is identical to many other similar businesses (restaurants, barbershops, etc.). Good execution guarantees success, at least at some level. Startups have no precedents, and even when they are well built their business models remain risky, because no one has ever done it before. They might even be attempting something people think is not doable. Startups are built to experiment in these conditions of uncertainty, to evolve and experiment rapidly, and then, once they've found the "repeatable and scalable business model" that works, scale rapidly. Doing this well requires Chutzpah.

My definition of a startup is: "a company that is challenging existing solutions and conventional wisdom, while developing a product or a service based on a hypothesis of what the future will look like and how people and organizations will behave." Not coincidentally, it is very close to Dr. Inbar's definition of Chutzpah, focusing as it does on challenges to the existing order.

One last note: A startup is not a PowerPoint presentation. A startup is not a hypothetical business model that's repeatable and scalable. It is a business model that must be tested and proven in the real world in a sequence of phases, from technology research, to product development, to testing the product in foothold markets, and ultimately to scaling it. I will discuss this process in more detail in Chapter 13: The Three Phases of Startup Growth. The salient point for now is that a startup isn't an idea—it's a business that is rapidly experimenting and iterating.

Not every innovative idea is a startup, but behind every good startup there's an innovative idea. The difference between an idea and a startup will become obvious as we discuss validation, solution development, market traction, team-building, and the other product-market activities that must be done before and during the early stage investment or incubation period.

2

THE FIRST RULE OF CHUTZPAH—CHALLENGING REALITY AND THE STATUS QUO

Be a free thinker and don't accept everything you hear as truth.
Be critical and evaluate what you believe in. —ARISTOTLE

This aspect of Chutzpah is a mental position, a state of mind in which the entrepreneur thinks, "I don't have to accept reality as it is. The current solutions are not good enough. They are not answering current needs. They don't provide a solution for real pains in the market; there must be a better, faster, more effective way. I will find it, develop it, and market it."

At times, as we are well aware, challenging reality may sound almost comical or delusional. Imagine telling everyone that "I can do this thing better than Google." Yet as we also know, some people *do* end up doing something "better than Google." When Google started, its founders, two college kids, had the Chutzpah to say, "We can make a search engine that will be better than Yahoo's or anyone else's."

This is certainly not to suggest that investors should give money to any entrepreneur who shows up with a plan to make a better search engine, missile interceptor, or social network. But be aware that the attitude of taking nothing for granted, of disbelieving the conventional wisdom, of challenging the way things are done, is essential for a startup.

ISRAEL'S IRON DOME, a missile-defense system that shoots down rockets fired at a certain area, has had the almost miraculous result of allowing people to live their lives normally, even as thousands of rockets are fired at them. In many ways it has changed the reality of life in Israel, and the realities of the missile threat from its neighbors. It wouldn't exist if its creator hadn't challenged reality as it was perceived by the weapons industry. When Dr. Danny Gold, then head of MA-FAT (Administration for the Development of Weapons and Technological Infrastructure, a joint body of Israel's Ministry of Defense and the IDF), broached the idea, the Israeli defense establishment and its US counterparts thought he was crazy. The Iron Dome flew in the face of deeply held assumptions about what missile defense can and cannot do, about its costs and capabilities.[1]

Rockets are cheap and easy to make. All you need are steel pipes, some fertilizer, a little TNT, and a simple detonating device. It is estimated that Qassam rockets, the rockets that are fired at Israel by the thousands from the Gaza strip, cost about $800 each.[2]

Before Iron Dome, Qassam rockets posed a serious threat to large parts of Israel. In the summer of 2006, approximately four thousand rockets were fired by Hezbollah at northern Israel from Lebanon, resulting in forty-four civilian deaths. Whenever a rocket was launched, a million citizens hid in bomb shelters (most houses in Israel have one) and their lives came to a screeching halt. In Israel's south, about eight thousand rockets and mortar bombs were fired at Israeli civilians between 2000 and 2008. Israel clearly needed to do something, but what?

"When I started this endeavor, the scientific community was skeptical," says Gold. "When you think about it, it does sound like science fiction, the idea that missiles could intercept other missiles in flight. . . . But I am happy to say that in this case science fiction became a reality."[3]

That "science fiction" is changing the political reality in the regions that were affected by the missiles. "What's important about the system is that it lets the political and military systems plan—the military can act with time on its side, since the civilians are protected and . . . there are no victims on the home front."[4] Political analysts are unanimous in viewing this anti-missile system as a game changer to the region's geopolitical calculus, since Israeli civilians are protected, can go about their lives, and as a result the military and political branches can decide to ignore attacks, if needed.[5]

One of the system developers, cited anonymously, described the incredible challenges that had to be met. "Since the Qassam rocket is made of amateurish materials and systems," he said, "its trajectory is non-coherent and rough. Sensing and intercepting something that small in such a noisy environment, at close ranges where most defense systems don't work, is like trying to intercept a Coca-Cola bottle flying faster than the speed of sound. That sounds crazy, right? We were told to do it and have a system ready in less than thirty months. Most weapons development projects, mind you, take much longer than that. And we did it at a tenth of the usual cost."[6]

IT IS A cold winter night, even in the desert around Be'er Sheva. A crowd of about 150 has come to listen to retired brigadier general Danny Gold give a talk at a cyber meetup. The event, funded by local investors, companies, and the municipality, is part of the effort to establish Be'er Sheva as a technology ecosystem.[7]

Gold begins by showing videos of traditional air defense systems and of robotic cars. They are interesting but everyone is waiting for the real deal. At last, Gold begins talking about Iron Dome. Gold says that real-life amateur videos of Iron Dome interceptions are far better than those taken by the system's developers; he shares them straight from YouTube during his talk. There are many such videos on the internet, because when people realized the system worked, they began to ignore the government's exhortations to seek shelter from falling debris and stayed on the street to watch and film the show.

Gold has "before" and "after" videos to show us. The first is of the pre–Iron Dome days. We see a crowd of children and adults during a celebration—perhaps a birthday—outside a building that houses a kindergarten. A siren sounds and everybody runs for their lives, taking shelter in the building. After fifteen seconds, there's not a soul in sight. The "after" video was taken on Tel-Aviv's beach promenade after Iron Dome became operational in 2011. As the siren sounds, some people continue bathing in the sea while others huddle along a small concrete wall, sitting on the sidewalk but not bothering to crouch or cover their heads. Some people do look for shelter but slowly; the panic is gone. Up in the sky, two wispy white clouds mark a successful interception.[8]

Gold's favorite Iron Dome video was taken in Be'er Sheva in 2012, by a videographer hired for an outdoor wedding reception.[9] At first, you see the guests standing under the open sky, eating hors d'oeuvres on small plates. When the siren sounds, they walk unrushed toward the wedding hall, obeying orders but with a sense of calm. Some choose to remain outside and continue eating. The camera then turns toward the sky. That night, Hamas operatives, beginning to comprehend the power of Iron Dome, had tried to find its breaking point by launching many missiles at once. As the rocket interceptors dodge and dart, forming semicircles while they seek the incoming rockets and determine their vectors, Gold narrates the footage: "See that rocket—it looks like the system lost it, but it did not. And see the rocket it decided to ignore? It can tell which ones are going to make it and which will falter or drop into the sea. It knows how to go after the right ones."[10]

THE IRON DOME'S inception dates back to 2004, when a joint body was established to investigate Israel's missile defense options. "The idea of intercepting and destroying missiles occurred to me. It was considered almost hallucinatory, out of touch with reality, and I didn't expect we'd get funding, but I decided we'll look at interception, no matter what," Gold recalls.[11]

In 2005, Gold solicited ideas from leading global defense companies. "We received twenty-four proposals, and we couldn't find merit in any of them. None of them looked like they could work in the long run."[12] So Gold's team defined an internal architecture they thought could work, lining up private investors who were willing to back the project in case government funding didn't come through, a fairly creative approach to the question of government support—and one that is full of Chutzpah.

"We wanted to develop the system from a civilian's point of view," Gold tells the Be'er Sheva crowd. "The military looks at missile threats from the point of view of an army base. It thinks of protecting a small area so it can continue fighting. We wanted to break that mold of thinking and see how an entire city can be protected—an area with a radius of ten to fifteen kilometers [about six to ten miles]. No one had done that before. The system we had in mind needed to actually intercept the missile. It couldn't deflect it and send it somewhere else, as other systems did. To be cost-effective, it also had to be able to tell which missiles are defective or about to hit a non-populated area so as not to waste an intercepting missile on them."[13]

Conventional wisdom about missile defense implied that Iron Dome's goals couldn't be met. As a result, Gold was critiqued for dismissing systems that used lasers to deflect missiles. But those systems were physically huge—they required an area the size of a football stadium to operate. Their laser technology also required "line-of-sight" to intercept rockets, which meant they could only operate in fair weather. Gold thought that was unacceptable, that something better could be done.

Partnering with Rafael, a local defense technology company, Gold and his team set to work, even though they hadn't received official approval. "I told Rafael not to worry, that we will get funding later on," he said, in defiance of every regulation.[14] It took two years, till 2007, for a formal budget for the project to materialize. The system's developers were counting on US funding, too, but in 2008 an American team determined that the project was not feasible.[15] Yet Gold persisted, convinced of the validity of the idea. "It always takes the political and military establishment a long time to think about what they want to do, and in the meantime, we started to create a solution," he explains.[16]

In 2009, Israel's State Comptroller issued a scathing report about Gold's and MAFAT's rulebreaking. According to the report, Gold "acted contrary to Defense Ministry regulations when he decided, in August 2005, to develop Iron Dome . . . a decision that is under the authority of the IDF Chief of Staff, the Defense Minister, and Israel's Government, before these bodies could authorize the project."[17]

Referring to the State Comptroller's critique, Gold says, "I believe I did the right thing. It's true that I didn't wait for the long bureaucratic process that can take several years, but I used my authority in MAFAT to do what I should have done—start working."[18]

Just one year after the Americans said "no" to the idea of funding the project, Iron Dome began showing great results. In 2009, the US team visited again, saw an interception, reversed its position, and issued an OK for the system. Funding was approved at last.[19]

All that was water under the bridge by 2011, when the system was deployed. It has since intercepted thousands of rockets. In 2012, Dr. Gold won The Israel Defense Prize for the same project he was criticized for three years before.[20]

ONCE YOU LEARN what single-use plastic does to the earth and to the seas, you can't unlearn it. Yet, every time you go to the supermarket, you face a dilemma—no matter how strongly you want to avoid the use of plastic packaging, most commercial products are sealed in it.

Speaking to the press in January 2018, Frans Timmermans, the vice president of the European Commission, said that single-use plastics "take five seconds to produce, you use them for five minutes, and then it takes five hundred years to break down again." He added, "Fifty years down the road we will have more plastic than fish in the oceans. . . . We are going to choke on plastic if we don't do anything about it."[21]

Daphna Nissenbaum is the CEO and cofounder of TIPA®, a company founded to provide fully compostable flexible packaging. Its goal is to create packaging that behaves just like an organic material, breaking down safely after use.[22]

TIPA®'s R&D launched in 2012. "I always wanted to do something entrepreneurial," Nissenbaum says. "I once read research about successful people who failed eleven times on average before achieving success. I also read that the idea for your venture is right under your nose; you just have to notice it."[23]

Nissenbaum conceived of her idea as she was preparing her children's school lunches. "I had an argument with one of my children about the water bottles they used to take to school. I kept asking them where yesterday's bottles were, since they hadn't been returned. I wondered whether they tossed them in the trash every day. The world's wasteful practices didn't make sense to me. One day, I went for a run and thought, *There must be a better solution, one that is not based on harmful plastic.* My first thought was to look at an apple. When I eat an apple, and throw away its core, it becomes a part of nature again; no pollution was inflicted on the world. Just as the apple core breaks down and turns into soil nutrients, we can create packaging that does the same."[24]

Nissenbaum was a software engineer and was managing an academic research center at the time. She knew little about plastics. "Actually, I knew something," she says. "I knew that water bottles made from a bioplastic material called PLA, which is derived from corn, existed, and that some supermarkets offered biodegradable bags. I thought, *Why can't I create a compostable package that can contain water—something that you can take to school or on a run and then throw away?*"[25] What Nissenbaum discovered was that the compostable solutions that existed then in the market were limited in their properties and were not suitable for packaging, which must be durable enough to provide shelf life and endure supply chain journeys.[26] So Nissenbaum set out to found the company that would later create the much-needed viable compostable package.

Nissenbaum founded the company together with Tal Neuman.[27] "We hired some designers to produce mockups for the packages and two experts in the bioplastics field to locate the right materials for our mission to produce fully compostable packaging. Six months later, when we had the designs in place, Tal and I met with the bioplastics experts, who both reported that the material we sought was not in existence and that we should put the project on hold for a few years until the technology will be developed or more advanced."[28] Giving up was not an option. "The challenge remained—I saw corn-based water bottles and biodegradable bags. Surely we can take the two materials and find the ultimate compostable packaging solution."

Nissenbaum and Neuman set to work. They secured the services of a researcher from a plastics institute and raised initial funding from angel investors. In 2012, the company won first place in a cleantech startup competition run by Calcalist, an Israeli financial publication.[29] "This was a boost," she recalls. "We decided to hire our own full-time researcher and began registering patents." In 2013, the company raised a Series A round from Greensoil.[30]

YET CONVENTIONAL WISDOM in the plastics industry still viewed TIPA® as something impossible. "Everyone in the plastics industry tells you the same thing," Nissenbaum explains. "Compostable packaging doesn't work; the material is weak, it has a short shelf life, it's not transparent enough, it smells bad, and isn't fit for packaging. Bigger and stronger companies than us tried to do what we were doing and have failed."[31]

Yet Nissenbaum and Neuman persisted and, gradually, the core idea of the company evolved. "We discovered that rigid packaging can be partially recycled while most flexible packaging cannot. Therefore, we decided to focus on the most pressing issue at hand and turned our attention toward creating fully compostable technology for the flexible packaging industry. The idea was to use existing compostable materials to create a film that will have enough strength and transparency to protect packaged and fresh food. It wouldn't be easy, we knew that, but it was worth the effort. Just think about all the flexible packaging you see at the supermarket," she says. "It isn't recyclable, let alone compostable. Think of all the snacks that are on sale. Since their packaging mixes several types of materials together, it cannot be put into recycling streams. So you have a packaging market of about $100 billion a year and growing, in which just 5 percent of the materials gets recycled. All of the rest gets incinerated, buried in landfills, or dumped in the sea. Every piece of plastic that has ever been manufactured is still here with us. This is a problem we need to face—there is nowhere to put all this trash."[32]

"I had to come to terms with the fact that the problem is so much bigger than I had originally envisioned" says Nissenbaum. "I had the naiveté of someone who doesn't know the market. You hear people's disbelief and you work to show that the solution is possible. I thought at each point that if we have come this far, we should continue. The fact that we received investor funding was also a catalyst. Giving my word that I would see this project through propelled our motivations. Just like an obstacle course, you see the first obstacle in front of you, but the many others waiting are initially hidden, and you encounter new obstacles almost every day. My way of tackling new obstacles is to remember how we overcame even more difficult ones in the past, and to keep moving forward. We took what we had achieved and created the first generation of the product, and from there, worked to create the second one."[33]

Today, TIPA®'s fully compostable end-to-end packaging solutions are available throughout Europe, Australia, and the United States.[34]

3

THE SECOND RULE OF CHUTZPAH—DOMINATE THE MARKET CATEGORY YOU ARE AFTER OR CREATE A NEW ONE

All men can see these tactics whereby I conquer, but what none can see is the strategy out of which victory is evolved. —SUN TZU

A startup can challenge an existing category by offering a better way to do something or define a new category by finding a way to do something new. In either case, if a startup wishes to succeed, it must aspire to eventually lead its market category.

In 2003, JVP identified a market gap that required new innovation in the business intelligence (or BI) sector, a domain that, at the time, had clear market leaders such as Business Objects and Cognos.[1]

At the time, BI projects—analyzing a corporation's raw data to discover business insights—were dauntingly complex, cost millions of dollars, and took years to implement. Special consultants performed them and the fruits of their labors—business analytics, reports, and insights—were only accessible to top management, never reaching midlevel managers or department leaders, who were running business on a day-to-day basis but not getting the right information and knowledge from their BI systems.

That's because information is power, and those who have power don't like to share it. There were other reasons, too: the high cost of implementing BI solutions, the need to adapt them to the needs of different stakeholders in the enterprise, inability to run the reports, and lack of attention from the IT department. JVP saw the opportunity and looked for a strong solution to solve the problem. While looking at an Israeli company in the space, and performing a competitive analysis, JVP came across Qlik Technologies (Qliktech), located in Lundt, in the south of Sweden. Qlik Technologies disrupted the industry of BI. It thought differently. It had the Chutzpah to believe that business intelligence projects should be simpler, cost less, and reach more people and more companies. Its founders believed that anyone who needs data should be given the tools to analyze it.

At the time, Qlik Technologies was a small local player, whose sales strategy was driven by selling professional services around their core engine, while serving customers who were within a four-hour drive from their headquarters, mostly in Scandinavia and northern Germany. While the company was weak in select areas (business development, sales, and marketing), it had the right ingredients from a technology and product perspective.

Things happened quickly with JVP. JVP's Enterprise Software Partner, Haim Kopans, met with Qliktech's team and was astounded at how well the company's product performed. An investment in the company immediately followed. It was one of the quickest due diligences that JVP had ever performed.

The story of the Qliktech investment is also a story about the impact and scale that a venture capital investment can provide. Qliktech's sales strategy was limited by its resources. It had Chutzpah on the product level, but not in its go-to-market.

JVP immediately began working with the company to devise a wider business strategy approach, growing the company from a local

Swedish player to a global market leader. Since all of JVP's companies came from a small local market, the fund knew how to instill a global market approach to companies and matched Qliktech with a venture partner in the US. The company relocated its headquarters to the US and the company began to consistently and upwardly scale.

The rest is history. With Erel Margalit, JVP's founder, overseeing the Fund's investment in the company, in July 2010, Qlik Technologies had its Initial Public Offering, and its first day closing valuation was nearly $750 million.[2] JVP continued to believe in the company's potential and worked to realize it by continuing to serve on its board and providing strategic guidance. In the two years that followed, Erel worked very closely with the management of the company to keep maximizing value, up until the point JVP sold its entire position, in what is known in the industry as a *home run*.[3]

KOBI ROZENGARTEN SAYS that rule-breaking Chutzpah and domination of a new market usually go together. Rozengarten tells the story of how he came to work with Saifun, a flash memory startup that was founded in 1996 and went public on the NASDAQ in 2005. He had been thinking of joining another startup as its CEO, "but then I met Dr. Boaz Eitan, Saifun's founder, who was already an important person in the world of flash memory. He told me about his idea. Basically, the technology was revolutionary—it quadrupled memory and cost ten cents instead of a dollar and a half. He said, 'Come join me, we'll raise money, let's start working.' Then he asked me whether I knew Siemens, since he was supposed to meet them later that day."[4] Siemens is one of the world's largest producers of energy-efficient, resource-saving technologies and a leading supplier of systems for power generation and transmission as well as medical diagnosis.[5]

Kobi joined the meeting, and the people from Siemens asked what it would cost to license the technology. "Boaz and I hadn't discussed this before," Rozengarten says. "At the time, $100,000 sounded like a fortune. So when Boaz says, 'Kobi, how much is a license?' I say '$10 million.' That was Chutzpah."[6]

"Later I overheard someone asking Boaz why he had brought me to the table. My response was way too expensive, he said; it sounded outrageous. Boaz told them they were wrong, and that the price of the license wasn't $10 million, it was $10 million per module, per technology generation. That was Chutzpah too."

Rozengarten says that a new generation of licensing deals in semiconductors was spawned as a result. "You can say our pricing was crazy, but that was the lowest price we ever gave for a license. We created a new world of licensing. It became a religion for us, and it was the result of the understanding that we were able to provide incredible value to our licensees, by enabling them to make more memory at a fraction of the cost."

The technology was still in its infancy and it took quite a few years to fulfill its promise. "A licensing model in itself is a kind of Chutzpah," Rozengarten says. "You're selling something that isn't fully developed, using the other person's money to develop your technology. The business model is upside down, but it's there, waiting for us to realize it."

4

THE THIRD RULE OF CHUTZPAH—FORESEE THE FUTURE AND INNOVATE TO MEET ITS DEMANDS

It's difficult to make predictions, especially about the future.
—DANISH PROVERB

"**T**here is nothing new under the sun" says Ecclesiastes 1:9. A similar quote is famously (and falsely) attributed to Charles H. Duell, the commissioner of the US Patent and Trademark Office at the turn of the last century: "Everything that can be invented has been invented."

Driven by Chutzpah, startup entrepreneurship presumes the exact opposite. They believe that there is always a better solution, that there are new needs to be met, and that there are constant changes that require constant innovation. For a true entrepreneur, the world is rife with new possibilities.

Entrepreneurs are part futurists and part prophets; they are constantly foreseeing "new somethings under the sun." They have firm insights into where markets, industries, technologies, consumer needs, and enterprises are headed. They then formulate a hypothesis and bet on it.

This vision of the future is not based on starry-eyed fantasies but on hardheaded assessments of the effects of future device and chip costs, broadband availability and connectivity, what the future holds for consumer behavior and preferences, and changes in the ways enterprises will work.

Navajo is a company that was identified by my JVP Media Labs partner, Haim Kopans. When the company was founded, the conventional wisdom was that large enterprises would avoid using the Cloud because of security concerns, and that no security solution could possibly render it safe. Navajo thought otherwise. Two years later, it was clear that enterprises were moving data to the public cloud, and Navajo's security solutions were sound. The company was acquired within two years of its funding, by salesforce.com.[1] The forecast for the cloud cybersecurity market is to keep growing and to reach $13 billion by the year 2022, so one can appreciate how Navajo foresaw the future and became one of the pioneers of that market.[2]

MARK GAZIT IS CEO of ThetaRay, a leading artificial intelligence–based big data analytics company that helps financial institutions drive advanced detection of terrorist financing, human trafficking, narco-trafficking, money laundering, and other malicious acts. Its Intuitive AI technology replicates the poweful decisionmaking capabilities of human intuition to uncover "unknown unknown" threats facing banks.[3] ThetaRay can find unknown malicious behavior that a bank doesn't even know to look for. Gazit has had a long entrepreneurial and executive career, including Group CEO and President of SkyVision, a global telecommunications company that he took from a startup to a global company with operations in more than fifty countries on three continents.[4] In 2013, he had just finished his role as general manager of Nice Cyber & Intelligence Solutions, a company that provides software and hardware solutions to government agencies worldwide in the areas of information intelligence and cyber.[5] At that time, he began looking for his next challenge.

"I knew that the future is not in collecting more data but in finding the needle in the haystack of data," he says. "I had a hunch that big data analytics—especially to prevent cybersecurity attacks—was going to be the next big thing and I know how to turn ideas into a business. I began looking for companies with technology that can support that."[6]

JVP was increasing its focus on cybersecurity investments, and was adding the cyber dimension to its Labs incubators. JVP introduced Gazit to the two professors, Ronald Coifman and Amir Averbuch, who had developed an algorithm that could detect "unknown unknowns" in data.[7] The claim sounded outlandish—an ability to detect anomalies in the data without having any prior knowledge of the data wasn't just detecting a needle in a haystack, but determining whether it was a needle at all—but Gazit joined JVP in checking out their research. Averbuch is a world-renowned expert in applied and computational harmonic analysis, big data processing and analysis, wavelets, signal/image processing, and scientific computing. He had been a researcher with IBM's TJ Watson Research Center in New York. Coifman is a faculty member at Yale University and one of the world's leading mathematicians.[8] He was awarded the National Medal of Science by President Clinton and is a member of DARPA's Advisory Board and the National Academy of Sciences.[9]

"So how do you create a company based on intellectual property that sounds like science fiction—discovering things you do not know you do not know?" Gazit continues. "At the time, people told me the algorithm sounded great but they didn't have the ability to tell whether it would work. I couldn't tell whether the algorithm works. JVP told me they had my back; if the algorithm doesn't work, we'll search together for a different IP that does. But the algorithm worked. Soon, it became clear that one problem the technology could address was attacks on critical infrastructure—like Stuxnet."[10]

Stuxnet is a computer worm that attacks the programmable logic controllers that are used to regulate industrial machinery and critical infrastructure, such as pipes, and—in the case of Iran's nuclear program—the centrifuges used for uranium enrichment.[11] Stuxnet was deployed against Iran's Nantaz facility in 2010 and caused its centrifuges to spin so quickly that they tore themselves apart.[12] Stuxnet also invaded Nantaz's command and control system and prevented it from noticing its effects, a little like placing a picture in front of a security camera in a *Mission Impossible* movie.

"There is a huge lesson in the Stuxnet attack," says Gazit. "The lesson is that we know what to look for in attacks on computer systems, but we won't know what an attack on a centrifuge looks like until it's too late. That's the unknown unknown, and many systems in the world—operational, financial, and industrial—are vulnerable to it. Instead of modeling infrastructure systems to see what their ordinary operation is and what is out of the ordinary, which will take too long and won't cover all the bases, you can just put the data into ThetaRay and look for anomalies."[13]

How does ThetaRay actually perform its magic? The core technology uses rule-free (or context-free) analysis, meaning its algorithms crunch thousands of parameters, mapping out frequencies of occurrences on different dimensions regardless of their nature (this is why it's called rule-free). It can, for example, identify a spike in activity on a bank's computer system on a day when its elevator was shut down as irregular, while keeping a low rate of false positives. In this way, ThetaRay can detect anomalies that are undetectable by classical monitoring of systems and networks.

Soon after ThetaRay was founded, General Electric, which is, among other things, the world's largest programmable logic controller company, made a strategic investment in it.[14] Suddenly, detecting unknown unknowns became mainstream. The anomaly detection market is growing dramatically, and is forcasted to grow from $2.08 billion in 2017 to $4.45 billion by 2022. Like Navajo, ThetaRay also had the Chutzpah to try and forsee the future, and build the company when the anomaly detection market was in its infancy.

5

THE FOURTH RULE OF CHUTZPAH—THE MARKET NEEDS IT (EVEN IF IT DOESN'T KNOW IT YET . . .)

People don't know what they want until you show it to them. . . .
Our task is to read things that are not yet on the page. —STEVE JOBS

E yal Gura is one of Israel's more prolific entrepreneurs—Gura has been a venture investor at Pitango Venture Capital, makes angel investments, teaches entrepreneurship at the Zell program in Israel's IDC in Herzeliya (where he is also a board member), and was recognized as a young global leader by the World Economic Forum.[1] Today, he is cofounder, chairman, and president of Zebra Medical Imaging, which received funding from Vinod Khosla's Khosla Ventures, aMoon, Johnson and Johnson, OurCrowd and Salesforce cofounder and CEO Mark Benioff, InterMountain, Aurun Ventures, and others.[2] The premise behind Zebra is that with an aging global population and a rapidly growing middle class in emerging markets, the demand for medical imaging services is far outpacing the supply of radiologists. To solve this, Zebra teaches computers to read medical images with better-than-human accuracy. Its algorithms help providers analyze millions of imaging records to understand the risk profiles of their patients, detect and predict diseases, and assist in building and managing preventative care programs.[3]

In 2016, Zebra unveiled two new algorithms to help predict and prevent cardiovascular events such as heart attacks. Later that year, Zebra and Israeli Clalit Health Services also introduced an osteoporosis detection algorithm that calculates bone density using CT scans that were performed for other purposes, without the need for additional procedures or radiation. In 2018–2019, Zebra secured three FDA clearances for its products and signed a deal to deploy its products with the largest care provider in India.[4] Slowly but surely, Zebra is disrupting the landscape in radiology.

Do you know that you can get into serious trouble for using stock photographs without obtaining a license for them? Many small internet sites have found this out the hard way, by getting letters notifying them of copyright infringement.

The idea behind PicScout, one of Gura's previous ventures, was to index copyright-owned pictures and then scan the internet to detect copyright infringement. "We tried to raise money from a venture capital fund," says Gura. "They said the market was too small—and they were right. So we bootstrapped the company." The idea was to establish the technology and then use it to prove that it had value, or as Gura put it, "Get money from customers on a per-success basis, get lawyers that have experience with copyright infringement on the internet, do everything that is required."[5]

The PicScout plan was progressing well, says Gura. "We had just finished proving—in Israel—that you can track illegal use of pictures that belong to agencies and verify that they were plagiarized. We proved that you can actually be awarded damages for that. We were ready to tackle the world's largest stock photo agencies, like Corbis and Getty Images, and make them our customers." The PicScout service would have enabled the world's largest stock agencies to scan the web for plagiarized images and request their removal, as well as to extract some form of punitive damages from the offenders. PicScout was eager to sign on its first international customers. There was one problem: Getty Images was adamant that they had no need for the service.

"They gave us all kinds of reasons," Gura says. "They said that they license their pictures to large corporations and that corporations do not plagiarize pictures. But we knew for a fact that their pictures were being used illegally. I think that there are situations where what needs to be done for the company's well-being is obvious but they don't bother to pursue it. This was one of those cases."

Gura then smiles and explains that he still managed to meet with many people at Getty Images. "If someone said no, I would find another person I could connect with and come through the window to meet them." After this had been going on for quite some time, Gura and his cofounder, Ofir Gutelzon, began to realize an uncomfortable truth: they had built a service that worked but that seemingly didn't have an easily scalable market.

After more than a year of unsuccessful attempts, they were struck by an idea. "Photographers whose photos were licensed through Getty get royalty statements from Getty. This was the data point we were missing," says Gura. They could compare how widely the pictures were being used on the internet with how much royalty those pictures were generating for the photographers. If the royalty payments were too low, then the pictures were being pirated. "We managed to get in touch with about a hundred photographers—representing about ten thousand pictures—and found a lot of pirated pictures as a result, enabling us to prove our claims at last and show Getty the magnitude of the copyright infringement and lost revenues."

Then, they decided to take a radical approach to getting Getty's attention—a display of public Chutzpah. Computer security firms sometimes plant a virus in a potential customer's computers and then discover it. PicScout did something similar.

PicScout issued a press release that said that Getty's images were stolen four times as much as any other player in the photography market.[6] "This was pretty obvious, since they were four times bigger than any other player in the market," says Gura, smiling.[7] But the announcement had its intended effect. Getty Images management was asked what they were doing to catch those plagiarists.

"We received a very angry email from Getty's CEO, Klein," says Gura. "It said something about Israeli aggressiveness. It wasn't nice. In return, we sent him a huge basket of fruit, and we've been friends ever since. I brought a group of young entrepreneurs to meet Klein a few years ago. He told us that the trick we did was not as successful for him when he tried to do it with a bigger company."[8]

In 2011, Getty Images acquired PicScout, making it its R&D center and incorporating its Image Processing and AI innovation into its business.[9]

THE INNOVATOR'S DILEMMA is a 1997 book by Clayton Christensen that argues that large companies are too focused on the current needs of their best customers. As a result, they do not adopt new business models or technologies that can meet those customers' future or unstated needs—and they forfeit the even larger market of unserved customers. Corporations that make this mistake are vulnerable to disruption by smaller, startup firms. The solution is to innovate and disrupt themselves.[10]

Large companies definitely do have the funds and the manpower to innovate on a large scale. But they rarely deploy them, which is why the right startups can so often eat their lunch.

It's not simply that those companies are shortsighted. Large corporations are held accountable by public markets. Their quarterly financial results are closely tracked and they are expected to show constant and sustainable growth. This means that they can't embark on just any project that crosses their minds—they have to be focused and make wise choices when allocating resources. Additionally, they are not always excited about innovating, since that may mean cannibalizing their existing business. So when you next hear about a startup that is revolutionizing an industry, it isn't necessarily a sign that the multinational was stupid and shortsighted; it probably was not.

From the point of view of a large incumbent corporation, startups aren't always competitors; they can be a bellwether of change—an innovation bandwagon the established company wants to jump on. Corporations often look to acquire startups that are disrupting their industries as a form of risk management and a way to resolve their innovator's dilemma. For a startup, it is important to understand a giant competitor's strategy—to know what it is or isn't focusing on and why, what it would choose to develop in-house, and what it would prefer to collaborate on or acquire.

In the last few years, multinationals have begun investing in seed-stage companies, through corporate venture arms or other mechanisms. Companies such as Intel, Qualcomm, Microsoft, Google, Facebook, Alibaba, Cisco, Coca-Cola, Procter & Gamble, EMC, and others are actively collaborating with accelerators, incubators, and VCs in order to be close to early stage innovations.[11] Some corporations, like Cisco, have mastered acquisitions as a form of product development and growth.[12] Naturally, this strategy also presents risks. An acquisition may be lost to a competitor, and even if the deal is won, integrating a company may turn out to be a significant challenge.

The financial services sector is undergoing a massive wave of innovation called Fintech. Digital cryptocurrencies such as Bitcoin are beginning to gain legitimacy, electronic wallets are being launched, stock trading has been democratized, and more.[13] Startups are disrupting everything that is finance, from lending to payments. Prosper (previously known as Billguard) uses crowdsourcing to detect fraudulent charges; CreditKarma offers loans online; Behalf (previously known as Zazma) finances small businesses by paying their expenses for them.[14] Banks and other financial institutions can't or won't innovate on all these fronts because they are highly regulated, conservative businesses. Many prefer to track the various startups that are active in the space, see how they grow and evolve, and then buy the best one.

This same logic also applies to how some companies are going global. Groupon clones turned up all over the world after the company had its initial success in the US.[15] Groupon acquired many of them as it sought to go international.[16] Was its model stolen or was this a great market entry strategy—buy the best local players and be spared the effort of entering new markets and competing with whoever got there first?

This brings us to the conclusion that the market expects Chutzpah: all markets do, even in cultures that are stifled by acquiescence and authority. The market expects Chutzpah and will acquire the companies that have the audacity to identify and dominate a new market, whether they do so silently and under the radar or boldly and in a grand manner.

6

THE FIFTH RULE OF CHUTZPAH—BEND THE RULES

Learn the rules like a pro, so you can break them like an artist.
—APOCRYPHAL QUOTE

C hutzpah is about bending rules. The rules can pertain to what is physically possible or what is considered "good practice." One implicit rule of commerce is that nothing should be given away. Chutzpah-laden startups have turned that rule on its head repeatedly, declaring that something that was previously for sale is now free. Such are the origins of Waze, the world's largest community-based traffic and navigation app. It was founded in 2008 and acquired by Google in June 2013 for $1.15 billion.[1] Israel has had a few exits that were larger than $1 billion, but Waze is unique in being Israel's first consumer-oriented startup to reach a unicorn valuation.[2] This is significant, since the conventional wisdom in Israel's investment community was that Israeli companies could only build billion-dollar companies in the business-to-business (B2B) space.[3] Israel's own market was too small and remote to reach that level with a consumer-facing (B2C) proposition.

The term "unicorn" was coined by Aileen Lee of Cowboy Ventures to describe a startup tech company with a valuation of over $1 billion.[4] Although startups worth more than $200 or $500 million may be huge successes, the $1 billion mark seems to be a psychological threshold for investors, consumers, and the press. The chance of becoming a Unicorn is only about 1 percent.[5]

Uri Levine, entrepreneur, cofounder, and former president of Waze, tells the story of the app's origins. "Ehud Shabtai, one of the founders, got hold of a GPS and began to develop an add-on to it. The GPS's platform was a PDA [Personal Digital Assistant such as Palm Pilot]," he comments. "Doesn't that sound prehistoric?"[6] The add-on allowed its users to share the locations of traffic cameras, so they could avoid getting tickets. It was a success, and Shabtai began distributing it at various online forums for "pocket PC freaks." "The original map with the add-on became Israel's best navigation software, exceeding anything else by far."

But rules are rules. The company that owned and distributed the original map contacted Shabtai and told him his add-on was breaching the terms of use of their software license.[7] GPS was something that was sold, not given away, and the add-on shouldn't be offered for free either. Ehud Shabtai didn't like those rules. It was true that he needed a map for his add-on to work. But his solution wasn't to kill the add-on or sell it to a license holder. Instead, "he concluded that his greatest problem was that he didn't control the map itself—if he did, he could have worked on the add-on without requiring any consent from the company that held the license for the Israeli market. So, he began to think about how to create a map."[8] The answer was a crowdsourced map that tracked users' actions.

Uri Levine continues the story: "At the time, I was a consultant for another company that provided GPS software to cellular operators, and I was thinking about taking the data created by users to understand where there were traffic issues so that they could be directed to avoid them. The company I was consulting for didn't want that idea. They said it wasn't easy to understand traffic from the technology standpoint and that such an implementation wouldn't be able to determine reliable ETAs [estimated times of arrival] for every possible route. Without an accurate ETA, they said, people will never use it. I thought there was value in knowing where there were road traffic problems but the company thought that was a trivial idea. They claimed everyone knew where the traffic was in the morning."[9]

In 2007, Shabtai and Levine met. "Things started to fall into place. There were no free maps, but we knew we could build one by tracking user actions. But to have enough users to do that, and to get meaningful traffic data, the service would have to be free.

"It took us a long time to raise funds," Levine continues. "We went fundraising and investors disliked the idea, thought it was crazy. I was very fluent with the idea after several months and it seemed totally sensible to me, but the investors I spoke to were caught by surprise and didn't like it at all. No one will share their location, they said; there are privacy issues. They had every objection you can think of. They argued that there was no value to the user, that people will never download it, and that we will never reach a critical mass of users. But I was in love with the idea so I didn't really listen."

CYBERSECURITY FIRM CYBERARK is another great story of Chutzpah. In mid 2010, with JVP's co-investors in the company looking for an out, Erel Margalit stood by his belief in the company and its potential. Looking around and seeing the growing need for solutions to protect against the enemy from within, Margalit stood by his view that the company could go further, having the Chutzpah to convince the management and board to not succumb to purchase offers, or plans to list the shares in Tel Aviv. An already long-standing investor in the company, JVP increased its position to close to 50 percent, up from around 30 percent, buying out its skeptical peers, and welcomed another major financial group to ride the next wave. This would ultimately turn into one of JVP's best decisions.

Udi Mokady, the CEO and cofounder of CyberArk, told us his story about stretching the rules with Chutzpah. "The company was doing very well," he begins, "and in 2013 we began thinking about going public.[10] We were ready by June 2014, but war broke out in Israel and we decided to postpone the IPO for a while. In September 2014, the IPO window [the time when the market will favorably accept new initial public offerings] reopened. Then the bankers called us with what they said was bad news. It seemed that the Chinese retail giant Alibaba was also planning an IPO, which was expected to become the world's biggest ever. Alibaba's IPO is going to 'block the sun,' they said. No one can go public at the same time. I asked for examples of blocking the sun, they gave us some, and we huddled—myself, the CFO, and JVP's Gadi Tirosh.[11]

"We thought critically about this," Mokady continues. "Alibaba was going to become a huge company in terms of market capitalization; we were much smaller. They were in e-commerce; we were in security. It occurred to us that the Alibaba IPO could be an advantage, since there would be no one else in our market but us in this IPO window. And as it turned out, we were right. Road-show meetings were great; we presented to packed rooms. The CyberArk IPO was oversubscribed and became one of the best performing technology IPOs of 2014."

The moral of the story? "We just went with the entrepreneurial instinct, without obeying conventional wisdom," Mokady says. "An IPO is not an exit, but rather a milestone that helps with sales and brand recognition and allows us to further grow the company."[12]

THE GOOGLE LUNAR X Prize (GLXP) was a 2007–2018 inducement prize contest organized by the X Prize Foundation and sponsored by Google that challenged privately funded teams to launch a robotic spacecraft to the moon.[13] The first to do so would win a grand prize of $20 million. The initial rules were as follows: launch the spacecraft; soft-land it on the moon; and then send a robot five hundred meters on, above, or below the surface of the moon while sending high-definition video and still pictures back to Earth.[14] But the Israeli team SpaceIL had the Chutzpah to change the rules.

Kfir Damari, who has founded several startups in the fields of cybersecurity and space, is an entrepreneur, engineer, researcher, lecturer, and a self-proclaimed "proud geek." He served in an elite intelligence unit in the IDF and then pursued a BS and MS in communication system engineering from Ben Gurion University. Yariv Bash, Kfir Damari, and Yonatan Winetraub formed SpaceIL in 2010. The three young engineers would make Israel the seventh country in the world to make lunar orbit and the fourth country to attempt a soft landing on the moon; SpaceIL was also the first such attempt by a nongovernmental body.

"Yariv was a Facebook friend of mine and I saw a post he made, saying 'who wants to go to the moon?'"[15] The three met in a pub in Holon, a city that's part of the Tel Aviv metro area. "He told me that he first jokingly proposed to mount a camera on a meteorological balloon, fly it beyond the atmosphere, and call it The First Israeli Spaceship. But then someone told him, 'Why don't you do the real thing?' and sent him the link to the GLXP site." Bash's Facebook status came in mid-November 2010: the last day to register for the prize was December 31, 2010. About thirty groups had entered the contest, but they had all entered much earlier, since the prize was announced in 2007. To register, they needed to deposit $50,000 and submit a blueprint of the lunar lander they were planning. Given that they had decided to go for the prize six weeks before its closing, that they were penniless students, and that they had no blueprint beyond some back-of-the-envelope drawings made on a napkin in that Holon pub, it was unlikely they would manage to apply at all. Yet they did.

"I'm proud of the fact that we managed to rush everything and submit the application on time," says Damari. "My wife told me that the three of us must have been truly very confident in our capabilities to believe we could ever make it. To us it seemed like a no-brainer. We thought it would be a soft drink–sized spacecraft that would weigh five kilos, and that we could do this using $8 million and within two years. It looked like a risk worth taking, and I remember thinking that if we didn't succeed, I'd go back and live with my parents." Damari laughs and then says, "As the saying goes, ignorance is bliss. We had no idea what we were going into."[16]

The first challenge was raising the funds, and there were only six weeks to do so. Bash, Winetraub, and Damari began meeting people—academics, philanthropists, and businesspeople to try to raise the funds for the application. "We were lucky in a sense that there was this six-week deadline, because the people we met couldn't defer their decision to a later time. They couldn't say that they want to think about what we're telling them or that they would like us to check some things and return with an answer. The six-week deadline created a sense of urgency and the only thing they could do with our story was take it or leave it. Most of them understood there was no time to deliberate and immediately donated the money for the application, several thousand NIS [New Israeli Shekel] here and there." Damari says that by the time they had managed to raise the money, incorporate, and wire the application funds, it was almost too late. Although they would be wiring the funds on December 31, 2010, it was likely they would be received by the GLXP on January 1, 2011. Bash, Winetraub, and Damari contacted the prize organizers to verify that if they had proof of the wire transfer but the funds had not yet arrived in the US, their application would still count. They were assured it would.[17]

The team also broke two implicit rules. Contrary to most groups that had applied for the prize, they had decided that their moonshot would not be a for-profit endeavor but rather a nonprofit one. The other rule they broke related to what the lander was to do on the moon.

"At the time, it seemed as though the GLXP represented some sort of sound business case—you invest what we had thought was $8 million and can stand to receive a payout of $20 million, and we could possibly have a dialogue with our supporters as to what percentage of the return they would be entitled to." In reality, Damari says, there was no viable business case: SpaceIL was the only applicant to launch a lander and the project didn't take two years and $8 million; it took more than eight years and almost $100 million.[18] "If we knew, at the time, what costs and time would be required, we probably wouldn't have done this," says Damari.[19]

The decision to raise philanthropic funds and to attempt a project that would not necessarily create financial returns but rather educational returns led to bending another implicit rule. Damari explains that most companies were focused on building a rover. As late entrants and without many R&D funds, SpaceIL had to think differently but within the rules of the contest. They were committed to launching the smallest and lightest vehicle to ever reach the moon. Yet, the requirements of the prize required traveling five hundred meters, and that didn't work well with their plans. Sending a robotic rover meant that the spacecraft would have to hold the rover inside; moreover, they would have to design it and test it. But the team was committed to building a small, light lander: the smaller and lighter it was, the less expensive it would be to launch. What if, they thought, the spacecraft landed on the moon and then jumped the five hundred meters—fulfilling the prize's rules by traveling on the moon, but doing so cheaply and cost-effectively? They checked with the prize committee and were told that they could. By forgoing a commercial venture, they could forgo the rover, have the lander "jump" five hundred meters on the moon, and deal with a simpler challenge—it just required a novel approach to the rules of the challenge, and slightly bending those rules.

Other innovations involved using the power of gravity to save fuel costs to fly the lander. The Beresheet (*Genesis* in Hebrew) lander wasn't launched directly to the moon, but instead shared a rocket ride with two other payloads.[20] Since it could not take a direct path to the moon, the lander zipped around Earth in ever-increasing orbits until it could let itself be captured by the moon's gravity, saving costs and demonstrating a new method of reaching the moon that could be more economical.[21]

In incorporating SpaceIL as a nonprofit, the team said that their aim was to create a new "Apollo Effect"— to inspire the next generation in Israel and around the world to think differently about science, engineering, technology, and math. For all its technological excellence, Israel faces a severe shortage of scientists and engineers. SpaceIL was committed to using the potential prize money to promote science and scientific education in Israel, to ensure that Israel continued to live up to its reputation for excellence in these fields. As a result, it engaged in many educational activities, meeting over a million young Israeli students (more than 50 percent of the students in Israel), and encouraging them to think that SpaceIL might be about rocket science, but that it wasn't magic. The students were encouraged to think that they could also build the next spacecraft that would reach the moon. This outreach work was done by hundreds of volunteers.[22]

To further its educational mission, the founders also understood the importance of marketing and PR. "The PR firm we selected told us we had quite a lot of Chutzpah to interview them and others and choose the best one. After all, we wanted them to do pro-bono work for us. We wanted to do educational marketing—tell the story of science with the power of consumer goods marketing. We wanted kids and their families to talk about going to the moon."[23]

One of the first marketing decisions they made was not to call it an unmanned probe, which was the technical term for it, but rather to call it a spacecraft. *Spacecraft* captured the imagination much better, especially when it came to kids. The vision and the main message was "to bring the first Israeli spacecraft to the moon."[24]

Damari also talks about their efficiency. "At most we had two hundred and fifty people working on the project—when someone from *National Geographic* came to interview us, I learned that four hundred thousand people worked on the Apollo project. There were many challenges. For example, we combined young technical people who know how to make things happen with the people at Israel Aerospace Industries who were more conservative and cautious. They wanted to have super-redundant and super-robust technologies and we were less inclined to do so—we wanted to keep costs under control and control the weight of the lander. Eventually, we arrived at a happy hybrid of both approaches."[25]

The GLXP expired in March 2018, as none of the five finalists had been able to launch by the final deadline, which was extended several times. On February 22, 2019, the Beresheet lander was launched. It entered lunar orbit on April 4, 2019. The landing was planned for

April 11 and was broadcast on Israeli TV. In the final moments of the flight, a problem occurred, causing the lander to crash onto the moon.[26] Minutes before the expected landing, when the lander was about eight miles (thirteen kilometers) above the surface of the moon, mission control received a "selfie" from the lander, with the lunar surface visible behind it.[27] The final telemetry signal was received when the lander was 149 meters from the moon's surface.[28] Morris Kahn, who funded large parts of the project, said, "Well, we didn't make it but we definitely tried."[29] Given that no country had ever attempted a lunar soft landing in its first attempt (the US had sixteen launches before it attempted to land, the Russians twenty-two, and the Chinese two), the Chutzpah of the SpaceIL team paid off. Although the soft landing didn't happen, SpaceIL's mission to reach the moon was accomplished. Beresheet's attempt was lauded by many and was awarded a $1 million "Moonshot Award" by the X Prize Foundation in recognition of touching the surface of the moon.[30]

7

THE SIXTH RULE OF CHUTZPAH—SHOW, DON'T TELL

Don't tell me the moon is shining;
show me the glint of light on broken glass.
—ANTON CHEKHOV

This advice is usually given to fiction writers. In the world of high-tech startups it means that no one will believe you if you just say you're going to change the world. But if you provide living proof of what your product can do, people can't help but believe you.

This is evident in how Liran Tancman built the first CyActive proof of concept (POC), in which the algorithm correctly generated later generations of the Poison Ivy virus from its 2008 version, and in how ThetaRay markets itself. As Mark Gazit, ThetaRay's CEO, explains: "We charge money for the proofs of concept we carry out for customers; we call them proof of value [POV], and take care to ensure they get immediate value out of the process. I'm an amateur magician, but I always make sure to show how the magic works. Selling ThetaRay's technology is very similar—it's like selling magic. Sometimes they give us data without letting us know what its context is—financial, operational, or anything else—and ask us to find the unknown unknowns. We manage to do that. We once found a problem in the loan portfolio of a bank. It took the customer four months to conclude we were right. Nothing works better than proving your system works."[1]

PROVING YOUR SYSTEM works means much more than just running a successful pilot. When success depends on a network effect, you need to prove that you can create one, and that users are willing to pay for the product. TIPA®, the compostable packaging company, needed to not just show the materials it invented, but also to prove the value its packaging brought to brands.

As Daphna Nissenbaum explains, TIPA® was open about how their product worked, inviting customers into their lab and describing the properties. But that wasn't enough. "Even when you get the product to work, there are many more issues to tackle," Nissenbaum says. "You have to understand the industry. Packaging is a basic need for consumer goods companies; it protects their products. They aren't going to replace what already works for them that easily."[2]

She further explains: "We therefore focus on offering not only films and laminates, but a narrative for a cleaner world, which reflects positively on brands using TIPA®. TIPA® brings an up-to-date, visionary perspective on packaging, showing the world that fully compostable packaging can actively replace the conventional plastic contaminating our ecosystems. I truly believe that brands who adopt responsible and honest practices will grow their market share. By the time one of our customers, a healthy snack producer in England, placed their second order, it was triple the size of their first. When we asked them what had happened, they told us that since they began using compostable packaging, their clientele grew and they began selling in supermarkets that had previously refused to carry their products because of the conventional packaging they were using before."

Additional challenges still faced TIPA®, namely manufacturing the product on a global scale and choosing a business model. "Plastics manufacturing is a huge business," says Nissenbaum. "Production facilities run 24/7 on very expensive machinery. Now think of TIPA®. At the time, we didn't have many funds. We had an innovative, yet unconventional product. Who would allow me to use their facilities to manufacture a product that has not been previously tested to run on such machines?"

TIPA® didn't build its own plant. "We decided the most sustainable and efficient thing to do was to work with whatever machinery is already being used in the existing market. Whoever will buy from us will be buying packaging from the same packaging converters they are used to buying from. We decided that our goal was to become transparent to our ecosystem. We built a technical team that knows the conventional plastics industry so that we can promise the customer that we aren't just selling them the materials, but are offering them an end-to-end solution, from the beginning of the supply chain to its end, ensuring that the right certificates apply, and so on."

IN PART I I've tried to demonstrate how the mindset of Chutzpah can be implemented into the startup's actions and decisionmaking. Even though most of the entrepreneurs who were interviewed and quoted didn't necessarily realize that they were using Chutzpah as part of the way they were managing their venture, once asked about it, it was quite obvious to them that they have.

Even though the startups, the entrepreneurs, and the examples I've used are Israeli, the rules of Chutzpah and its principles can be implemented by any entrepreneur, and any startup, anywhere in the world.

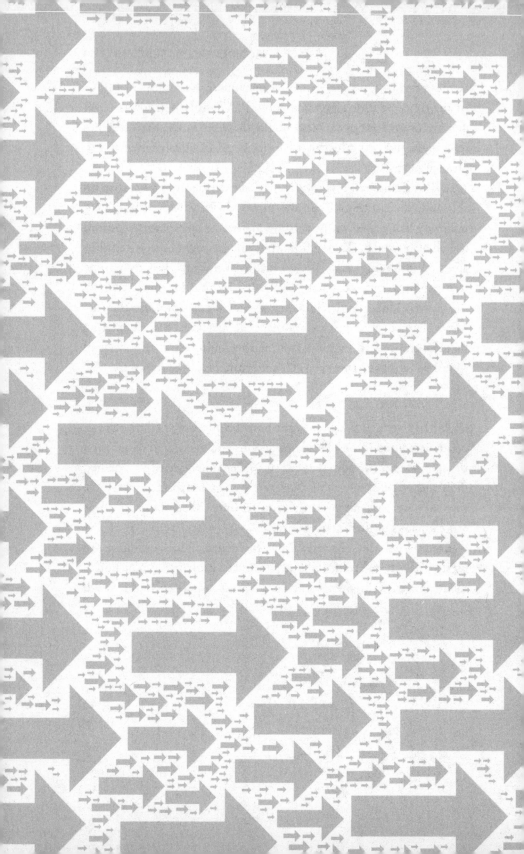

PART II
PRINCIPLES

8

COMPLETE THE MISSION!

If you're going through hell, keep going.
—DOUGLAS BLOCH

One powerful formative experience that Israelis have is mandatory service in the Israel Defense Forces (IDF), called "regular service." Everyone (almost everyone . . . there are some exemptions) is enlisted at the age of eighteen, once they complete high school. Men's regular service is thirty-two months long, and women's is twenty-four. When recruits decide to go into certain military professions or join an officer's course, they enter "permanent service." Even when they are released from active duty, many Israelis join the ranks of the reserves, training or taking part in active duty for three to six weeks a year until the age of forty-five and in some cases even fifty.[1]

Most Israelis absorb the same values during their service, and those values, especially as they relate to camaraderie, teamwork, work ethic, and management style, permeate civilian workplaces (along with military slang). "Mission Command," a doctrine that combines centralized intent with decentralized execution, is at the heart of the IDF's operational philosophy, and it has come to define the ethos of Israel's startups as well.[2] In a nutshell, it means that while the commanders define the goals of the mission, the officers in the field are empowered to take the initiative and choose whatever tactics are needed to carry the mission out.

I enlisted in the IDF for regular service, became an officer, and entered permanent service, commanding a combat unit as a captain for a few years in the regular service, and for another twenty years as a major in the reserves.

What the IDF engrains in you the most is not the importance of courage under fire, or the need to execute according to plan (although those things are important), it is the imperative *to complete the mission!*

You *must* complete the mission, even if nothing goes as planned: your communications network fails, you are short on ammunition, your weapons malfunction, your soldiers are wounded, and the weather changes unexpectedly. Since you are the commander in the field (even if you are a junior officer) and have all the immediate information, you must make decisions in real time, even if they don't fully fit the orders you have received. You are fully empowered and expected to improvise, come up with creative solutions to complicated situations, and do anything within your power (and within the law) to accomplish your goal. As the saying goes, failure is not an option.

This is also the way that the trainings and the drills are composed. Throughout the drill, there are unplanned "events" such as a lack of a certain ammunition, simulation of wounded soldiers, reinforcements that fail to arrive, new enemy maneuvers, moving an attack from daytime to nighttime, radio malfunctions and other communications failures, and so on. These events are created in order to challenge commanders, force them to make decisions in real time, and take new actions according to the revised situation. In order to do so, they need to be creative, improvise, meet challenges with what they have, and make sure they stay fully focused on achieving the goal and completing the mission.

N. is a colonel who for many years commanded one of Israel's elite Special Forces units. "When you have a special operation, it almost always begins as a mission impossible," he says. "But the Special Forces' culture is that all problems have a solution and that the mission must be completed. It's very Israeli."[3]

IDF commanders simply cannot imagine themselves picking up the radio and reporting that they have failed or given up. With authority comes responsibility; they are fully accountable for their results. There is a well-known saying in the IDF that encapsulates this: "*There are results, and there are excuses.*" You always want to be on the "results" side of the equation. Another well-known saying is, "*There is no such thing as 'I can't'; there is only 'I don't want to.'*" Excuses are not relevant. The only thing that matters is whether the desired outcome—the mission—was accomplished.

The Mission Command ethos carries over to startups. The QA engineer will work over the weekend, even if they weren't asked to, so that the deadline can be met. A customer success team will go overboard to make sure the customer gets what they want. N., the Special Forces commander, says: "The mission precedes everything, and people will give anything and everything. They have a complete identification with the mission, and a complete devotion to it. You don't abandon it in the middle, and you don't look right or left. It's a character trait. The people who don't have it are filtered over time and don't stick around."[4]

N. notes that there are sometimes "situations when the people on the team are not aware of the overall picture in which the special operation fits. The commander knows but the people on the team don't always know. All they know is that what they do is something that is extremely important for the security of the State of Israel, and they are highly focused on their mission." This is rarely the case in civilian life, but the mindset of completing a mission is extremely relevant to any startup at any stage. Any good entrepreneur will have that virtue, regardless of whether they served in the army. This management style and culture that is unique to the IDF can and should be incorporated into a startup's culture, no matter what country it happens to be in.

Like combat units, startups work in dynamic and constantly changing environments—new competitors, new technologies, and new business models arise constantly; changes in personnel and in distribution and marketing channels can throw off the best-laid plans. Just as soldiers do, the startup needs to react to these changing circumstances in real time and with a high sense of urgency.

THE MISSION SHOULD BE CLEARLY DEFINED

When we talk about the missions of a company, we aren't talking about its larger purpose, as it is described in its mission statement. We are referring to specific tasks and goals that must be achieved. Such a mission may be traveling to a potential customer with a technical team, figuring out what their issues are, and resolving those issues on the spot. It might be engaging with potential customers at a trade show, or hiring the best VP of Sales that the company can find.

Some startups do not make the effort to clearly define what the tasks at hand are, leaving individual employees with the almost incomprehensible task of figuring out what to do or how to prioritize their tasks. Management by missions means that the organization is forced to define its priorities, objectives, and the means to achieve them. A general statement such as "we will have the best product" is not a mission. Defining a feature that will make it the best product in the market, and specifying the time frame and budget within which it should be developed, tested, and released, is.

This focus on defining the mission and outcome creates clear key performance indicators (KPIs) for every level of the company—what needs to be done, by whom, and when. Everyone in the company at any level knows what their mission is, what the priority is, the fact that they will be measured by it, and in some cases also compensated accordingly (annual bonuses are often given based on KPI performance).

MISSIONS REQUIRE PLANNING

Before starting its actual work or even raising funds, every startup should have a detailed operational plan. That operational plan includes many smaller "sub-missions" that are clearly defined and measurable. It should provide clear answers to each of the following questions:

1. What needs to be achieved?
2. When should it be achieved?
3. Who does what in order to achieve it?
4. Who is accountable for it?
5. How much capital is required for it?

The plan must be ambitious but realistic, and its assumptions should be based on actual market knowledge.

Every plan needs KPIs, and they should cover all the core aspects of the business: product, revenues, head count, development, distribution channels, strategic deals, and so on. KPIs should be assessed annually, quarterly—and sometimes even weekly or daily. At the same time, a startup should beware of defining too many KPIs. The company as a whole might have three to five KPIs that it will assess on an annual basis, out of which smaller, departmental KPIs can be defined.

WHEN MISSIONS AREN'T ACCOMPLISHED

Just like a commander who doesn't want to be in the position of reporting that he or she didn't accomplish the mission, a CEO should dread coming to a board meeting and explaining that he or she did not meet his or her KPIs. Missing KPI targets can exact a price—losing market share to a competitor, revenue shortfalls that may lead to layoffs, or eventually shutting down the company.

All this isn't to say that plans and reality will match up 100 percent. They don't. There are always difficulties and surprises along the road, and these need to be embraced and dealt with. Moreover, the company may have very little influence on some changes that occur in the market. But the company as a whole and each of its individual units should strive to be flexible, responsive, and quick to react so it can still complete its overall mission, even if its environment is constantly changing.

BE A LEADER, NOT A MANAGER

The IDF's battle cry is "After Me!" No one will charge into fire just because an officer tells them to. But when commanders conquer their own fear and lead a charge into gunfire, soldiers will follow them. Effective leadership turns on earned trust and respect. When commanders repeatedly show that they can make clearheaded decisions in times of stress and that they are not afraid to put their own lives on the line, their soldiers will trust them with their lives.

Leadership is more important than management, in the military and business alike. There is a saying that managers do things right, but leaders do the right thing. Doing things right might not suffice to complete the mission, but when one does the right thing, the chances of success are that much higher.

MILITARY AND COMBAT EXPERIENCE AS AN IMPORTANT TOOL FOR ENTREPRENEURS

Uri Levine of Waze says, "I'm a graduate of the Intelligence Corps, yet today, when hiring CEOs, I much prefer a combat officer to a technologist. This is where you learn values in the army. A combat officer has real proven leadership, the ability to deal with stress, and when they lead more than a few people, they will also have a great managerial capability. People like this never give up, they are devoted. They may not have business finesse but they know how to manage people. People like this also know they need a technologist since they don't have the background. In the army, you're not afraid of excellent subordinates; you build your people to replace you as you move on, and therefore these people have no problem bringing people that are better than them and helping them grow. That's a good attitude."[5]

FAST DECISIONMAKING— IMPORTANT FOR A GOOD CEO

Levine says, "I read research that shows that good CEOs have quick decisionmaking with a high rate of internal conviction. Companies that do this succeed more. The best HR organization in Israel is the IDF. They get almost 100 percent of the population and they get them for a short time. Their best HR practice is the sociometric test—asking what everybody knows. Just ask your people who's good and who's bad—who would you like on your team and who would you not want on your team. Listen to your people. This model is very powerful.[6]

"A startup is always in combat mode," Levine continues. "Employees don't have to know about all these crises, but the CEO does." Someone once asked venture capitalist Ben Horowitz how he slept at night when he was CEO of Opsware (formerly Loudcloud) and he replied: "Like a baby—I woke up every two hours and cried."[7]

"But you have to persist," Levine says. "You can grieve all night, but in the morning, you have to start again."[8]

MAKE DECISIONS ON YOUR FEET

The IDF allows a lot of freedom, flexibility, and responsibility to the commander on the ground. N. says: "Since we know that the battlefield is a kingdom of uncertainty, during a special operation there is a complete freedom to the commander to act. They know the task, and even if it means changing the plan, they are well trained to do so and complete their mission."[9]

A battle cannot be micromanaged, and neither should a startup. Boards of directors need to accept this. There is a thin line between positive involvement and assistance and actually managing the company on a day-to-day basis. This line cannot and should not be crossed. The CEO must receive all the tools, authority, and knowledge needed to succeed. Board members should always help but they shouldn't get into the bits and bytes that will transform the CEO from a leader into a manager. If you feel that you cannot trust your CEO, don't micromanage them. Replace them instead.

COMPLETING A MISSION IS A MINDSET

One may argue that since most countries don't have compulsory military service—and even in the ones that do, it usually does not come into actual practice—these military-related references would not be relevant or applicable to entrepreneurs around the world. But in my opinion, if you take any successful entrepreneur from anywhere in the world, he or she will have mission-driven characteristics, regardless of any military experience.

Completing a mission is a mindset that any entrepreneurs should adopt. A mindset to improvise when needed, to tackle challenges in new and creative ways, and not to give up when things do not go according to plan. They usually won't. Keep your eyes on the ball, focus on the mission, and make sure you do everything within the set of tools you have, with the team you have, and the budget you have, to complete the mission.

9

ON PASSION AND FAILURE

A ship in the harbor is safe,
but that is not what ships are built for.
—JOHN A. SHEDD

The cold statistics show that the majority of startups fail. According to a Harvard Business School study by Shikhar Ghosh, 75 percent of venture-backed startups fail.[1] Moreover, only 6 percent of venture capital–financed companies are responsible for 60 percent of capital return.[2]

According to CB Insight, the top ten reasons for startups to fail are: no market need (42 percent), ran out of cash (29 percent), not the right team (23 percent), got outcompeted (19 percent), pricing/cost issues (18 percent), user unfriendly product (17 percent), product without a business model (17 percent), poor marketing (14 percent), ignored customers (14 percent), and product mistimes (13 percent). Since many startups offered multiple reasons for their failure, the above exceeds 100 percent.[3] With those kinds of odds, why would anyone join or found a startup? Why jump into a pool in which there is a huge likelihood that you will drown? Why go on a crazy operational and emotional roller coaster when you know in advance that your chances of success are so low? It seems irrational.

VCs build portfolios of startups, so their risk is reduced. Though some companies inevitably fail, the ones that don't will more than make up for the difference. But entrepreneurs bet everything—their time, their reputation, their capital, and their quality of life—on one company.

Despite these statistics, startups continue to be founded and eco-systems built. What's driving that clearly goes beyond rational calculation. There is a power that compels talented people to start their own companies rather than go to work for large, successful, and secure multinationals. This power is called passion. In fact, it is more than that: it is an *irrational passion*.

FALL IN LOVE
WITH THE PROBLEM AND
EMBRACE THE MARKET PAIN

When Uri Levine of Waze talks about his reasons for funding companies, he wears his emotions on his sleeve. "I always begin by looking for 'the pain,'" he says. "I allow myself to actually become angry at things that are no more than annoying for other people, and then I begin thinking what can be done about it. It doesn't matter if it's about hating to stand in traffic or in line, or anything else that comes to mind. You really have to fall in love with the idea, and simply not listen to what people are telling you. . . . So many people told us at the beginning that Waze would never work."[4]

This passion is not optional; it is one of the key factors of future success. First, because passion is contagious. It is what investors are looking for, it is what talented people are seeking, and it is what the press wants to write about. It also has a positive effect on potential clients, business partners, and distribution channels. Passion is hard to define, but there's no need to do so. You know it when you see it, just as you can immediately tell who has "star quality" on *American Idol* without having to define exactly what that quality is.

You cannot fake passion. It isn't about waving your hands or speaking loudly about the company. It is something that emanates from within, from your deepest, truest, innermost self. If you don't feel this kind of passion, you should be brutally honest with yourself and ask if this startup is really the thing that you want to build. Will this idea really revolutionize the way things are being done? Is this the company that you are willing to sacrifice so much for?

The prospect of a big exit isn't a passion. Money alone won't give you the kind of motivation you need to make it through the rough patches, nor should it be your sole motivation for starting a company. An exit is one possible outcome for building a good company that grows into an excellent one. But your core motivation must be a true desire to change something, to challenge the status quo, to see where the world is going and come up with solutions that most people or enterprises don't yet know they will need. You need to care deeply about cyber, media, enterprise software, medical devices, renewable energy, agricultural technology, water solutions, smart cities, pharmaceuticals, virtual reality, education technology, or whatever field your startup is in. You need to feel the pain of the problem you are solving and fall passionately in love with the solution that you are offering.

This passion is important for another reason. If you are banking on a relatively "safe" idea, one that everybody likes and agrees is good, then you may not need passion—but your idea is probably mediocre. A really innovative, creative, radical idea, one that can create a true paradigm shift in the market, is almost certainly highly risky and will be received as "too crazy" or "impossible to do."

Your passion and strong belief in the idea, as crazy as it may sound, will be the engine that moves it forward, allowing you to defy negative feedback and skepticism. Obviously, not every idea that gets criticized is revolutionary, but all revolutionary ideas will be criticized. The passion of the entrepreneur is the force that allows them to succeed.

TIPA®, the compostable packaging company, had to overcome many failures before it achieved its first success. Daphna Nissenbaum says, "Today I know that many companies fail to bridge the chasm between R&D and actual manufacturing. The initial story which helped us win the startup competition in 2012 was a fairy tale that took years to actualize. The reality is that processes in this huge, industrial market aren't simple. We needed to move our materials from the craft phase to a phase of mass production, and to be able to repeat the process. It took a long time before we reached a stable manufacturing procedure with a clear understanding of which machines would reliably produce the same product consistently. In 2014, we began working with a manufacturing facility in Turkey. We flew our teams and raw materials there four times, and we failed four times in a row. It cost us a lot of money and I had to report to the board that we had nowhere to manufacture. It was a difficult period; it was tough for me and for the team. But we regrouped, formed a task team, painstakingly found two new manufacturing facilities, and we eventually made it. We're already producing our thirty-second batch with them."[5]

All this proves the adage: *You have only failed if you have given up: until then it is called learning.* Despite these difficulties, TIPA® managed to meet its KPI of having its products on the shelves by 2016. By early 2018, dozens of products were being packaged with TIPA® solutions and sold to hundreds of thousands of consumers around the world.[6]

Summing up the TIPA® experience so far, Nissenbaum says: "I must say that there are many failures and that the process is a crazy trip with many ups and downs. You need to have a certain character. You know you'll fail and you know you will have enormous difficulties, but you have to persist, understanding that not everything will succeed."[7]

Nissenbaum's story makes an important point: you can't *just* bring Chutzpah to the table. Persistence, grit, and the willingness to do incredibly hard work are absolutely necessary. Also, the wherewithal to weather many failures, small and large.

ON TOP OF this irrational passion, an entrepreneur must be ridiculously ambitious and truly want to build a company that can be a category leader. Without this ambition, the startup will not move fast enough to become the first in its category. Good entrepreneurs have a high sense of urgency and competitiveness. They feel that they need to run fast, then run faster, and then accelerate in order to lead the race. It doesn't matter if they have a direct competitor or not, they should always assume that someone, somewhere, is building something very similar to what they are doing, and they need to beat that someone. Without this sense of urgency, you may build a good business, you may be even be number two or three in the market, but you will never become a global category leader.

DEALING WITH FAILURE

"What goals would you be setting for yourself if you knew you could not fail?" The question was first posed in print by Robert Schuller, an evangelical minister, but there is food for thought in it for people in the startup world as well.[8]

Speaking of an inability to fail, Kfir Damari of SpaceIL says: "I've always believed that if there is something you want hard enough, you will be able to achieve it. Because you can either succeed, or you make a conscious decision to stop trying. This isn't really failing and I've believed this ever since I was a kid. I knew my family would support me; I thought nothing bad could happen."[9] In real life, SpaceIL faced multiple funding issues and its lander ended up crashing onto the moon after missing the GLXP deadline. "It was hard. I remember paying the caterers for a 2011 event with Shimon Peres"—then Israel's president—"and thinking at the same time that I will need to terminate the employment of SpaceIL's employees because we didn't have the money to pay their salaries. Eventually, another donation was received." Yet Damari thinks the fact that Beresheet didn't land on the moon also serves SpaceIL's educational mission. "We showed the children we met at schools a video of a drone we used for experiments— only we showed one of the many experiments when it crashed. We wanted to convey the message there are a lot of failures along the way. After the crash of our spacecraft, I got a lot of feedback that parents, children, and educators spoke about failure and about the fact that you need to try really hard. I think that has great educational impact."

One of the simplest definitions of failure is "lack of success." But, in order to know if your company has failed or not, you have to know what its success metrics are. Is it reaching the break-even point? Achieving profitability? Distributing dividends? Gaining market share? Being acquired by a larger enterprise? Having an IPO on NAS-DAQ? Each company will probably have its own definition of success, set by its founders, board, investors, and shareholders, and this definition may also change because of timing, market opportunities, and new risks. This is why failure can be subjective and relative. There are operational failures that happen as you build the company, such as product failures, not hiring the right person, not meeting the business plan, or not meeting the revenue targets and other KPIs you've set yourself to achieve. These failures can be temporary and more anecdotal than fundamental; they can be fixed and overcome. However, there is one event that is an objective failure: when you can't afford to keep your doors open anymore, and the company has to shut down.

A STARTUP IS A
JOURNEY OF FAILURES

Uri Levine from Waze says, "A startup is a journey of failures. The only thing that matters is how fast you recover from them. If you are operating under the fear of failure, you will break. The ones who are not afraid of failure continue to try until they succeed or run out of capital. You should make sure that you did everything within your power to address the failures, the issues, and the challenges. The thing about failing is how quickly you can get back on your feet. You try all the time till you succeed or till it's over. And you also need to ask yourself whether the problem-pain you wanted to tackle is still valid. If it is, it's still worthwhile to solve it, despite having failed this time around."[10]

There are endless reasons why a startup may fail. There are many variables startups have no control over, such as radical changes in the market, new competitors that took a better route, new technologies that have disrupted the market, wrong distribution channels, changes in customer needs, or regulatory shifts and tariffs. Other issues may be lack of a product-market fit, or that the initial hypothesis of where the world was going simply missed the mark. Other elements might have been within the startup's control but just as hard to manage, such as hiring the right people, making the right product changes when necessary, building the right partnerships with the relevant players, crafting the right business and pricing models, having the right go-to-market strategy, not burning too much of the company's cash too soon, or simply not giving up too early.

But when we analyze why a startup has failed, we find there are two main reasons. The first is because the startup didn't listen closely enough to what the market was saying and didn't pay attention to its various signs. When we say "the startup didn't listen," we include its management, board, employees, advisors, and every person who was involved with the company. When we say "market," we don't mean what the investors were saying, or the feedback from people the startup wasn't targeting. The market is potential clients, users, strategic partners, distribution channels, and any other player that is active in the category. You may have very smart people on the company's board, you may have an excellent team, you may have very experienced investors, but the market is always smarter. Only the market will tell you if the product is right, if your solution has a meaningful competitive advantage, if your pricing strategy is valid, and what the real sales cycle is. Only the market will tell you if your initial hypothesis is correct or if it needs to be updated, changed, or adjusted. Dismissing these signals is ignoring reality. And since the market is dynamic and constantly changing, the vast majority of startups will need to make changes to the product in order to get the right product-market fit on an ongoing basis. As Leon Megginson summarizes of Darwin's *Origin of Species*, "It is not the strongest of the species that survives, nor the most intelligent ones that survive. It is the one that is most adaptable to change."[11]

Many would guess that the second reason for failure is the people, that the "team wasn't right," or "there were ego-management issues." But this is only partially true. The reality is that these issues rarely make the difference between success and failure. What *does* make the difference is if the CEO and the management do not make difficult personnel decisions, or if they make them too late. Some people simply don't belong on a team. They need to be removed from it. So the second reason startups fail is wrong decisions made regarding the team.

FAILURE IS AN EVENT, NOT A PERSON!

The Hebrew for "venture capital" literally reads as "risk capital fund." It is an apt name: venture capital is a high-risk business; most startups fail.

Though company founders, boards, investors, and employees sometimes make fatal mistakes, a healthy high-tech ecosystem doesn't treat failure as a person, but as an event. This is an important distinction, because it has a major effect on people's motivation to start companies. If potential entrepreneurs believe that they will be branded as failures for the rest of their lives if their startups shut down, then they won't even consider trying and will probably find more secure jobs. On the other hand, if they know that the environment will be supportive no matter what happens, they will be more inclined to take the risk. When we say "environment," we mean everyone: the social environment (girlfriend, boyfriend, husband, wife, friends, brothers, sisters, parents, and so on) as well as the business environment (investors, potential clients, employees, and so on). Most investors will not reject an entrepreneur who has failed out of hand, since they know that person is actually more experienced than a first-time entrepreneur, and has probably learned some painful lessons.

"I have a startup called Refundit," says Uri Levine. "It deals with VAT refunds for non-EU tourists in Europe. In 95 percent of cases, people can't get the VAT refund for goods they have purchased overseas. The interest of the country is to have tourists spend more with the VAT exemption, but bureaucrats are slow to refund. I tried to set this up two years ago, before I founded Refundit and it didn't work, but now I've decided to try it again. A second-time entrepreneur has five times the probability of success. Experience is so dramatic. I don't care about the failure. I care about what you've learned."[12]

Levine concludes: "Dealing with stress and having investors that can deal with stress is very important. In 2010, Waze was running out of money. Then Google released a navigation feature and our investors were ready to throw in the towel. Other VCs said they wouldn't even remotely consider investing in us. But we didn't give up. Why? Because the problem was big and worth solving and because the team was amazing. Many startups do get to the last dollar and still pick up and survive. Waze's technology is amazing but that's not the main thing. What makes our algorithms so great is that they pack two years of failure into every line of code."

Various studies show that the success rate of entrepreneurs is higher on their second venture.[13] It makes perfect sense since second-time entrepreneurs are coming with all that they have learned from their previous startup. They are more experienced in various aspects: in structuring the company, in hiring the right people, in prioritizing the tasks, in developing new technologies, in going to the market, and in managing the funding, just to name a few. They are less naïve, they understand the dynamic of a startup, and hopefully learned from past mistakes. So even though no one likes to fail, it is by no means a projection for future trials. On the contrary, if one has failed but decided to try again with the same company or with a new venture, their chances to succeed are higher.

There was a sign I once saw near a rock-climbing wall that summarizes it in a nice and accurate manner: "Failure is a lesson learned. Success is a lesson applied."

10

THE THREE-PERSON MULTINATIONAL

You have to think big to be big.
—CLAUDE M. BRISTOL

Why should a technology startup aspire to be a multinational? Compared to early stage startups, multinationals are altogether different beasts. Multinationals are huge lumbering giants: a food company like Nestlé, a mining conglomerate like Rio Tinto; or a tech monolith like Cisco or Microsoft. These companies began operating outside their home countries after long periods of sustained growth; they didn't become citizens of the world until they had already achieved massive scale.

Yet I would argue that any startup should cultivate a multinational state of mind from its inception. This may be Chutzpah, given the miniscule size of the startup, even a delusion of grandeur, but it is an essential ingredient for success, especially for non-US based startups. This attitude underlies most of the success stories in Israel's startup nation.

Being a multinational startup means that only R&D and management can be local, and that is also subject to change as the startup grows. Everything else must be focused on the world.

- The product offering should appeal to a global market and address a global need.
- The startup's go-to-market should focus on large markets and not a local market, even if the local market is relatively large (such as the UK, Germany, Brazil, or Russia).
- Startup operations should be multinational too. The team should travel constantly to the market, even if it's far away; key hires in sales or business development should potentially come from the geography the company is targeting; and the startup should consider relocating its management team, and in some cases, its entire team there. Waze moved Noam Bardin, its CEO, to Silicon Valley while the rest of the company stayed in Israel.

THE BENEFITS OF GOING MULTINATIONAL EARLY

UpWest is a Silicon Valley–based seed fund that was founded in 2012 to bridge the geographical and access gap between very early stage Israeli startups and the US market. It was founded by Gil Ben-Artzy, Shuly Galili, and Liron Petrushka, all Israeli expatriates. Uniquely (in Israel, at least), UpWest started as a for-profit accelerator that received equity in companies in return for its involvement and funding, but has since evolved to an early stage seed fund.[1]

Ben-Artzy says that Israel-based companies risk losing touch with customers and competitors alike if they don't spend meaningful time in the US early on. Yet moving the entire company to the US is mostly not an option, since Israeli companies build using their existing relationships in the Israeli startup ecosystem. "Moving everyone to the US would be beneficial in terms of company structure—everyone stays together, but who will you hire in the US? Will you have access to the same deep stream of talent that flows out of the IDF? You have no advantage in recruiting good people in the US. Moving may even adversely impact the quality of the product."[2] The ideal solution, concludes Ben-Artzy, is to keep part of the company in the US and part of it in Israel. The uniqueness of UpWest's approach is that it encourages companies to touch the US market much earlier in the process and to do so more extensively—accelerating the product-market fit by bringing the company's founders or other members of its senior team into Silicon Valley.

"Today you don't need a lot of money to prove stuff—the main issue our fund aims to solve is market access. Our investment thesis is to help Israeli founders get to market quickly." Asked when the optimal time to connect with the US market is, Ben-Artzy says that companies should come to Silicon Valley when they have "something they can show someone," but that something has to be more than a PowerPoint presentation.

UpWest's portfolio founders are much older than Ben-Artzy and his partners originally expected. "We thought that our startup founders would be around twenty-five years old," Ben-Artzy says. "Then we found out that the youngest applicants were twenty-five but the average age was people in their early thirties. Founders we back are paying a hefty personal price for spending significant time in the US, but they do so because they have a deep belief in their startups' likelihood of success. We invest in founders that truly believe that the market proximity UpWest provides will help them.

"Each year we meet with close to a thousand startups, but invest in only seven to ten of them. We invest in startups with a prototype, with a beta, with a first product or first customers (even paying customers). Some of the founders we backed have already raised some funding before us. What they all want is market proximity."

UpWest's offices are in Palo Alto, but it also leases a large residence in Menlo Park. "Founders asked us where they will live when they first come to the US, so we rented a house," Ben-Artzy explains. "When you land at San Francisco airport, you can live in the UpWest house and work in our office the next day. We immediately send you out to meet customers, partners, and people that know your business and will help you build it."

"Once entrepreneurs land at the house and arrive at UpWest's offices, the process of connecting with the market enters a certain rhythm," Ben-Artzy continues. "There is a setup phase where each week has its main motifs. We set up office hours, talks about user interfaces or user experiences, fundraising coaching, and so on. But our focus is to see an empty office—as the founders should be in meetings most of the time with potential customers and partners."

Ben-Artzy says that when UpWest began as an accelerator, they ran three cohorts a year, each lasting three months. As to which companies were chosen, "we look for large, interesting market opportunities targeted by a team that has context that is relevant to it. One of the companies we invested in, Honeybook, wanted to go after the US wedding market with a go-to-market strategy that focused on wedding photographers.[3] That made a lot of sense for the Israeli wedding market. Once they came to the Valley, they discovered an even larger market opportunity in offering business management tools for creative freelancers and entrepreneurs. They could not have discovered this opportunity in Israel."[4]

NON-LOCAL DEFAULT

Indeed, one of the rules that guides almost all startup investments in Israel is to go outside the local market and establish a business presence in the target market as quickly as possible. Startups don't incubate themselves locally, waiting until they come of age to enter the global market. They go after the global market before securing their initial funding, and the default location they choose is usually the US.

There's another angle to the global mindset in the early days of a startup. If the company focuses on the local market, it may make the mistake of making the competitive analysis only versus local competitors. This, almost by definition, will lower the competitive bar, because there's a good chance that your biggest global competitor is not coming from your local market.

Setting the highest competitive bar is the only way that a company can win the market. It needs to be on top of everything that is going on in its space, and make sure it does everything possible to beat the competition, from every possible aspect—technology, product, distribution, marketing, and so on.

The imperative to go multinational quickly is so ingrained in the investing culture that Israel-based investors avoid Israeli companies that only go after the local market. No matter how successful a company is in Israel, its marketplace is too small to support the kind of scaling that is needed to make a venture capital investment worthwhile. This doesn't just go for Israel. Startups may gain traction in larger local markets like Germany, France, the UK, and Brazil, but they risk ceding the international arena to a competitor and thus missing out on the opportunity to become a category leader.

This line of thought is so prevalent in the Israeli investment market that we have a code name for it: "the three-person multinational." It may sound audacious, full of Chutzpah, or tinged with more than a hint of megalomania. But this is a must for a startup company to succeed, especially one coming out of a small country. Later in this book I discuss in detail how this can be achieved by working with large multinationals; this chapter is focused on the realities of going multinational at such an early phase.

WHY GO GLOBAL?

Size: For Israeli companies, the answer is self-evident. Israel's population is 7.9 million, or 2.5 percent of the population of the US. Compare that to the San Francisco Bay Area's 7.4 million people. Would you invest in a startup company whose market was limited only to the San Francisco Bay Area or to the population of the city of London (8.3 million people)? Probably not.

Location: If you are an American artist growing up in a small town in the rural west (Jackson Pollack, for instance, who was born in Cody, Wyoming) and you want to make it big, you move to New York

City. When you come from a small country in the Middle East and you want to make it big, you go after a large market, typically the US (but not always, as we'll see later).

Proximity: Companies need to be close to their core market and to their clients. In the technology world, the core market in most cases is the US, regardless of whether the company is going after businesses or consumers. Access to the core market ensures:

- An ongoing dialogue with users and clients and better product feedback. Without these, the company's product can be a figment of its founders' imagination
- Being able to keep a close eye on the competition
- Better access to PR and media opportunities
- Better access to investors, mentors, and potential partners that can give the company a better value-add (and a better valuation)
- A larger network of supporters

Ben-Artzy describes the proximity issue from the standpoint of a young startup company, located in Israel and traveling often to the US: "Many Israeli entrepreneurs come to the Valley for a week to immerse themselves in the market. That week is definitely amazing for them. They tell us that they have managed to get more work done during that one week in the Silicon Valley than they had managed to do in the past six months. The problem is the day after: when they come back to Israel, usually no one in the US remembers who they were. To avoid this, the company should plan on multiple touch-points with the global market, traveling often, and touching its eco-system as much as possible. At a later stage, establishing the HQ of the company in the US market may be a must."[5]

Culture: There are some things you can only know once you're immersed in a culture. Serial entrepreneur Eyal Gura says that the Gifts Project, a startup that was founded by his wife and brother and initially funded by him, would never have been thought of if they hadn't lived in San Francisco, where people buy presents in different ways than Israelis do.[6] A social commerce platform that enables multiple friends to pitch in toward an item for a birthday or some other occasion, the Gifts Project was acquired by eBay in 2011.[7]

This principle extends to almost anything that has to do with a startup's product, from its user interface and value chain to the realities of how people conduct their businesses and their personal lives.

LOCAL ISN'T GLOBAL

Local success is no guarantee of global success. Local corporations may use software or hardware that is nothing like what their US counterparts use; they may have idiosyncratic needs. In Israel, for example, Hebrew is read from right to left. This means that our computers must be configured differently.

Check, a mobile bill payment company, was sold in May 2014 to Intuit for $360 million.[8] Intuit makes software that helps US consumers and businesses manage their finances; Check's product complemented their offering.

In Israel, consumers do not use personal finance tools that are anything like those offered by Intuit or Check. For example, they use neither software nor paper to "balance their checkbooks"—this simply doesn't exist. If Check had started out by serving the local Israel market, would its offering have gotten any traction in the US? Most likely not. Capturing a local market in a small country is not only *not* a proof or indication of a similar success in global markets (or at least in the US), it may also derail the company, wasting time, resources, and focus.

"Let's say you are a security company coming to the US with funding from UpWest," says Ben-Artzy. "After four months, your beta customers are from the likes of Facebook and Intel. When you begin fundraising, you now have the local proof that you are tackling a big and meaningful problem and that the best companies in the world vouch for you. Had you stayed in Israel, you might have built a product in two years based on a remote hearsay of what the Facebooks and

Intels of the world were looking for. Your time is the greatest asset you have. Spend it wisely."[9]

Touching the market early can eliminate a big part of the guessing game for companies. "For instance, one company we invested in raised a seed round of $700,000 prior to our involvement, and built a beta product that fit the largest customer they could get in Israel," Ben-Artzy says. "They assumed that US customers needed the same thing, but when they came to the US they discovered that the segment they were after didn't want the product they'd developed. They therefore changed the target audience, updated and changed the product, so at a minimum, we saved them six to nine months of wandering around and building the wrong product. The mistake of building the wrong product is very expensive and you can't recover from it unless you had initially managed to raise a significant round of financing."[10]

CyberArk is trusted by the world's leading organizations, including more than 50 percent of the Fortune 500, to protect against external attackers and malicious insiders. "I went to an event a few years ago, and was introduced to the audience as the 'fifteen-year overnight success,'" its CEO and cofounder, Udi Mokady, relates. "I'm actually proud of this fact even though some people see that as an oddity. We really were a late bloomer."[11]

Mokady cofounded the company in 1999 with his boyhood friend Alon Cohen. "Alon came up with the idea, a digital vault. In 1999, the main dogma for security software was separating the corporate network from the internet with firewalls. We thought about firewalls as doors, and while doors are an absolute necessity, they aren't enough. If you have to let someone into your house for some reason, you don't want them roaming freely into every room, or opening your drawers and cabinets so they can check out what's inside. Additional barriers are needed to protect your most valuable belongings, like a safe for your jewels. Humans are curious by nature. For example, people who have access to sensitive data may snoop around where they shouldn't. IT adminstrators, for example, may read management emails and check salaries. This isn't hacking—they are using their existing authorization to look at what they shouldn't. Alon has a personal stake in this. When he was in charge of systems and security at the IDF Central Data Processing Unit, he wrote a love letter, which he encrypted on his computer, and a fellow soldier hacked his computer and circulated it. CyberArk created a digital vault in which companies could keep their most valuable or sensitive digital assets—salaries, options, business plans, financial results, intellectual property, and more."[12]

But CyberArk's customers found different uses for the vault. After it raised its initial funding, it began working with Israeli companies as beta customers, mainly local legal and accounting firms. "These companies weren't using the digital vault as prescribed; they were excited about tangential use cases for the technology" Mokady says.

"But the Israeli market use cases misled us," Mokady adds. "This isn't an Israeli phenomenon—you're always misled by the local market, even if you're a French company in France. It truly is easy to find customers in your local market. In Israel the product—we had started calling it the network vault—was selling, but it never took off outside Israel and we drove ourselves into the ground trying to figure out why. In retrospect, the answer is simple. We needed rapid adoption to create a network effect where many people adopt the product at once. In Israel, which is a small country where people know each other, it was very simple to create a network effect. Banks in Israel adopted it for secure communications between Israel's many banks, then the local insurance companies joined the bandwagon, and so on. But the US banks wouldn't even consider it. We had some early sales in the US, but they misled us into thinking we could break out early. We worked well—when we made a sale, we made sure we understood the use case and then moved to cater to that need, but as time went by the money started to run out."

Mokady moved to the US in 2000, and the company raised an A round.[13] But after the September 11 terror attacks, US funding dried up. "We returned to the Israeli VCs for funding because we knew they were more resilient to terror and wouldn't stop investing."[14] In 2002, two Israeli funds (JVP and Vertex) made a B round investment in the company.[15]

"As time passed," Mokady says, "we noticed that US companies were buying the product for the original uses we had envisioned—protecting sensitive information. They were also using the product to store passwords and the information they needed to manage IT resources."[16] The Israeli market had pointed the company in one direction; US customers in another. In 2005, six years after the company was founded, it decided to stake its future on privileged access security.

"That's why we're a late bloomer," Mokady concludes. Their investments in the early product were paying off, now that the market was moving in that direction. "There were new regulations inspired by the Enron scandal and then the Sarbanes-Oxley legislation kicked in. Organizations were required to better control their IT networks. Horror stories also surfaced. After a network administrator working for the city of San Francisco was fired, he blocked network access for all city employees. People were starting to worry about admins who go rogue."[17] At the same time, another lesson was setting in: external protection isn't enough, because attackers can and will infiltrate the network. The Edward Snowden breach was the Super Bowl ad for CyberArk because in an interview from his hiding place in Hong Kong, Snowden said that he could steal state secrets because he had privileged access.[18]

When the 2008 recession struck, the company did well. As other companies laid off staff, Mokady says proudly, "We decided not to be lean and mean and we didn't let go of even one employee. We did cut management salaries, but people knew that we were loyal to our team. Loyalty is a strong company value and I think its origins are Israeli—'don't leave anyone behind.'"[19]

NONLINEAR GROWTH

Traditional growth strategies take a linear approach in which a company grows like a person, from childhood through adolescence, until one day it is eighteen and can vote, and later when reaching twenty-one it can be served alcohol. A startup doesn't have the privilege of developing at a natural pace, but needs to fast-forward through its childhood and then scale exponentially.

To understand why growing fast is an important requirement for a startup, let's examine the difference between a "new" company and a startup. For instance, imagine establishing a new type of dining experience for hamburgers. The first restaurant opens in Tel Aviv, with plans to grow to ten branches (franchised, perhaps). You then move across the Atlantic and plant one such hamburger restaurant smack in the middle of Manhattan and then grow some more, possibly covering the entire US in a distant future. How is this company different from a startup? The answer is that it isn't designed to spread like wildfire. It's one hamburger restaurant and then another—its growth is linear.

To grow fast, a company needs to offer people something they need, but it also needs to be able to reach them quickly and in a scalable way, before the competition does. The need to secure real estate limits the pace of growth for the hamburger chain. That's why you don't see software startups selling door-to-door; they sell from a website, or on the phone, or through channels and partners. More importantly, selling software doesn't require a storefront. A startup's business model must present a good strategy for rapid growth. If it doesn't, the company is new, but it isn't a startup.

Startups need to rush because if they don't someone else will, no matter how non-trivial their technology or personnel is. Skipping the local market altogether can have exceptional results. Intucell, a provider of self-organizing network (SON) software, which lets mobile carriers dynamically adjust their cellular grids to maximize mobile traffic speeds and minimize dropped calls, was founded in 2011. Intucell's SON uses big data to assess the state of a network and then lets the carriers' towers communicate with each other. That way they can expand or contract their cells in real time so that users get better mobile reception. During the due diligence for Intucell's series A round (in which $6 million was invested), its investors checked its technology with AT&T and not with local companies.[20] This connection with a large provider that was interested in the service proved to be extremely valuable. AT&T bought the software from the company, creating a cascade of events that resulted in Cisco acquiring Intucell in early 2013 for $475 million in cash.[21] Going after Israel's local carriers would not have had the same result.

Adi Pundak Mintz, an angel and a venture partner in Canaan Partners Israel, works with many early stage startups. He argues that the sooner a startup moves to the US, the sooner it can exit through acquisition. Buyers don't materialize from nowhere—they are usually someone who knows you and has done business with you. In real life, you meet your potential buyer months or years before the exit, and being present in their local market helps quite a lot.[22]

CAPTURING THE TOP OF THE HILL

Simply put, startups cannot afford to let a competitor win the race. Startups should always target being the number one company in their category. Even in cases where the company sees a market with a need and its competitive analysis comes up with a clean slate, it can't assume that the market "void" will last long. If there's a market need or a gap, someone else will also move to fill it. A sense of urgency is therefore crucial for any startup, no matter what space it is operating in, and should be embedded in the company's culture

The analogy we often refer to in Israel is as follows: if several army units are vying to conquer the top of a hill that hasn't yet been occupied, the unit that gets there first has the highest chance of staying there. When a new technology category emerges, dozens of companies will strive to dominate it. The effort and resources expended to remove an incumbent from the top of a hill are much greater than the efforts that are needed to seize an unoccupied hill. In some cases, the company defines a new category, and thus invents the hill, so occupying it at first is relatively simple. But very soon it will need to be defended. Thus, your startup can never stand still, and should always protect its position by further developing the product, increasing its market share, and constantly creating new competitive advantages through R&D, marketing, and business development.

GOING INTERNATIONAL ISN'T SIMPLE OR EASY

Of course, moving to the US isn't easy. "The way I see it," Pundak Mintz says, "a move to the US is typically coupled with the receipt of funding from a US investor. What happens is that you have an Israeli company that is good at product and can perform quick and dirty R&D to get to a minimum viable product [MVP]. With the move to the US, there is a sudden cultural shift. You need to hire people in a different culture. I personally think that the chance of success for those hires is 50 percent—and you need to hire them without the benefit of your own professional, academic, and social networks. Without a US VC, it is very difficult to find good people to hire. If you still have two US hires out of your first three after two years it means you are doing a good job. But even if you don't move the company or the management to the US, you will probably need a US office. Once you have secured more capital in a B or C funding round, and if the customers are geographically there, you should probably move."[23]

Pundak Mintz elaborates: "Your initial US hires must be 'Israeli-compatible.' Being Israeli-compatible means that you have the right to offend but you don't get offended yourself. Something about the Israeli tonality can be offensive, so you need to hire people who don't take it personally. For an American, Israelis are unpredictable people—and those new US hires want process and consistency. The Israeli unpredictability and lack of process are great for the minimum viable product stage but aren't that great when you want to scale the company. Additionally, a company in the Valley and a company in Israel have a time difference that is almost unworkable—and as time goes by, the US staff may begin thinking, *"Those #@%* Israelis!"* This is the cost of a split organization and you have to be able to deal with it. I actually believe that as New York develops a stronger startup ecosystem, Israeli companies may be better off moving there, since its relative proximity [compared to the US West Coast] reduces the costs of a split organization."

"On the other side of the coin," Mintz continues, "the Israeli team can begin feeling like second-class citizens. If they were hot shots in the company before their CEO moved to the US, the new US people make them feel somewhat downgraded. A bigger question mark is whether everyone has to move to the US. Maybe for a smaller company, planning for a smaller exit, you'd rather not relocate but only travel constantly to the US. In any case, people tend to forget how remote from the market they are and under-invest in travel. To work well, people need to meet often. There really is nothing like a face-to-face meeting."[24]

Investors told CyberArk to hire an American CEO in 2004. "That was the fashion at the time," says Mokady. "The idea of an American CEO didn't work for us," he adds. "There was a great disconnect between the US operation and the Israeli development center. Sometimes it looked like an 'us versus them' mentality was at work—I overhead people saying 'they don't get it' when referring to the Israeli part of the business. It was mostly a cultural gap. When an external CEO is parachuted into the company without the cooperation of the founders, the CEO naturally suspects everything to do with the founders. This taints his approach to the entire Israeli operation. Also, the going was tough; this was a very difficult time for the company. The day I became CEO, the disconnection between the Israeli team and the US was ended and we could streamline product feedback and actual development."[25]

"Hiring salespeople in the US is very tricky, especially as their profession is sales and they are selling themselves as salespeople to you, the Israel CEO," says Shahar Kaminitz, cofounder and CEO of Insert, which was sold to Pendo in 2017, and founder and CEO of Worklight, which was sold to IBM in 2012.[26] "I hired the wrong people the first time around and I didn't know what was preventing them from selling—maybe the sales cycle was too long, maybe they needed to ramp up, or maybe they weren't up to it. Either way, a year went by that was very dear for the startup."

LOCAL STILL HAS (SOME) MERIT

All that said, there are things that can be done in the local market even when it's not the company's main target. For instance, it can be used for proof of concept, to test the technology and ensure that it actually works, to test a hypothesis, or to try out a product in a certain vertical. Yet, transitioning from local success into your target market isn't just a matter of copy and paste.

Another scenario that justifies local efforts is when the international customers can be approached locally. Israel has an enormous amount of subsidiaries or branches of large-tech multinationals: Intel, eBay, EMC, IBM, Google, Microsoft, Apple, Deutsche Telecom, SAP, TI, and many more (over five hundred of them).[27] This is unusual for a small country, but it creates a potential pathway to the global market. The startup trying to go down that road must tread cautiously, however. Some multinationals give their local organizations a lot of independence—which means that selling to them may not result in a sale to the global organization. But then again, it can catapult a company into becoming a global best practice for the whole company.

Eran Wagner, an entrepreneur-turned-venture-capitalist, moved to the US in 1998, when the company he founded, Xacct Technologies, needed to be present in the San Francisco Bay area. But not all companies have to. "You actually needed to plant your people in the North American continent to do business in the US, to begin sales there. There was no way around it. I didn't know what marketing was when I moved, and I knew very little about raising money from a VC."[28]

"The need to move to the US has an entirely different dynamic today," says Wagner. "There were some groundbreakers in Israel, who began selling remotely and generated a lot of market momentum through the phone, about ten years ago. Companies began demonstrating you can prove a scalable and repeatable business model from phone sales in Israel. This changed how investments are made and validated. There are more Israeli entrepreneurs in America now, and more shared infrastructure, such as accelerators and workspaces. Information disseminates faster. The need to move has become less critical."

THE MAKING OF A UNICORN: WAZE

"Israel had been written off as only being capable of producing small exits—not global internet brands," says Waze's CEO, Noam Bardin.[29] He then echoes the conventional wisdom about Israeli unicorns in the consumer space: "As technology moves from application to content, the weakness of Israeli entrepreneurs is that they don't get the American consumer. We can do chips, security, telecom, but nothing consumer-related—we don't 'get' US consumers." Yet, Israel created Waze—a unicorn—and a unicorn that went after the consumer market.

While Bardin's formative experiences in Israel made him a different type of consumer than Americans of the same age—Israel had only one television channel in the 1970s and 1980s, few computers, and little exposure to the biggest American consumer brands—that is not the case with Israelis who are coming of age today. Bardin argues that the global consumer experience is flattening (to paraphrase Thomas Friedman's *The World Is Flat*).[30] As consumer experiences across cultures become more similar, consumer values become more transferrable, especially in the software and mobile spaces. This, together with additional Israeli elements—specifically, a culture built on rapid iterations and a natural cultural affinity with the lean startup movement—makes Israel-based consumer unicorns a possibility.

How did Waze manage to get US consumers and become a target acquisition for both Facebook (as was rumored) and Google? Among the many things Waze did right was moving its management (i.e., Bardin) to the US on time. "Unicorns," argues Bardin, "should be close to or in Silicon Valley—what makes Silicon Valley so unique is its concentration of people who have actually seen a unicorn in the wild. Seventy percent of unicorns were based in Silicon Valley. This ecosystem of entrepreneurs, engineers, product managers, marketers, PR people, investors, mentors—this, I believe, is the secret sauce of Silicon Valley."[31] While Israel is also beginning to have its share of people who have seen unicorns with their own eyes, touching the Valley is a must. Therefore, a startup needs to have dual presence—both in Israel and in the US.

"Splitting up a small company across seven thousand miles, a ten-hour time difference, and a twenty-four-hour connecting flight is one of the worst things you can do. It adds tremendous execution risk," says Bardin. "But the only thing worse is not doing it. Between the execution risk (that is within your control) and the risk of not being there (which is out of your control), I choose the former. I want to choose the risk I take."[32]

Bardin chose to live outside Silicon Valley's Israeli enclaves—he wanted exposure, and as surprising as it may sound to those unfamiliar with it, Silicon Valley is similar to Israel in size, informality, and interconnectedness. "You will meet many experienced industry people who are happy to help, introduce, connect, and mentor. Some of my best connections were the parents of kids in my daughter's class," says Bardin.

Gil Ben-Artzy echoes this sentiment. "The risk everyone is trying to manage is that of being remote from the market—the risk that your competitors are closer to customers, the risk that the market is moving and your competitors will notice where it is going before you do. There is also the risk that your competitors will raise more money than you can. The risk of splitting the company across two continents isn't simple to tackle, but at least it's in your control."[33]

Ben-Artzy argues that the best solution is to "keep your R&D in Israel and the rest in the US. That way you remain close to the market and you can hire the best tech talent in Israel. The risk you are taking is that not everyone in the company is on the same page, and overcoming this gap will require a substantial effort. But this type of risk—company, culture, and communications—you can actively influence. You will need to deal with issues related to managing a team on the other side of the world, but at least you're not taking the risk that you will miss the market because you are detached from it."[34]

Yet Waze did not go immediately to the US. It first took care to meet some critical milestones in Israel. "We always wanted to go global," says Uri Levine, "but the Waze pilot was in Israel and geographical proximity was important. Our developers were also users of the platform and talked to other users. We could try stuff, make mistakes, and fix them really quickly. Trying to do this internationally would have been too risky."[35]

"One of the first challenges," Levine adds, "is understanding the value you provide for your first users. If you don't understand that, you can't go anywhere. First users are different than early adopters—they are innovators. They would drive around with a GPS and the Waze app and compare them. They were very excited about correcting the map and feeling that they were in control of their traffic experience. People that write in Wikipedia and comment on forums are like that—they are deeply invested in their hobby. They aren't looking for a reward, but for recognition that they are good at what they do."

An application like Waze needs to reach critical mass before it has enough users for its map to be complete, its traffic data meaningful, and its ETAs (estimated times of arrival) reliable. The term is borrowed from nuclear physics, where it refers to the amount of a substance that is needed to sustain a chain reaction. Waze's first critical mass was in Israel. "To achieve that," Levine admits, "we had to 'cheat' along the way. Before we were generating our own traffic data, we used data from a fleet management company so we were able to provide value to users. It made the Waze experience look real. You came to a traffic jam and it looked like a traffic jam in the app too. We wanted the experience to be good in at least eight out of ten cases. If a user drove somewhere and there was no road on the map, we sent them a message the next day telling them that if they open the app, they will see that the road has been added. That way they felt like Waze was progressing."[36]

"We knew it was time to expand when we could not learn anything else here in Israel," says Levine. At last, the company was ready for the world, but things didn't work as planned. "We went global in 2009, but it didn't work. People downloaded the app, but their experience was bad; they thought it didn't work. The map wasn't created quickly enough, and the people who tried the app stopped using it. We worked on many iterations in 2010, but sometimes even the fixes didn't work. In some countries, we did well, and in others poorly.

"In each country, we began with 10 percent retention. It's like moving water around with a sieve. When you get to 30 percent, the people that stay recruit many new people and the sieve becomes less porous. The trick is to speak to the people that didn't continue to use your app. Don't talk to the people that converted. Talk to the people that didn't.

"We added gamification. Ninety percent of people didn't care, but some people did and drove for the points and that helped improve the map. The big jump of Waze in the US was in the summer of 2010. The main highway in LA was going to be closed for maintenance, and the media dubbed the expected traffic jam 'Carmageddon.'[37] ABC TV used us for real-time data in their coverage, which put us in the news.[38] We offered our data to TV channels in other markets, and some of them put us on the air three times a day. It took all of 2010 to make the US map good."[39]

Levine offers a contrarian view—not to go to the US as your first global market. "After you've conquered the local market, you need to go to a large market you can win, markets like Brazil, Mexico, or Indonesia. You need a market where you can work public relations to your advantage, where user acquisition is cheap, and there is low competition. It turned out that Waze's earlier successes were in the Czech Republic, Ecuador, and Slovakia. Even though we've never specifically targeted these countries or made any special efforts, it simply happened and it went very well. We understood that Waze works best where there are no alternatives. The US isn't simple, and it's also expensive; you can't launch a consumer app without a lot of capital, and thus you should only do it when the company is ready and at the right timing."[40]

THE OPERATIONAL IMPLICATIONS OF HAVING A THREE-PERSON MULTINATIONAL

At least in its initial phases, the company may not have a thorough understanding of the mentality, language, or culture of its target market. Product and market research and especially competitive analysis, the cornerstone of a good plan, can be done using the internet. The rest will require travel. The implications of this are unavoidable. Your startup will need:

- **More capital:** A three-person multinational should have a very significant travel budget. The core of the model we're discussing in this book involves constantly touching the market, testing initial versions of product offerings with customers, and soliciting market feedback. This can't happen if you're trying to save on travel costs.
- **Someone on the team with international experience:** One question you will need to ask very early on is whether your team has international experience. Have any of its members worked at a large multinational enterprise? Have they operated overseas? Did they sell to multinationals? Did they live abroad? Can they speak the language well enough to be able to present and sell? Do you have someone who can open doors, network, and get to the right people, at the right organizations?

From the investor's standpoint, it is important that the entrepreneur is able to cross the cultural barrier and understand what they are hearing. Having experience in the US is a plus. If they don't, the work of the investor will need to be hands-on. Many early stage Israeli investors accompany founders to their first business development meetings in the US. A less-experienced entrepreneur may not know how to interpret the phrase "it's interesting." It can mean what it says, but it can also be a polite refusal.

I once worked with an entrepreneur who had a meeting with eBay in the US and they had expressed, according to him, an interest in a business deal. Whenever we talked about his company's progress, he reminded us that eBay was interested—how could we be worried over product-market fit? Finally, we asked him to contact eBay and schedule a meeting to move things forward, and to make sure they knew we were coming all the way from Israel just to speak to them. eBay's response said it all. They said we shouldn't make the effort, as they still had many internal discussions to conduct and issues to resolve, and it was not a top priority—that was their way of saying no.

You can't expect all the members of the team to have strong experience in the target foreign market. But one of them has to. The skill gap can also be addressed through the advisory board, or hiring someone local, effectively outsourcing local experience and local knowledge. However, this should be done carefully, and without ceding control of important aspects of the company to someone external to it. Investors can help with this as well, by leveraging their contacts with relevant multinationals.

SPEAK ENGLISH!

Have you ever wondered why, even though Tolstoy's *Anna Karenina* and Dostoyevsky's *Crime and Punishment* were both written in Russian, so much of their dialogue is in French? This reflects the reality of life in the nineteenth-century Russian aristocracy, in which French was widely spoken and conferred social status on the speaker. French governesses were imported to teach children the language.

English is the *lingua franca* of the technology world, and startups should speak it. Being a three-person multinational also has a linguistic impact on the day-to-day business of the company. Most Israeli startups manage all their documents in English: product requirement descriptions, presentations, agreements (including employment agreements), emails, everything. This makes it much simpler for a foreign investor to join later on. If they want to track board resolutions, contracts, past presentations, or any other materials, that will be no problem. Presentations are in English, even if they are subsequently explained in Hebrew. Emails are sent in English. Staff become immersed in English and overcome any fear of the language they might have. Like French with the Russian aristocracy in the nineteenth century, English is a marker of prestige—sending emails in Hebrew is as uncool as it would be if Vronsky spoke Russian at a tea party.

And one small piece of advice: when you use a second language as the first language of your business, there are some things you have to be wary of. Don't translate idioms literally. Don't assume that all metaphors, slang, and similes are universal. Don't say, "He's in a movie," when you're talking to an American (the Hebrew meaning of the phrase is that a person is living in their own private fantasy; an American won't necessarily understand that), and don't say, "You don't understand" (meaning exactly that, but saying so directly is considered very rude in the US). Don't assume that because you've been emailing in English for the past three years, you can freely communicate in English slang—some things are best left to native speakers.

WHEN TO MOVE AND HOW

Generally speaking, the company should consider moving some or all of its management team to the target market fairly early on—ideally, about twelve to eighteen months after being funded. This is a strategic decision that will impact the company's business, its understanding of the market, and even its valuation at later rounds.

Bardin, Waze's CEO, recommends moving the CEO or founder. This person should be able to take any meeting, make decisions on the spot, and go into in-depth discussions with anyone, from investors through partners and marketing people. Because of the distance and cultural issues, Bardin emphasizes that the person moving to the Valley should not be a new hire. "At Waze, I moved to the US after working with the team in Israel for eighteen months, so we already had a pretty good relationship and trust. This is key. Do not underestimate it. The founders and I still had our share of misunderstandings, but overall, they were contained and we could openly discuss our issues based on the relationship we had developed. This is why you cannot hire an American business development person or CEO. They will be sitting out there alone and have no idea what's going on with the company. There will be constant misunderstandings, miscommunications, and frustrations. Only a founder or CEO native to the company's starting point will have the trust of its team back home."[41]

As to that person's job description, Bardin comments, "It will include flying back and forth every four to five weeks. Nothing beats face time and you must preserve your relationship with the team, bringing them your feedback, hearing their feedback, eating dinner together, going out, and maintaining personal bonds." He admits it is challenging, but insists that it's a must. On the other hand, Bardin recommends flying key members of the Israel team to the US and vice versa, so they will get to know the product and network with their peers. "At Waze, every new hire must fly to Israel early on and spend a week working there. Nothing can replace spending time together, going out as a unit, and feeling like a true part of the team early in your tenure."[42]

An additional consideration for the timing of the move is the extent to which the company's goals and products are clear. Launching from the US beats making a product launch from Israel, and raising an A round from foreign investors is easier when one of the company's founders resides in the US. "You can probably raise an angel round without physically being there, but the odds of raising an A round from a top-tier investor is very low unless you have a local presence. Make sure you are well established and connected before you start your A round search. It is much easier for investors to swallow an 'I live in Palo Alto and the tech team is in Israel' than 'I will move after I raise my round and can only meet on the twenty-ninth,'" says Bardin.[43]

Once there, the main point is to go out and meet the locals. "It is very easy to sit alone in an office in Palo Alto every day and not meet anyone, but then you might as well have stayed at home. There are lots of events to go to and people to meet. That's why you are here!"

11

DANCING WITH MAMMOTHS—HOW STARTUPS CAN THRIVE BY PLAYING ON THE SAME FIELD AS TECHNOLOGY GIANTS

Be so good they can't ignore you. —STEVE MARTIN

Beyond state-funded military research and development, technology training in Israel's intelligence services, and the existence of leading universities like The Technion, a significant part of Israel's success as a startup nation is due to the fact that many of the world's largest and most innovative tech companies opened subsidiaries and research centers in the country early on, some of them almost forty years ago. The initial impetus toward establishing a presence in Israel typically came from Israeli expats, who were longing to return home from the US. They, in turn, convinced their companies, with a dose of Chutzpah combined with an extreme form of local patriotism, that setting up shop in Israel would be a great move. For many of those companies, Israel was their first foreign development facility.

Take Intel. In 1974, it established a small office in Haifa, an hour's drive from Tel Aviv, where the microprocessor for the first IBM personal computer was developed.[1] In the 1980s, Intel set up a huge fab in Jerusalem, which became responsible for a large part of the company's output.[2] With ten thousand people, Intel is Israel's largest privately held employer today.[3]

Dov Frohman is the reason Intel came to Haifa. He began his career at Fairchild Semiconductor; and then followed Gordon Moore, Robert Noyce, and Andrew Grove into newly founded Intel. In 1970, he invented EPROM (Erasable Programmable Read Only Memory), a key innovation that led to the personal computer, since it enabled memory chips that were both nonvolatile (i.e., will not erase when the power is off) yet reprogrammable. (Other nonvolatile chips were capable of being programmed just once.) Intel founder Gordon Moore called Frohman's invention, for which he was awarded the IEEE's Edison Medal, "as important in the development of the microcomputer industry as the microprocessor itself."[4]

When Frohman decided to return to Israel, he convinced Intel to let him set up the design center in Haifa. The year of its founding is worthy of note—in 1973, Israel had fought the Yom Kippur War, which traumatized the nation with a reminder of its vulnerability. The following year, 1974, was bleak, with social unrest, unhappiness with the ruling elites, and a strong sense of disillusionment. Nevertheless, Intel took the risk. In 1991, when Israel was under Scud-missile attack, Frohman made the decision to keep Intel Israel open, against the government's advice. In a *Harvard Business Review* article, "Leadership under Fire," Frohman justified his decision, arguing that Intel Israel needed to prove to its parent company that it could operate no matter what military threats it faced.

> In subsequent years, whenever we got any pushback about doing major projects in Israel, it was always helpful to remind our colleagues that, as the experience during the war had demonstrated, "Intel Israel delivers, no matter what."[5]

The role of these multinational tech companies goes far beyond developing local talent and fertilizing the startup ecosystem. Multinationals are gateways through which local startups can build an international presence. They do this by rapidly iterating on a product side by side with an innovation-hungry multinational. Most startups seem to skip this path, fearing a bear hug from the larger player or coercive contracts that will leach value from the startup. But large-tech companies highly appreciate startups and don't necessarily want a cut of the deal. Some base their innovation strategies on startups as much as on their internal R&D divisions, and are even establishing local accelerators that have been game changers in the Israeli ecosystem over the past five years.

Let's look at Microsoft as an example. Microsoft's Israeli center, its first outside the US, was established in 1991, immediately after the Gulf War.[6] In 2012, Steve Ballmer, Microsoft's CEO at the time, said that Microsoft employs more workers per capita in Israel than anywhere else on earth, and that "the range of innovative things that Israel is doing is remarkable . . . there is always something to challenge us here, or one that we can acquire."[7]

In 2012, Microsoft opened its first accelerator ever in Herzeliya, a coastal city north of Tel Aviv. This initiative was led by Tzahi (Zack) Weisfeld, the former Global Head of Microsoft for Startups.[8] Microsoft has since opened several other local accelerators in Bangalore, Beijing, Shanghai, Berlin, London, Sydney, and Seattle.[9]

Weisfeld says that historically Microsoft provided tools and support to startups through programs such as Bizspark. But it didn't open accelerators, which have created a much more robust dialogue with developers and early stage companies. From a superficial point of view, it isn't easy to understand why Microsoft would have created the accelerator in the Tel Aviv metropoline. "It was established as a not-for-profit endeavor—people were asking themselves whether this makes sense—to do all this work to make the accelerator work, and just for 'marketing,'" says Weisfeld.[10] For companies entering the Microsoft accelerator, there really are no strings attached. Microsoft doesn't take a stake in them and it doesn't force them to purchase

Microsoft services or commit to using them. Companies get credits for Microsoft services (such as the Azure cloud platform) but they don't have to make use of them. Yet, Microsoft manages the local accelerator so well that it is one of the most sought-after accelerator programs in Israel, and possibly the best.[11]

"The question we asked ourselves," Weisfeld explains, "was how we can bring Microsoft back into conversations with the best developers. We wanted to expose developers to Microsoft and also work the other way around, so that Microsoft will be exposed to new breeds of developers. . . . The initial idea was to create a program for connecting to the developer world."[12]

Weisfeld began by checking models that worked. "I went to Boston and met with accelerators there and it immediately struck me that this was a model that can create a lot of value for software entrepreneurs and for Microsoft. At Microsoft headquarters, they told me I was crazy and that we will fail miserably. I insisted."

The program Weisfeld set up is cohort-based, with a lot of mentoring and a demo day. Almost eight hundred startups went through the program, raised about $4 billion, and sixty-six of them exited (six through IPO).[13] The program doesn't require any financial commitment from startups. "We don't want to take equity in the startups," Weisfeld emphasizes. "The value we derive is far greater than the investment we could have made. We get exposure to an ecosystem and a culture."[14]

Weisfeld says that the value of the program to Microsoft is fourfold: 1) **Bringing back Microsoft into the conversation**. 2) **Building long-term trust and relationships with the best entrepreneurs.** "We really mean this," Weisfeld says. "Sometimes people tell me our accelerator is a great marketing campaign for Microsoft, but I will tell you it is much more than that. We get the opportunity to develop a deep relationship with leading entrepreneurs. One of our companies, Appixia, was acquired by Wix. The two founders are truly formidable entrepreneurs. Once the acquisition was completed, I got a phone call from one of them. He told me we had done so much for him and that we never asked for anything in return. This is valuable for us. We had a four-time entrepreneur come to us and say that in the first weeks we helped him with numerous basic decisions about the company—and I'm humbled by this feedback, because people of his caliber could easily provide mentoring services to our startups and not the other way around." 3) **Bring the best startups in the world to work with our platforms.** "We don't force anyone to choose our platforms and the Microsoft Azure Cloud," Weisfeld notes. "We just expose them to what we have. Appixia, for instance, had never worked with platforms like ours, but the exposure made them reevaluate some of their technology decisions. We've had people rewrite their code in C# so it could work with our platforms. We couldn't get this dialogue with developers beforehand." 4) **Create a feedback loop for Microsoft.** "The world is changing," Weisfeld says, "and the role of companies like Microsoft is changing too. We see thousands of applications a year and we choose just 2 percent of them. People come in from Microsoft's headquarters in Redmond to hear what the entrepreneurs are doing. I can sometimes see light bulbs go off in their heads. Sometimes our companies detect showstopper bugs or provide Microsoft product teams with valuable interactions." Weisfeld sums up: "The lesson is that an accelerator isn't a front for business development; it is the real thing."

CRAZY HEAT AND CRAZY ISRAELIS

Guy Horowitz is a General Partner at Deutsche Telekom Capital Partners, who was representing the German giant in Israel and has recently moved to the Silicon Valley. We met at a café on a very hot and humid day in late August. "Why should Germany come to Israel for technology in this crazy heat?" he asks. "It's because of those 'Crazy Israelis' who want to come back to Israel after working in the US—people who are important enough for a large-tech company to open an Israeli branch for. That's how Dov Frohman brought Intel to Israel and that's how Moshe Lichtman brought Microsoft. These branches would not have been opened otherwise, but they managed to prove one thing—there is a lot of talent in Israel. That's why large corporations like to build centers here—it's easy to get the initial talent, and talent brings more talent (their friends). For a large technology company, coming to Israel is a really easy way to get access to great talent."[15]

Horowitz's initial role in DT Israel was as a technology scout. "What does a large technology company (like Deutsche Telekom) do when they don't have global R&D and they want access to innovation? They send a scout to Israel. Now the question is, who should this scout be? Should you send a Swede, a German, or an American to Israel, or would you hire someone local? Most of the multinationals that have scouts in Israel hired locals. A local comes into the job with their existing Israeli network. I believe that at the beginning, it is less important to know the intricacies of the Deutsche Telekom business than it is to know the right people in Israel. In the past few years there is hardly a multinational technology company that doesn't employ a person here with the charter of scouting. Almost all the large technology companies have one, unless they have already acquired an Israeli company, which then plays a similar role.

"The CEO of DT didn't want an office that represents DT's interests in Israel; he wanted to bring innovation into the company. He said, and I quote, 'It is obvious that innovation won't come from within the company.' When searching for innovation, there really are two places where you must be personally present: Silicon Valley and Israel. But there's one important difference. In Silicon Valley, Deutsche Telekom is a strong European brand, but it is one of many. Americans don't need the European market for their innovation— they have a large enough local market and enough people in their own time zones. Innovating for Deutsche Telekom is not on the top of their minds. But if a startup in Israel gets a visit from Deutsche Telekom, they stand up and salute, and do whatever it takes to line DT up as a customer. Innovation for Deutsche Telekom will certainly be on the top of their minds, and the spillover effect for DT will be considerable. But before that can happen, the scout must make DT accessible. I am something like an ombudsman."[16]

"A lot of what I do as a scout is facilitation," says Horowitz. "People ask me who should they speak to and I point them in the right direction. Scouting isn't just about finding interesting investment opportunities, it's about contributing to the ecosystem. I am there to answer questions for investors too. I help them understand what the status of a startup is in the context of Deutsche Telekom. The things I am proudest of are helping companies that were about to have a door shut in their faces get the access they needed. For instance, Deutsche Telekom didn't put a certain company on its shortlist because it was considered too small and undercapitalized. I helped them get onto the shortlist, which helped them get an investment, and for me that's a success. It also creates a cultural change at Deutsche Telekom, which is a form of spillover."

Horowitz explains: "Innovating for a large company is a long and painful process, there is no way around it. Large corporations don't take your innovation as it is and give you a big contract. You work hard to convince a champion in the large corporation, then you change the product to fit its needs. Decisions take a long time and that champion may change roles and suddenly everything you've done becomes irrelevant. But if you master the process, then winning a contract with Deutsche Telekom in certain technology sectors is both possible and incredibly valuable."

Why Israel? "People have a saying that in some cultures *entrepreneur* is French for *unemployed*. In Germany, stable employment is almost sacred, and in such an environment the perceived price of a startup (and especially a failed startup) is seen as too high. In Israel, even the waitress in the café has an idea for a startup. Entrepreneurship is everywhere."

EMBRACE EXTERNAL INNOVATION

Yinnon Dolev, Head of Sompo Digital Lab Israel and previously Director of Partnerships at GE Predix, knows one or two things about the moves when a startup begins dancing with a corporate gorilla. Today, he heads Sompo's digital lab in Israel. Sompo Holdings is one of Japan's biggest non–life insurance providers, providing services to more than twenty million customers across Japan. To grow innovation and improve customer experiences, Sompo launched three digital labs in Tokyo, Silicon Valley, and Tel Aviv.[17] Prior to Sompo, Dolev was part of GE's scouting team in Israel and headed its accelerator-related activities, focusing on software developers and entrepreneurs so they could create and commercialize solutions with GE as a partner.

Dolev explains how both companies played in the Israeli startup space: "We're always scouting for companies that match certain investment themes that we are interested in, like manufacturing, big data, insurance products, and more. The actual list of investment themes is continually changing."[18]

Dolev mentions that in his experience the decision to look for startups comes from a conscious decision by large multinationals to embrace innovation from startups, something that wasn't a common practice in the past. "Why are huge multinationals doing this? Seven or eight years ago no one in the companies I've seen enter the space was actively looking at external innovation. It was all about building innovation internally. But companies realize they don't have a monopoly on innovation and that there are great ideas that can come externally. Additionally, companies realize that innovation isn't just about their core products, but about the entire ecosystem they are selling into. If you're selling into an industrial plant, you need to consider the entire infrastructure around it. You have to acquire the holistic understanding that is a part of true innovation."

Dolev comments that the rapid pace of innovation in financial technologies, the internet of things (IoT), software, and analytics, is making large companies much more "startup friendly." "When I started working at large multinational corporations, we mostly thought of startups as poor little things we could help here and there. Today it is a totally different world. As part of the scouting activities I'm involved with, I make sure to involve senior leaders to act as mentors to startups and I expect to have more, since our people love to get involved with innovation. A lot of the pioneering scouting and startup work done in Israel has inspired other companies to use the same model for innovation hubs all over the world."[19]

Dolev explains that there are several ways large companies can engage with startups. The first is through investments made by a corporate venture capital fund. Such investments are made when the startup's activity is strategic for the multinational. "It doesn't mean that the startup needs to be working with the multinational on a solution, but the product should be something that's related to themes that the multinational is working on, something the multinational would like to access in the future. In order to make an investment, there needs to be an internal sponsor."

The multinational can also have a basic relationship with the startup, buying its product for internal use or to be distributed as part of a solution. This is typically applied to later-stage companies. But most importantly, corporations are looking for startups to add to their ability to disrupt traditional industries. Multinationals typically operate an acceleration program with a goal of combining a startup's innovative product with the corporate's commercial scaling capabilities. "For instance, startups can be the applications that are built on top of an ecosystem a multinational is trying to develop," Dolev says. "Startups like this because they can cooperate with a large multinational, and when this is done within an accelerator, there is no funding, and no fixed term for being in the program. The value is in the cooperation."

Asked whether startups fear being swallowed by the multinational or prohibited from cooperating with its competitors, Dolev answers: "Five years ago, a startup's biggest paranoia would be: 'How can I prevent a huge multinational company from stealing my intellectual property?' But it isn't like that today. The biggest fear that businesses big and small have today is that they are wasting time and effort. They want to get their ideas to the market as soon as possible, rather than worry about how to protect them. We're very open with the companies. You can do pioneering work with a multinational and we'll work hard to make it happen, but we can't make promises. But we do give you access to our units and to our customers. The value of that access can't be overestimated. When I started doing this, I was sure startups would require a contract with the multinational before they began development work. But when I spoke to startups, they just wanted to be in events with key stakeholders, get exposure—they were sure they'd know how to progress from there. We work hard to deliver just that.

"Don't be confused—multinationals have a lot of internal innovation, and healthy internal competition," Dolev adds. "Their research generates a lot of value. But multinationals need to know that there are a lot of great solutions out there. Sometimes 'build' is the wrong answer for a multinational; sometimes 'partner' or 'acquire' makes more sense. The organization recognizes that it is risky to build everything in-house, since you may end up building yesterday's product. Another risk is creating something that is too niche-focused and not generalized enough."

DANCING WITH GORILLAS

GE invested in ThetaRay. Dolev tells that story: "In 2012, the era of the industrial internet was just beginning, and we knew that cybersecurity was something Israeli companies knew really well. JVP's Yoav Tzruya called us in to take a look at ThetaRay. I asked the ThetaRay people to meet with our Chief Security Officer. I remember being on the phone, listening to them—they had traveled to the US to pitch him. Twenty minutes later—after a math conversation I could barely understand—the CSO sent me a text message saying, 'I'm all in.' Initially, ThetaRay was focused on cybersecurity, but we gave them an industrial data set since they are an all-purpose anomaly detection platform. They identified many issues in the factory, long before we were able to notice them with other means."[20]

"The person you are dealing with at the multinational should always be very happy with your work," says Mark Gazit, ThetaRay's CEO. "They can't lose their job over some mistake you make. And the proof of value you have with them must shine."[21] That's why ThetaRay did its proof of value with a local bank before it moved its unknown unknowns detection technology to the financial sector. "A friendly beta with a local customer is cheap and simple. You need to be aware it may not be relevant to the needs of other customers you may have, but you can afford to have some issues. It won't harm your reputation or your internal person, who is frequently referred to as 'your champion' inside the organization. When I go outside of Israel, I can't possibly afford a bad proof of value. If I have a failed proof of value with a US bank, then I can't have a POV with any other US bank after that—they all meet and compare notes. We take care to set expectations and never fail. This actually goes against the cultural grain of being Israeli. There's a joke in which someone asks an Israeli, 'Can you play the cello?' and the Israeli responds, 'Sure, let me try.' I'm also like that, but I have to resist that urge—we can only work when we are ready. There will always be mistakes, but when you go for a big POV or a large multinational, you can't afford to fail."[22]

Having a multinational investor or partner can be a great shortcut to global markets. This should, of course, come at terms that aren't detrimental for the company's marketing and business activity. It should leave it free to do business with other customers as it wishes. The company can then use the corporate investor as a customer, a design partner (i.e., a customer that is very involved in product definition), or a distributor, without having to worry that it will be limited in what it can do in the future.

"Working with a strategic investor like GE is a commitment and they get to set the rules," says Gazit. "A small movement by a gorilla can completely overrun you. It is like a large warship and a small boat beside it. But GE understood our concerns and worked with us. The access we get is amazing. I was invited to a dinner with Jeff Immelt, GE's chairman at the time. I thought the dinner would be in a huge ballroom and that I would only get to shake hands with him. Instead it was me, him, and six leaders of very large companies, talking about security and cyber issues.

"Our ability to work with the giant is what makes the difference," Gazit continues. "It is important to listen, carefully. There is a reason God gave us two ears and one mouth. That is how to work with corporates. Startups are either afraid of big corporations or very disparaging toward them. The best thing is to take them seriously."[23]

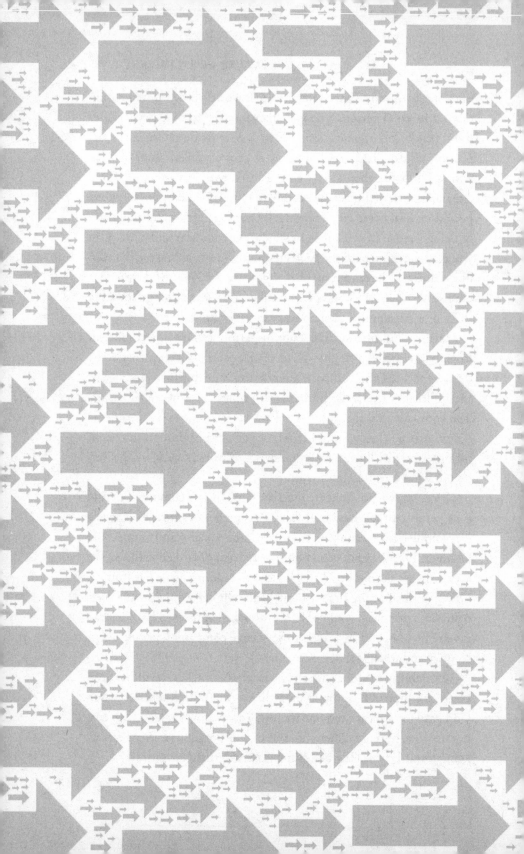

PART III
PRACTICE

12

THE EARLY STAGE
INVESTMENT CONTINUUM

In investing, what is comfortable is rarely profitable.
—ROBERT ARNOTT

On many occasions, I've heard people using the words *incubator, accelerator, company building,* and *micro-fund* in various contexts. When it comes to early stage technology companies, the meaning of the words vary significantly across different countries. This chapter focuses on the differences between the various early stage investment vehicles.

THE EARLY STAGE
INVESTMENT CONTINUUM

Startups are funded through an equity investment, in which the investors get shares of the company in return for providing it with capital. The inherent riskiness of the startup's undertaking—a business that is in an exploratory mode—makes debt financing an improbable option, since you can't realistically assume that a company without a product or actual revenues will be able to service its debt. That's why most investments are done in return for equity, or a stake in the business. If the business shuts down, the investors get nothing, but if there is an exit, they get a share in the upside.

"A lot of the work in an early stage company is to remove the question marks about the company," comments angel and venture investor Adi Pundak Mintz about his work with early stage startups. "The part I like best is the first two years—there are many unknowns, but you are building the company's DNA, creating the first presentation to customers, having the first board meeting, getting to a beta with a customer and demonstrating that the product has value."[1]

"For me, a good seed round is $1 to $2 million. It's a magic number, since it gives the company six quarters to prove something—get to initial product/market fit, show a minimum viable product [MVP], and demonstrate repeatability and an offering methodology. In my experience, a company needs more than a Series A to get to a true product-market fit. I think that number is more in the $5 million range. After the product-market fit phase, the company may need another $10 million to get to the right 'unit economics' that will allow it to scale significantly. Companies should know they won't solve all their issues with the series A funding, but they should complete as many pieces of the puzzle as possible to make an investor want to write a check for the next round of funding."[2]

Equity financing is provided by several types of players, from angel investors, through accelerators, incubators, micro-funds, venture capital funds, and sometimes by crowdfunding. It is important to mention straightaway that the "early stage investment continuum," which is the subject of this chapter, isn't about pitting one model of early stage investing against the other. It is a way of showing how they all intersect, supporting startups as they grow and gain momentum.

ANGEL INVESTING

Angels are individual investors (or a group of individual investors) who provide funding and often advice. Sometimes they are former entrepreneurs whose companies were sold or went public, who want to invest in startups and to support other entrepreneurs. Unlike accelerators, incubators, and venture funds, the help Angels offer is unstructured, varying from intense support, with the Angel spending considerable time with the company, to a hands-off approach. This is because Angels don't have a "back office" setup. Historically, Angel investments were considered a good choice to fill the gap between "friends and family" investments and full-blown venture capital support. Today, just as startups come in all shapes and sizes, so does the use of Angel investing.

Some call Angel investors amateurs. They are certainly not business amateurs, but investing may not be their main line of business. That said, many Angels perform as much due diligence as a VC would. In some cases, they are interested in more than financial returns, using their investments to stay abreast of a market they have previously been active in. Angels usually invest between $50,000 and $200,000. Some invest only in the initial round, and others participate in follow-on rounds as well.

Some Angels pool their funds, creating an "Angel group" or an "Investment Club." These groups act to give advice and support to startups in a more structured way, leveraging the power of the group for a better filtering process and investment decisionmaking.

"To be able to raise a Series A fund, what you really need is some proof that the dogs will eat the dog food the company is selling, and that it can provide it in a repeatable and scalable way," says Pundak Mintz. "However, some investments are fit for Angels only, so the first step you need to make is to decide whether the company is 'VC grade' or not.[3]

"To figure out whether a company needs Angel or venture financing, I try to wear several hats during a meeting. I try to imagine the company's Series B round and then do some backward math to its

Series A and seed round. It's like going at a maze from the end to the beginning. What is a VC-compatible company? It should have innovation that is big enough to move the needle for a VC, together with a certain type of entrepreneur with a certain star quality. This implies a certain projected exit, of course. One of the ways to understand whether this is a VC game or not is to simply ask the entrepreneur what they believe will constitute a success story for their company. Are they looking for a $10 million exit or a $1 billion-plus public company?"

Many companies that aren't VC compatible, or aren't VC compatible yet, can be a good investment proposition for Angels. "If the company isn't VC compatible, the question then becomes whether it can break even early," Pundak Mintz continues. "Angels are happy if some of their investments end up raising VC money, but for them, low-level acquisitions or breaking even early is also a good result. I believe that, in some cases, this is also a good result for an incubator, meaning that there is an entire field of companies who don't play the VC game but are still good technology investment options."

CyberArk's Udi Mokady tells a story about the Angel group that funded his company in its early days: "We raised money from Angels and we still call them Angels to this day. They participated in all the rounds we had and were great to have on board. One of them sits on our board today. Originally there were four of them, but one of them was very harsh during our first meeting. It was a dissonance, because the other three were so respectful. We took some time to think about it. We were beginning a long journey that would have many ups and downs and already there was tension. That wasn't what we wanted. We told them we would pass on their investment. They took him out of the team and the remaining three stayed."[4]

ACCELERATORS

Accelerators such as Y Combinator, Tech Stars, and 500 Startups, also known as pre-seed or seed accelerators, are programs that have several (typically two or three) "classes" or "cohorts" per year, in which a group of startups enters the program at the same time, usually after a filtering and selection process done by the accelerator. In the case of the top programs, only 1 to 3 percent of applicants are chosen. The main objective of an accelerator is to build the pre-seed startups in such a way that it will take them from pre-seed status to being able to raise seed funding.

The companies graduate together, usually after three to six months, on a "demo day," an event in which they make presentations to potential investors. If they are successful, they should be able to raise funds not long after, typically a seed round (but some exceptional companies manage a Series A round). The accelerator sometimes provides the company with a small cash investment, up to $150,000, enough to support it while it is in the program. Some don't invest any capital at all but do provide in-kind benefits and value, such as office space, mentorship, and other services. In both cases, it is in return for a share of equity, typically around 5 to 10 percent.

In some acceleration models, the accelerator does not take any equity. Such is the case with corporate accelerators or university ones.

Accelerator programs give entrepreneurs access to a network of mentors, as well as advice and training on a wide range of topics, from technology to achieving product-market fit, as well as how to fundraise, on what terms, and from whom. Some accelerators host dinners where prominent startup founders speak about their experiences. The interaction is usually confidential and the talks go unrecorded. This rule exists so that the founders won't just talk about the "bingo" moment when they got the model right or the hard work that preceded it. They are expected to speak openly about the difficulties they had along the way and their mistakes, challenges, and near-misses.

Accelerators usually offer one-on-one interaction, focused around office hours with the accelerator managers and with external mentors they bring as part of their model. Entrepreneurs can get advice on any topic, from strategy through pricing and design. In essence, the accelerator is a highly structured way to mentor and direct pre-seed companies so they can gain the ability to raise a seed round.

"When you look at accelerators and early stage company formation, very interesting things are happening," says Adi Pundak Mintz. "The background is that many barriers to entry are falling: it takes less time and less money to develop a technology product. The stuff you can accomplish today with half a million dollars required two million dollars a decade ago. This means that the market has different expectations of an early stage company. Accelerators then come into this environment of lower barriers to entry, and completely change the rules of the game. To my mind, they are a methodical way of giving many companies small sums of money and taking them through a defined process, giving them the little fuel they need to start and perhaps create a great fire. When you give companies money and a place to stay and many in-kind services, you help consolidate a process of business definition, development, and networking. Doing this in a cohort means that the participants are surrounded by a marketplace of ideas and initiatives. There are their peers and also a community of people who can help them—mentors, corporates, and other important contacts. There is the saying 'it takes a village to raise a child.' . . . In this case the village is the accelerator."[5]

"Accelerators allow people to experience startup entrepreneurship as a learning opportunity that almost replaces going to graduate school," Pundak Mintz concludes. "Instead of working or studying as a young person, accelerators offer a third way of developing and they make the cost of failure miniscule, almost positive. In effect, accelerators commoditize or standardize the path to entrepreneurship."

INCUBATORS

Incubators follow right after the accelerators; they are the "post-accelerator" vehicle. If accelerators are focusing on startups at their pre-seed phase, incubators are focusing on startups at their seed stage. While the main objective of an accelerator is to bring the company to fundraise their seed funding, the main objective of an incubator is to bring the company from seed status to a Series A investment.

Most companies begin as a dream or a vision ("wouldn't it be great if [fill in the blank]"), then the company building begins. The pre-seed and the seed investment are supposed to fund the dream phase, but if the company doesn't provoke some initial interest from the market, the chances of it going on to raise an A round are small. *A dream is what you sell in the seed stage. A company is what you sell in round A.* The incubator's role is to assist the startup in moving from the dream phase to the operational phase, from a vision to a company.

Moving from a "dream company" to an operational one is one of the most challenging and crucial phases in the life of a startup. When the seed money is finished and the company can't raise a Series A round, the company is in trouble. Some people call this "the valley of death" or the "Series A crunch," meaning that the startup did not manage to show enough market traction to convince A round investors to get on board. Around 60 percent of companies that raise Pre-Series A funding fail to make it to Series A or beyond.[6]

"One of the ways to think about Israel's startup ecosystem is to depict it as one enterprise funded by many investors," says Pundak Mintz. "This enterprise generates nearly a thousand new startups a year—and several hundred of them have managed to prove something that is interesting enough that they are able to get to the next level of funding. After that, tens of them get the next check. These are the companies that are mature enough for a Series A round."[7]

This is exactly where incubators fit in: to help companies build a team, create a differentiated product, and plan a go-to-market strategy that validates the market. Even if a startup has a perfect pitch, it is typically lacking in one or more of these areas. Incubators start where accelerators finish.

Incubators also offer more capital. More capital provides the company with more time compared to the brief stint at an accelerator. An incubator is a distinct form of early stage investing that combines the rigorous program often offered by an accelerator with considerable funding, typically between $500,000 and $1.5 million. This funding should last at least eighteen months, the average time a startup will spend at the incubator, and in most cases, it is taken through a highly structured process. This will be explained in depth in the next chapter.

Commenting on the difference between incubators and accelerators, Liran Tancman of CyActive says, "The obvious difference between an accelerator and an incubator is funding, of course. An accelerator gives you many apples to eat, in terms of the depth of the program and the support. But it doesn't give you the teeth to eat the apples, because you don't have the money. Just like cars can't work without fuel, startups need money to grow."[8]

Incubators occupy a unique position on the early stage investment continuum, between accelerators and venture-backed Series A rounds, and somewhat alongside Angel investing. The incubator provides the time, money, and program that lets startups leapfrog the extremely difficult and deep chasm between an early idea and a fundable company.

SERIES A ROUND

"Series A Round" is the common term used to describe the stock offered by a company in its first venture capital round. Typically, the amount invested ranges from $2 to $10 million, giving the company runway for a period of eighteen to thirty months in which it can develop its products, establish some market presence, grow its employee base, and develop its business operations. The investment typically gives the Series A investors 10 to 25 percent of the company's stock.

Before a company can raise its Series A round, its core pillars need to be in place:

- The **product** should be in beta phase or general availability.
- The **market** should be initially validated (through design partnerships, beta customers, or other forms of market traction).
- A **go-to-market plan** needs to be in place (hopefully with some proven sales and marketing personnel as part of the team).
- The **management team** should be in place or identified.

If the company has proven an initial scalable and repeatable business model, and has initial revenues that prove the product-market fit, the chances of raising its Series A round are high (although there's a good chance that additional rounds of funding Series B, C, and D, may still be needed).

In most cases the investors want to know what use the proceeds will be put to. Such uses can include research and development for the product, building or expanding the sales team, engaging with business partners and distribution channels, and, of course, expanding the company's human resources. All of these should enable the company to grow, scale, and gain more market traction and market share.

Series A investors check whether the company is ready to scale, whether it knows how to do so, and whether the plan is a fit with their risk profile. They typically do not look to be involved with the company on the execution side (truly being part of the team), but rather apply governance through a board position to make sure the company is on the right track. In many respects, the same logic applies to raising Series B and C rounds as well.

There are exceptions, of course. Sometimes the company was founded by a successful serial entrepreneur and can raise an A round just based on an idea they have, since they have already proven that they know how to successfully build, develop, and exit a startup. In other cases, a company may have a unique, innovative, and breakthrough technology, or a very strong intellectual property that will enable it to raise a VC round A funding. Sometimes the product is in a sector with product or technology characteristics that require considerable funding and where there is no way to launch simply and cheaply. An example of such an expensive sector is semiconductors, which are notoriously costly to develop.

A NOTE ABOUT COMPANY BUILDERS, MICRO-FUNDS, AND CROWDFUNDING

There are other vehicles existing in the market that are not as common as the above, but are worth mentioning.

Company builders: As the name suggests, these are pre-seed vehicles that are involved from the conceptualization of the company. The managers are usually highly involved and take a full part from the ideation phase all the way to recruiting the team, building the product, and launching it to the market. Some company builders have in-house capabilities such as R&D, design, sales, business development, and marketing. These services are given to the companies being built, each service at the timing that suits the company. Since these startups are being conceived there, and most of the seed-capital is coming from them, the company builders usually take a significant equity in the company, and in some cases even take the position of cofounders.

Micro-funds: This is a vehicle that is structured like venture capital, but the total size is not as large as the common VCs. The average size of a micro-fund would be $20 to $50 million, and the average initial check will be around $250,000 to $750,000. Micro-funds usually invest in pre-seed or seed stage startups, and try to be highly involved with the development of their companies. Similarly to large VCs, they usually leave an allocation of 40 to 50 percent of their fund for follow-on investments, so they can keep their position in the company.

Crowdfunding: Online crowdfunding platforms have become alternative places for startups to get funding or at least prove market traction.

Companies can post product pitches at crowdfunding sites, regardless of their development status, as long as they are described properly and without misleading information. Returns for the investors are in most cases not financial—the owner keeps 100 percent ownership of the company. Investors get credits, perks, and a product.

3D printers were funded through crowdsourcing, which brought the product to the attention of the general public. In rare cases, the amount of funds raised by crowdfunding are no different than a Series A investment. Formlabs, an MIT spin-off, raised nearly $3 million on Kickstarter from over two thousand backers, which allowed the company to grow from a three-person team to thirty-five people.[9] Backers got printers shipped to them and Formlabs later received a large Series A round of $19 million.[10] The company has raised a total of $103.7 million in funding over seven rounds and in 2018 it has became a unicorn with a valuation of over $1 billion.

Crowdsourcing removes some of the barriers to funding by enabling companies to prove consumer interest early on. This is especially interesting in certain segments like consumer hardware—such as a new type of earphones for example. Consumer hardware products can find it almost impossible to get access to funds through VC or an Angel—who will want hard data on consumer acceptance, unit costs, distribution channels, and go-to-market. Crowdfunding makes it possible to get an early read on all four.

The diagram below shows the Early Stage Investment Continuum:

ACCELERATOR	INCUBATOR	VENTURE CAPITAL— A ROUND
• Up to $150K investment • A 3–4 month structured process • Next target: to fund a seed round • Startup maturity: very low	• $500K–1.5M investment • Semi-structured process • Next target: Series A funding • Startup maturity: low	• $2–10M investment • Unstructured, board seat if applicable • Next target: Series B or early acquisition • Maturity: moderate
Angels, company builders, micro-funds, and crowdfunding: average of $100–500K investment in a low–moderate startup maturity with the goal of reaching Series A or breakeven.		

*In all the stages above, there is also an option for a strategic investor to join the round. This usually means an enterprise that is interested in the technology, the product, and the proposition, and wants to have equity in the venture.

It's important to note that the company's "runway" (i.e., the oper-ations period funded by the investment) may last from several months to a few years, depending on the amount raised and the company's spending rate (also known as "burn rate"). But time and money aren't the main differences between the potential funders, and it's not that some startup founders are lucky and get venture capital money and the rest don't. Each model focuses on a different stage in the contin-uum, from "the big idea" to a "repeatable and scalable business model," and each phase poses a different risk-reward profile and in-vestment thesis.

INVESTMENT BUSINESS MODELS—FROM the accelerator through the incubator to the venture capital fund—are about fitting investors and investment types with companies. Startup investing occurs in "a marketplace for innovation—for people seeking innovation and the people that are creating innovation," says Pundak Mintz.[11] Deutsche Telekom Capital Partners' Guy Horowitz, who used to be Deutsche Telekom's technology scout, explains the marketplace for innovation from the point of view of a large company: "What drives giants like Deutsche Telekom to scout for technology innovation isn't just about discovering this innovation or that. What's import-ant is creating a spillover effect. When Deutsche Telekom gets access to the Israeli innovation ecosystem, it, too, becomes accessible, cre-ating a chain of innovation both inside and outside the company, in a way that is meaningful to us. We know that innovation of that sort just can't happen at Deutsche Telekom, and we know we can access it here."[12]

One of the core questions an investor has about a company is how well advanced it is in proving its underlying idea and how quickly it can show market traction that will support that thesis. This is because any early stage investment is about taking a startup from point A to point B, and then to points C and D, each phase further proving that the startup can execute on its vision. Point A is where the company is now, and it matches a certain amount of funds it can raise from a certain type of early stage technology investor in the innovation marketplace. When the company reaches point B, it will be able to raise more funds along the investment continuum line, perhaps from a different type of investor. The funds required by companies typically grow as they progress from phase to phase. As the companies grow, so do their staffs, and the burn rate becomes higher.

Investors fund startups so that the startups will begin to prove their business model, by moving from point A to point B. If the startup's business model is proven to be repeatable and scalable, it is safe to assume that future funding will be provided. The closer the company is to proving its model, the more value investors will associate with it and the more money it can raise; it also follows that the company's valuation will be higher. This is one aspect of the early stage investment continuum—the more proof, the more funding. Proving the model can be many things: it may be getting to a critical mass with millions of users; selling to several enterprise clients who think the product is interesting and valuable; getting to breakeven; becoming an industry standard; or just getting enough traction in the market to make a convincing case for the next funding round. This "proof" is one of the key factors when choosing the investment type.

Liran Tancman, the cofounder and CEO of CyActive, describes the process of fundraising—from both venture capital funds and JVP's incubator—and the proof he and his partner were required to provide in the process. Since Tancman and his cofounder, Shlomi Boutnaru, were aware of how inexperienced they were, and weren't sure their pitch was good, they "decided to first go to all the venture capital funds where there was a very low likelihood we could raise money."[13] They wanted to practice.

At that point, Tancman and Boutnaru had a PowerPoint presentation, and one they both recognized as fairly geeky, maybe too geeky. "These people can waste your time by not deciding to invest, so we thought we might as well waste their time, too, and begin learning how to pitch," says Tancman. "Shlomi also insisted that we go to an investor meeting only if we understood what we did wrong in the prior meeting we had with an investor, and only after we made sure we fixed it." They were testing the waters and learning to swim at the same time, and their plan of action is a highly recommended one for first-time entrepreneurs.

Yet the presentation and the iterations didn't take them far. "About six months passed and nothing happened. At a certain point, it became evident that we could not raise money without a proof of concept. If there is one thing I learned in the Intelligence Corps, it was that to make people believe in an idea, nothing helps more than a quick and dirty POC." Luckily for Tancman and Boutnaru, Israel's government supports innovation. They applied for a Tnufa Grant. The Tnufa Program, funded by the government's Israel Innovation Authority, is designed to encourage and support entrepreneurs in their initial efforts to build prototypes, register patents, design business plans, and so on.[14] Grants are up to 85 percent of the approved expenses for a maximum of $50,000 for each project. Just as Tancman and Boutnaru sensed they were getting stuck, they received a letter in the mail saying they had qualified for Tnufa funds. That grant and the POC that it paid for are what drove JVP to make its initial CyActive investment, culminating in an exit less than eighteen months later.[15]

As Tancman and Boutnaru began having meetings with the managers of the incubator, they honed their story. "The meetings were valuable," says Tancman. "JVP's Yoav Tzruya de-bugged our pitch with their questions and rejects, so by just listening to them we got better and better." It wasn't just their pitch that got better; they refined the ideas behind CyActive. "Once the startup begins working, the initial idea doesn't stay the same and it doesn't change slightly. Once you begin, the idea undergoes substantial changes."[16]

Funding decisions aggregate a host of factors, such as the investors' expectations of the company, the risks involved in it, what level of involvement it will require from investors, and whether all of the above fit specific investor preferences. But for purposes of mapping the early stage investment continuum, the main questions are the status of the company pre-investment and the expectation of where that investment will bring the company. An early stage company should plan not only the current round of investing but also the next one, and should make sure that each funding round is sufficient to bring it to the next one.

13

THE THREE PHASES
OF STARTUP GROWTH

*Only those who will risk going too far can possibly
find out how far one can go.* —T. S. ELIOT

Now that we know what kinds of funding and services are available to startups during their earliest phases, it's time to take a deeper look at what happens during their incubation.

To understand this process, it is important to remember that early stage companies must finalize their product, launch it, and get initial market traction very quickly. That is virtually the only way they can raise a Series A round. Getting there requires a diligent and thorough process of experimentation, covering all the different moving parts of a technology startup: the vision, the product, the business model, the go-to-market, the distribution channels, and the many underlying assumptions supporting them. This constant process of tweaking and refining the product and the value proposition occurs in three phases. Everyone who is involved with the company—the founders, its management, the board of directors, and the advisory board—has a role to play during the process. When it is done well, it lays the foundation for a successful company.

One of the ways to get the most out of the incubation period, which is usually eighteen to twenty-four months long, is to break it into three distinct six-month phases, each of which is a step in the direction of the Series A funding round. These three distinct phases are applicable to any seed or post-seed company with financing of $1 to $2 million that's supposed to support twelve to twenty-four months of operation; they aren't applicable just to incubator-funded companies, but to any company whose funding and state are similar.

SOME PREREQUISITES FOR INCUBATOR FUNDING

Companies and their investors must be in substantial agreement on what the company's vision, strategy, and go-to-market are. Before an incubator invests in a company, it would expect to have a mutually agreed-upon operational plan that will take the company through the next eighteen months. The plan should be aligned with the time and financial constraints set by the investment itself.

As Liran Tancman explained in Chapter 12, the process of fundraising typically sparks a continuous process of evolving the product vision and operational plan, as well as a full-fledged proof of concept (or more, when the market demands additional proof prior to investment, for instance the ability to create user interest, deploy beta product with corporate customers, and more). This means that when the company receives funding, it is already equipped with an operational plan and a product vision. It doesn't, however, mean that those plans can't and won't be changed. As we'll show in this chapter, the three-phase process involves experimentation, changes, and in some cases even pivoting.

On day zero, the company's management and its investors should see eye-to-eye on the strategic choices and opportunities the company is facing, what the company is, and where it is supposed to fit in the value chain. The company's plan should combine an ambitious vision with a detailed operational plan and objectives; the end result should make the company—if everything goes well—a category leader in its space. The plan should contain the high-level goals and lower-level tasks required to achieve them, including the measurement and tracking of these goals and tasks.

Some people believe that the vision and the operational plan have no connection, that the vision is a theoretical and aspirational exercise, and that the operational plan is the actual plan the company is committing to. This is not the right way to map the relationship between the vision and the operational plan. The vision is what drives the company's beginnings, and is at its core and DNA. The operational plan should be a translation of this vision into practical and operational actions. It should include an R&D and product road map, human resources plan, marketing plan, business development plan, go-to-market strategy, business model, and more.

Now let's see what each of the three phases consists of.

Months 0–6. Phase 1: Product Building

The first six months represent the "product building" phase. This phase is internally focused, with the company preparing those elements of the product that will allow it to prove that the market responds well to it. The most important thing to define at this phase is the MVP—minimum viable product. Eric Ries defines the MVP as "that version of a new product which allows a team to collect the maximum amount of validated learning about customers with the least effort."[1] Ash Maurya, the author of *Running Lean* and *Scaling Lean,* defines it this way: "The smallest thing you can build that delivers customer value (and as a bonus captures some of that value back)."[2] What "capturing some of that value back" means is that if there is a revenue model, then the MVP process should include getting paid by the potential customer as a tangible proof of the value of the MVP.

The MVP is not so much a final product as a strategy to enable fast testing based on quantitative and qualitative data. This doesn't mean that the product itself is minimal, containing just one feature, or that it is a super-simple eight-hour-coding project. The MVP can be demanding technologically and very ambitious in its use case and even feature set. "Minimum" means that it has the minimum subset of features that allow it to be deployed to possible early adopter customers who can then be engaged to generate feedback regarding the product and the revenue model.

Defining the scope of the MVP is a challenge, since on the one hand it should consist of enough features and demonstrate enough technology to ensure that the feedback from the market will be valuable. On the other hand, it shouldn't take too long to develop or be too expensive, nor should it include any great detours from the product road map. The company does not want to be in a position where the MVP was too minimal, and thus did not accurately reflect the end product. It also wants to avoid launching a product that may require significant iterations after the launch, resulting in wasted development efforts.

One may find this confusing. Why can't the company take a little more time and show a more fully developed product to its customers? Won't they be more receptive to that? The reason behind the MVP approach is to avoid investing in a product no one wants, or planning a go-to-market strategy that is based on underlying assumptions that cannot pass a reality test. Instead of approaching the market with a complete yet flawed product that took the full funding of the first eighteen months to develop, the company can test a partial product, get valuable market feedback, and save time and money. This way, the company will go to market with a better product and reach a better business outcome at the end of the same eighteen months.

As Steve Blank says, "A minimum viable product [MVP] is not always a smaller/cheaper version of your final product. Defining the goal for an MVP can save you tons of time, money, and grief."[3] He illustrates this with a great example. If you were to sell a service that consisted of photographs made by a drone—for instance, a service to farmers that would use the pictures from the drone to assess the health of their crops—the MVP shouldn't necessarily involve creating a working drone with a high-resolution camera mounted on it. For purposes of market feedback, it might be better to rent a small plane, take the pictures, and engage with farmers. That is why Blank concludes that the MVP is an opportunity for smart learning and not necessarily a cheaper product.

Eric Ries discusses how Dropbox dealt with their MVP: "Dropbox needed to test its leap-of-faith question: If we can provide a superior customer experience, will people give the product a try?" This is not the kind of question you can get a good answer to from a focus group. Customers often don't know what they want, and they had a hard time understanding Dropbox when the concept was explained to them. "Dropbox believed—rightly, as it turned out—that file synchronization was a problem that most people didn't know they had."[4] Once they experienced the solution themselves, they couldn't imagine how they ever lived without it.

The problem was that making the Dropbox product work seamlessly was no simple feat. There was no way the MVP could include all the features that would eventually be built into it. Instead, they created a three-minute video in which Drew Houston, the Dropbox CEO, demonstrated it to potential early adopters.[5] The results were amazing: the beta waiting list went from 5,000 to 75,000 almost overnight.[6] The Dropbox team now knew that it was developing something the market wanted, and not something that only their friends and family would use.

According to Eric Ries, the MVP is not just a product definition, but a process that consists of learning, building, and measuring.[7] This process requires effort and discipline. Rather than staying at the company's offices and developing more and more features, dreaming of a perfect product, companies have to subject themselves to a rigorous process that challenges their core assumptions. Rather than have a team of engineers play around with technology and make it work, they sometimes have to forgo the fun part and find an MVP (such as a video) that can prove it will be worthwhile to spend all the time that will be needed to play with the technology. This is how companies succeed, and it is crucial to make the process in this first phase an effective and a fruitful one.

Done well, the MVP and its resulting iterations can create traction with customers earlier and with a better chance of meeting their needs and expectations than would have been feasible if the company had waited for a finished product. Companies can be very creative in carrying out the MVP process. For instance, some companies create a webpage for a product that doesn't exist, to measure clicks and willingness to pay. For companies in the service business, an MVP may be an offer to manually perform a service that can later be performed automatically.

All of this needs to be measured with sound statistics-based analytics to verify each hypothesis. The early days at a startup shouldn't be chaotic, but rigorously structured to test its propositions via A/B testing and real-time market feedback. This is also when the company needs to invest in understanding its competition and their products at a very detailed level, so it can better understand the added value it gives its users, and refine the competitive edge it has or should develop in order to win. This competitive edge can be at the level of technology, the business model, pricing, features, user-interface (UI), user-experience (UX), or any other level. Product management and R&D management are extremely important during the first phases; the sales and marketing management will be more relevant in later phases.

It is important to note that in most technology startups there is an inherent tension between product management and R&D. The product team defines *what the product should be* and has a long list of requests; the R&D team defines *what the product can be*, given the time and resource limitations the company has. While R&D tends to prevail—limiting the product to engineering realities—the company's senior management team must tune the product road map between what can be and should be achieved, and it's better to lean on the side of aspirations. At the same time, it's important to remember that both sides represent a legitimate perspective—they both serve one company and one goal, and the tension between them should never be allowed to devolve into an unnecessary war of egos.

R&D should always bear in mind that the product has to be associated with a user experience and user interface, and that both are inseparable from the core value of the product. You cannot afford to only focus on technology and assume the rest is boring or inessential. Product management, on the other hand, should find creative work-arounds relating to real R&D limitations.

When developing the product, even at a bare-bones MVP level, the company should also consider infrastructure development. Most web software and mobile products require a scalable back end. Even though the product is new and in its beta phase, without a proper infrastructure it will not be able to scale massively and quickly. This is why the MVP development should address the cornerstones of the technology infrastructure, ensuring that the scaling process will be efficient.

The first phase ends with an MVP that will be used for initial validation. The company should be able to test its technology and obtain meaningful user feedback that isn't just about what's missing in the product but the entire product experience, proposition, pricing, and use case. This isn't to imply that the whole company needs to be launched. It can still stay under the radar in what is frequently referred to as "stealth mode," and its beta can be a closed one.

The extent of the beta or product pilot depends on whether it is a consumer or an enterprise play. For software or a product that targets enterprise customers, the goal is to be able to get a pilot with a potential client and have a product that is stable enough to enable its potential user to assess it and understand its value proposition. Sometimes the product will have to generate revenue for the process to be complete. For consumer-focused products the goal is to prove consumer interest through measurable parameters such as user engagement, user retention, the ratio between DAU (daily active users) and MAU (monthly active users), etc. Another important aspect of this phase is to try to learn as much as possible about future user acquisition methodologies and costs.

Months 6 to 12. Phase 2: Initial Market Validation

Creating the MVP in the first phase allows the company to continue refining its product and proposition in the second. Here the company should begin work on validating everything it can, such as customer acquisition channels, cost of customer acquisition, the length of the sales cycle, conversion rates, retention rates, engagement rates, etc. For a consumer product, six months may not be enough time to learn about lifetime and lifetime value of a user or customer, but it can give an initial hunch where the numbers are going, especially if users give up on the service or product after the first or second use. In an enterprise product, six months should be a reasonable period of time to enable a product pilot or a POC with a purchase decision at its end. It's worth noting here that to be efficient during the second phase, market preparations should have been taken care of during the first phase—i.e., finding potential pilot partners for an enterprise company, or preparing a marketing plan and defining a few optional user acquisition channels for a consumer-oriented product.

ONCE A COMPANY begins to receive feedback from the market and its users, it should iterate constantly. Iterations can be product changes or tweaks, UI or UX design improvements, performance optimizations, different business models, new pricing strategies, and so on. This is an ongoing process: you try something, get feedback, make changes, get feedback, respond, get feedback, make changes, and so on. This is a never-ending process in any company's life, but it is done more intensively at this phase.

One should beware of placing too much emphasis on the feedback of too few individuals or one enterprise. Not all the feedback you will get is crystal clear or meaningful. Some companies, typically enterprise-related startups, may become enamored with the feedback of one large enterprise customer. They should distinguish between input that represents a very private-use case relevant to one enterprise, and inputs that represent a large swath of the market and are likely to represent many potential customers.

Ido Yablonka founded a company called ClarityRay. Until very recently he was Yahoo Israel's vice president and general manager, and previously its head of ad security. "Our initial premise for ClarityRay was that ads on the web may cross the line and annoy consumers, thus compromising user engagement," he says. "Given that, we reasoned that users should be willing to spend a little money for an ad-free web experience. This was our theory and we thought it made a whole lot of sense, as did our investor from which we had just raised $500,000; yet, three months into the process, we noticed that users simply did not convert and weren't willing to pay for the removal of ads, at least not anywhere near the rates our plan required."[8] That ClarityRay's MVP wasn't working well was obvious. But what was Yablonka and his team supposed to do about it?

"We had to figure out why users weren't converting. One of our hypotheses was that, instead of paying us, users used free pirated ad blockers, considered an utterly negligible phenomenon back then. And yet, we had to verify—what else are we to do, go home? Critically and honestly investigating where you went wrong isn't an easy process: the uncertainty and moreso the reflexivity are emotionally challenging. Since we had the technical integration in place, we were able to rigorously measure how many people used ad blockers, thereby preventing publishers from realizing ad revenue. At the time, the industry's conventional wisdom assumed that these ad blockers were used by about half a percent of users, implying it was a nonissue, a rounding error. Yet, we discovered something that no one knew yet—that the actual rate of website visitors using ad blockers was a remarkable 10 percent on average, and in some cases as high as 60 percent. The problem we had set out to solve was in effect already fully solved by users."[9]

Yablonka and his partners now had to figure out what to do with this new knowledge and how to leverage it so they could make it into an interesting market offering. "Pirated ad blockers, pervasive as they turned out to be, were nothing short of an existential threat to publishers, which the industry was, perhaps blissfully, unaware of. The problem seemed to define a solution technological in nature. How do you block an ad blocker? We quickly figured out how to do just that, developed the product, and registered the intellectual property." Having decided to pivot and switch sides, ClarityRay then set out to reinvent itself, using a lot of Chutzpah in both its communications to the market and its product offering.

"Galileo got a device, the telescope, that gave him information arguably no one had before—and within days, in a sense, he knew more about astronomy than all humanity before him," says Yablonka. "For us it was the ability to see how prevalent ad blockers really were. But how do we best leverage that key insight? We assumed that there were ten competitors out there who were at least as smart as we were, concluding that market domination would likely belong to the first company to widely pop the ad blocker bubble, go public with the real problem size, and become synonymous with the pain—and that's exactly what we did." Their first act of Chutzpah was to publish research on the state of the industry, turning themselves from a "nobody" to a prophet of doom who couldn't be ignored. "This created a crazy amount of leads for us, including from high-end clients we were unlikely to reach otherwise, as well as a highly effective sales funnel," Yablonka says. It positioned the company as the leader in its space.

The next step was the product definition. The company developed a technology that discovered, in real time, what ad blocker the user had, and either circumvented it or sent a message to the user. Instead of simply trying to directly sell the product to publishers, it instead offered them a free report on how many of their users were using ad blockers. "I will give you a free report revealing a fundamental truth about your business—want to do something about it? Call me," says Yablonka. ClarityRay became profitable within a year and was ready to tackle a new problem. "We were integrated with many websites. We could audit their sizable accumulated traffic, and began to identify yet another, inverse problem—ad injections that don't belong to the page. These are advertisements that are being injected by third parties, taking advantage of the publisher's users without the publisher, or the users themselves, typically even knowing about it. Many companies before us tried to get users to buy and install an anti-ad-injection software, a challenging proposition as consumers were almost always unaware that they even had a problem. We therefore decided to also reveal to publishers how many of their users were seeing ad injections, coupled with smoking-gun screenshots. The response was so strong that we also started selling data, sometimes without the preventative product—selling publishers PDFs with insights about their overall ad security posture. There was no need for integration, and enterprise sales were typically frictionless, 90 percent were closed over the phone or Skype from my house, the remaining 10 percent from a few trips I took to the US." After two and half years and still with just ten employees, ClarityRay was acquired by Yahoo, forming its ad-security group.

BY THE END of the second period, the company is still working with an MVP, but the MVP should be radically changed and improved. By now, the company's board should be receiving a weekly dashboard from the company. Tracking key performance indicators is super important! Both the board and the advisory board should have been assisting the company in opening doors during this phase, as well.

The final result of the second phase is a beta product that incorporates all the market feedback and is ready for full launch. The business model should be fully validated and the value to the consumer or enterprise crystal clear.

Months 12–18. Phase 3: Market Engagement

During the third phase, the company is seriously engaged with the market; its goal is to generate real traction that will lead it into its Series A round.

Shahar Kaminitz is cofounder and CEO of Insert, a mobile engagement company (it was sold to Pendo in 2017). Before creating Insert, he had founded another company called Worklight. "I founded Worklight in early 2006," he says. "I knew enterprise software well. I had ten years' experience at Amdocs [a large Israeli global tech enterprise], where I held several roles that were all applicable to a startup—development, managing developers, managing the product, and sales to large clients in the US. Worklight was focused on simplifying the process of accessing information from enterprise systems. At the time, if you wanted to access a certain piece of information, you had to log in into the enterprise software that the company uses, go through many screens, and work hard to find that nugget you were looking for. At the same time, the internet made it really easy to find data, and I wanted to make enterprise data just as accessible and simple to find."[10]

Kaminitz spent some time researching the product and the market, and began work as a sole founder. "Although I believed my Amdocs experience made me well rounded, things weren't quite as simple," he admits. "As a startup founder, you're all alone. You manage the financial side of the business, time investment rounds, figure out the right burn rate, set up marketing, lead generation, sales, figure out how to sell, etc. These are hundreds of details that someone else does for you in a large company. In a large company, you deal with 10 percent of this. Someone else closes the deal with the customer, signs it, etc. Suddenly I had all these things to decide and figure out by myself."

After raising funds, Kaminitz hired a team and set out to develop the product. "During the first two years of the company's existence, I kept speaking to potential customers in the market, making sure we were getting validation for the product. It's an important process. You show your future solution—a prototype—and try to gauge whether the market is interested. The signs were great. I was told that the product was really cool—and the people saying that were my target customers in the organizations we wanted to sell to." Validation seemed to be by the book. "They say that the product is unique and that they've never seen anything like it and it's valuable for their organizations. All the checkmarks were in place."

Yet, as we'll show later, Kaminitz was getting the wrong signals from the market. Eighteen months later, he would be forced to pivot. As a result, he was very cautious about market validation when he started his second company, Insert. "When you go validating, customers will be very positive about what you are showing them because people are nice. They know you're showing them your dreams, and they don't want to ruin them for you. Verbal validation will always tend to be positive. I learned to rely less on what customers say and more on my instincts about the market."

But the most important lesson Kaminitz learned was about the importance of bringing a product to market early in the process. "You need to watch closely whether people put money where their mouth is," he says. "We released the product much earlier at Insert and without apologies about its preparedness—no talk about beta, etc. This gave us time to tune the product offering and tweak our pricing. We could see for ourselves whether people were willing to spend money as they had told us they would during the validation phase."

Worklight didn't release a minimal version of its product. "The Worklight product was ready after about a year of development," Kaminitz says. "I personally sold it, and later on hired salespeople. I approached all the people that had told me it's a cool product during the validation process a year earlier, but all that happened was we hit a wall. They still had issues accessing their data and they still said the product is interesting and unique, but as it turned out their issues weren't that urgent. Suddenly, I discovered that data accessibility isn't one of their top three concerns. This same response repeated itself over and over again. But the situation wasn't clear-cut. We had some sales to early adopters who liked the solution well enough to buy it, but that made it even more confusing, since these early adopters were big names and we didn't know if we should stop the product or carry on. We were doing well but we were stuck—we were generating revenue with big-name customers but were unable to really take off. Each sale required too much sweat."[11]

AT THIS POINT KPI tracking becomes even more important, since it can highlight whether the company is really progressing, and it will show you how Series A funders are likely to value it. A company at this stage should demonstrate quantitative KPIs that reflect the positive response of the market to its value proposition, and a couple of agreements with partners and distributors, initial proof of a business model, and above all, a well-rounded and passionate management team. Now the company begins recruiting marketing, sales, and business development people in earnest.

The validations that show market traction and that will be the most relevant for Series A funding should be concrete and real. General conversations with potential customers will matter less. Signed contracts and proofs of commitment matter much more. The nature of market traction varies, depending on the vertical the company is operating in. For instance, companies selling to enterprises should demonstrate traction with real enterprises. They should prove that the product is answering a real pain and addressing a real need that is significant and that isn't just a niche requirement. Consumer companies should have KPIs that prove consumer traction, such as conversion rates (i.e., downloads, active users, purchases, etc.), retention and engagement rates, user lifetime, DAU/MAU ratio (Daily Active Users divided by Monthly Active Users), and so on. It is also important at this stage to show the cost of user acquisition and, if possible, the lifetime value (LTV) associated with it, so that the company can demonstrate that it generates a positive ROI on its customer acquisition costs. If the company can show that it has figured out the basic "formula," and is looking for funding mainly to scale, its chances of completing a successful funding round are high.

The twelve-to-eighteen-month phase is also when the process of raising the next financing round begins in earnest. Before engaging with investors, the company should explore how much funding is required for its next round, what its goals are, and what it will use the proceeds for. Is it planning to reach breakeven with the funds raised? Get to the B round? Go to other markets or territories? As we've discussed in the previous chapter, the average A round's funding is usually in the $2 to $10 million range, but could be more. The moment the amount that is to be raised is defined, the types of investors that should be addressed will become self-evident. Companies should seek out investors that offer an added value on top of the capital they inject. A fund that has a proven record in a certain space, or that specializes in certain types of companies or verticals, or a strategic investor that can bring business partnerships to the table, is preferable.

The company—and not its existing investors or the incubator—should manage the process of finding the next round of financing.

The investors and the incubators should, however, assist the company in developing its pitch, investor presentation, and the best way it can deliver its proof of market traction. They should make introductions as well, but making sure not to spam their networks. Only the right and most relevant people should be approached.

An incubator, just like any other early stage investor, also needs to consider the signals it gives to the market. One of the strongest signals is the decision to make or not make a follow-on investment in one of its portfolio companies. Some incubators don't have the capital for a follow-on investment or they have a policy to never make one. But if an incubator that does make follow-on investments decides not to invest in a company as it is graduating from its program, it is sending a negative signal that makes the company's fundraising much more challenging. This doesn't mean that those companies will necessarily fail. They can reduce their burn rate till they improve their model, they can try to break even, and may eventually manage to raise a funding round.

PIVOTING

Entrepreneurs, investors, and companies don't always get it right the first time around. If startups are organizations in search of scalable and repeatable business models, a pivot is what happens when that search comes to a dead end.

Like ClarityRay, many companies reach a point where it is obvious that some part of their plan just doesn't work. Perhaps the product is not good enough, the user interface and the user experience are unengaging, or maybe the competition has a better product. There might be insufficient demand for the company's product. Perhaps the margins are too low, or the model isn't scalable.

Inexperience often leads to mistakes: companies find it difficult to tell whether the model isn't working because the sales VP is doing something wrong or because the product needs a new feature. But sometimes the issue is deeper and more systemic and requires a thorough rethinking of what the company is about and what its proposition is. This could be a time to cut your losses, but it's also possible that the company and the technology you have developed are still very relevant, but to a different audience and with a different proposition. If that is the case, then it's an opportunity.

A startup can successfully pivot when it changes directions but stays grounded in what it's already learned and made, keeping one foot in the past and placing the other in a new possible future. Over time, pivoting may lead a startup far afield from its original vision, but if you look carefully, you'll still be able to detect common threads in each iteration.

Many unsuccessful startups remain too attached to their original idea, not willing to reconsider alternative directions, or they just jump outright from one vision to another, completely different one. These jumps are extremely risky, because they don't leverage the validated learning about the market and customers that came before.

"Pivoting" isn't tweaking; it happens when something very fundamental about the company changes. Pivots can occur during each of the three phases, but typically happen in the second or third stage, when the product is introduced to the market and the company can see what works and what doesn't. They are what happens when a company takes the market's feedback seriously, and applies their core learnings to a different product, target audience, proposition, or business.

"MY DEFINITION OF a pivot," ClarityRay's Yablonka says, "is when a company begins as one thing and ends up as a different thing altogether as the result of a continuous learning process. Startups often feel that their original direction isn't working out. The question is what can be done about that. If you think there is a zero chance the company will succeed, you aren't pivoting, you are building a new company. To me, a pivot is a data-driven change, a change that is based on insights. If the startup isn't working, don't mystify the problem. State the problem clearly, identify the issues you don't know well enough, and use data to answer your questions. And beware of rationalizing your failure; the data isn't good or bad, it's just objective—hence, rationalizing your inability to succeed may result in missing an even bigger opportunity you didn't consider."[12]

According to Yablonka, to know whether you're doing well, you need to define success. "If you don't define success, you can't know that you're failing. In the ClarityRay case I understood my original assumption about ad blockers was downright wrong. Once we measured the real extent of how many ad blockers were out there, we knew where the opportunity lay, and that we should aggressively pursue it. It wasn't a dream or intuition. It was data and it was there."

Yablonka goes on to warn that pivots aren't simple. "Pivoting requires a lot of honesty. People may perceive pivots negatively. They ask themselves why they should believe your second story if your first one didn't work out. Employees naturally have a limited tolerance for pivots. Ideally, you should hire most of your employees after you pivot, once the existential problems are solved. Otherwise, you're left explaining to employees who left their previous jobs and took a pay cut to go after a very specific dream that, unfortunately, that particular dream is no longer viable, actually never was, but everything is all right as it just so happens that another dream is. They may understandably not be overly receptive to that."[13]

"Regarding investors," continues Yablonka, "it is a potential crisis, and to solve it effectively you need to address the risk, the very potential of a risk, ahead of time and openly. Create trust with the investors, have them know you're accountable, that you care at least as much as they do, if not more, and share your data with them. Make your decisions seem self-evident, naturally derived from the facts. You have to be credible at all times." Yablonka adds that entrepreneurs should be wary of becoming a dream-selling machine. "Many entrepreneurs work so hard to sell their dream to raise funds. While that is an important skill, the real role of the entrepreneur is different and much harder—to make dreams happen, which will only be possible through a disciplined approach predicated on truthfulness."

SHIMRIT TZUR DAVID, the cofounder and CTO of Secret Double Octopus, a simple and secure passwordless multifactor authentication solution, also had to face the question of going through a pivot.

"At first, our product was a site-to-site security solution with no need for encryption key, and we felt we had a great product in our hands. But a year in, customers weren't rushing to buy it. We met potential customers all the time. Everyone that saw our product understood that it was groundbreaking, but the problem it solved wasn't a high enough priority for them. We asked ourselves, what are people really afraid of, what security risk really bothers them? We were running out of funds, and needed to show some success stories for the next round, and we began thinking about pivoting," providing a better user experience with the same level of security.[14]

But how? "In your first course in information security you learn that, like in many things in life, there are trade-offs. If you want great security, you need to forgo some of the user experience. If you want a great user experience, you need to forgo some of the security. Our site-to-site protocol made encryption keys unnecessary. And by shifting to password-free security, we shattered a new paradigm. Security is great, unparalleled really, and the user experience is as good as it can get. This made people's jaws drop. And thus we made the shift.

"One developer continued to work on the original product, and we got two others to work on the new one. Once we had a working prototype and we saw that it was good, we made the full pivot. We don't sell the site-to-site product anymore. We received our first revenues from the authentication product in the fourth quarter of 2017, and it's selling very well."[15]

REMEMBER KAMINITZ? HIS Worklight startup had arrived at the traction phase but his product was hard to sell and he sensed it wasn't addressing a major concern for his customers. He was ready for a pivot, but what would it be?

"In 2007, the iPhone debuted and customers started asking me if we did anything in mobile. We were stuck in stagnant sales, and the technologies we had planned to use to 'consumerize' our product were looking dated, now that the smartphone was starting to mesmerize everyone."[16] Kaminitz says of this crisis point: "You have to accept that what you're doing isn't working and that you need to go and work on another product. Our deliberations about what to do lasted a relatively long time because there was something confusing about our early success. It didn't help that the initial company vision sounded real and convincing. It's easy to go after the classic excuses—we were too early to market, etc. Instead, I began to think about a pivot, going after the same vision, but in mobile—enabling mobility for enterprise apps."

Pivots aren't easy. "A pivot meant letting go of many company assets we spent a lot of capital and energy on: our positioning, marketing, and half our technology, even some of the people I had hired. We needed a mobile skill set, which some members of the team didn't possess. You have to terminate relationships with customers you were very proud of, and that took you a lot of time to acquire. It is a difficult reckoning. As a startup CEO, you sell all the time—to the market, to investors, to customers, but also to employees. You keep telling them that this is a great opportunity and now you have to tell them that it isn't going well. Why should my employees believe me? I was wrong the first time around, why should I be correct now? This can bring people to despair. The market doesn't care that you pivoted, but the employees certainly do. I felt I had lost several battles. Whenever someone asked to speak to me privately I was worried that they were about to leave."

Kaminitz also had to undergo the same process with his board and investors. "They were actually easy, because they were all experienced and had seen other companies that pivoted. Pivoting required more funding and our investors supplied it." After a new development effort, the pivot was complete. "We had new people, a new product, and a new positioning. We were now a platform for rapid development of mobile apps for the enterprise market. It's like beginning a new startup from scratch. The same development effort, the same validation. The same people telling me the product sounded like a great idea."

Things didn't flow too easily the second time around, either. "We got stuck again; the plot had another twist. This time, the product was ready, but the customers weren't ready for it. The product was supposed to make mobile development in the enterprise much easier. But this type of value proposition is something that sells only after you have already begun mobile development and seen how difficult it is, and how expensive over time. But in 2009, most organizations had not started to develop a mobile app, so the value we offered wasn't immediately apparent to them. We had the right product, but we were a little too early. So again, we had a tough year; revenues weren't any higher than those from the first product. One quarter we get a new customer, but then nothing happens in the next quarter. People say that although we've pivoted, nothing has really changed. As a CEO, all I thought was that I should persist. I was convinced that the product was right; we just needed to wait for the market. I also knew that another pivot was not an option. So I banged my head against the wall all through the first half of 2010, but then, in the second half, the market was ready and we began selling. 2011 was great."

In 2012, Worklight was acquired by IBM.[17] "IBM managed to really scale the product's presence in the market, doing things we could not have done, at an impressive scale," Kaminitz says.[18]

The lessons Kaminitz learned went beyond pivoting. "Being the sole entrepreneur at Worklight was not a good idea," he says. "The emotional toll was huge. I didn't have a cofounder that I could sit with and say, 'I think we've made a mistake. I think half our people are about to leave and I don't know what to do.' At Insert, I had cofounders and we had open and healthy relationships. These were people I've worked with in the past and with whom I could speak openly."

Asked for words of advice for startup entrepreneurs, Kaminitz responds that he has a mixed message. "There are two core things a founder should do for their company. On the one hand they need to hire the best people they possibly can, knowingly choose people that are better, more talented, and capable than the founder. The founder should then interfere as little as possible in how these hires work and do their job. Yet, on the other hand, the founder should also be aware that they alone will have no choice but to make two or three key decisions in the life of the company. Often, these decisions seem improbable or unreasonable and yet they will be the decisions that chart the company's future; their sole justification will be the intuition of the founder. As for the rest of the time, the founder should just focus on letting great people do their job."

14

BUILDING AND RUNNING AN EARLY STAGE INVESTMENT VEHICLE

Even though the future seems far away,
it is actually beginning right now.
—MATTIE STEPANEK

For most of this book, the focus was on the startups. This chapter and the one that follows will describe what it's like to start and run a small to midsized early stage investment vehicle for technology companies. We hope this information proves useful to you, whether you are thinking about starting an early stage investment vehicle yourself or want to know more about how they work so you can approach one for an investment.

Whether that vehicle is an incubator, a micro-fund, or a venture capital, it needs to have a planning process behind it. I will refer to incubators throughout this chapter, but the principles that are laid out apply to all early stage investment vehicles.

MAKING CHOICES: THEMES

You can't invest in everything; no one does. Investing in startups doesn't mean you will invest in everything that is technology-oriented, either—that would be casting too wide a net, and it can prevent you from adding value to your portfolio of companies. There has to be a commonality in the companies you choose, and that commonality is your investment theme.

The incubator's investment theme presents a choice of sector or subsector in which its companies will be active. Part of the sector and subsector choice is a result of conscious planning and yet, as the sector and market naturally evolves, the investment theme will change, too, acquiring additional meanings it may not have had when it was first chosen.

The investment theme is the focal point for the incubator's team. Choices of corporate partners, ecosystem development, management expertise, mentors, and almost everything else depend on it. The ability to bring real, tangible value to the incubated companies lies in getting the right people for the right investment theme.

There are two categories of themes: verticals and horizontals. The broad business categories such as—cybersecurity, fintech, healthcare IT, enterprise software, and so on—are all verticals. Horizontals are the core technologies that they make use of, such as artificial intelligence (AI), computer vision, predictive analytics, blockchain, IoT, robotics, materials, and so on,

You can also think of subthemes. For instance, a cleantech theme can have a water technologies subsector and an enterprise software theme can have a subsector focus on financial technology.

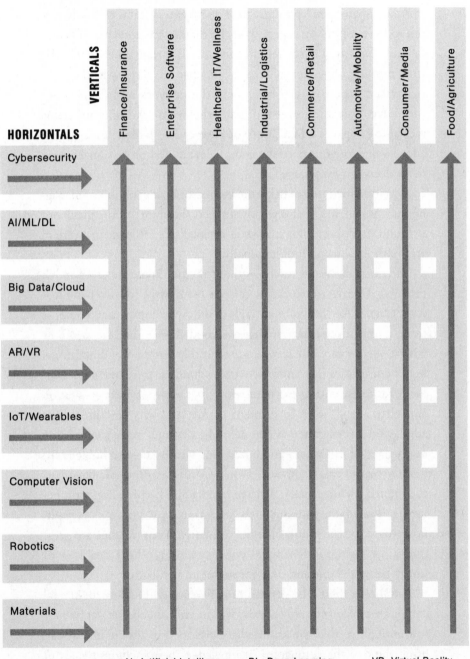

AI–Artificial Intelligence   DL–Deep Learning   VR–Virtual Reality
ML–Machine Learning   AR–Augmented Reality   MR–Mixed Reality

An incubator can have more than one theme, yet it is probably wise not to have too many, especially if the themes are unrelated. Becoming an expert in a space requires focus. Also, remember that, aside from funding, the main value of the incubator is its people, the experience and expertise they bring, and the network and connections they have. Spreading over too many themes or choosing unrelated technology spaces can dilute your expertise, which leads to less added-value for your portfolio companies and less professional investment decisions for yourself.

A well-defined theme helps the incubator do a good job of managing its investments. It also greatly impacts the ability of the incubator to brand itself, becoming known as a center of excellence in a certain area both locally and internationally.

The exact nature of the investment theme should be given much thought. An investment theme can't be too narrow for two main reasons. One, there should be enough deal flow of companies to choose from, and if it's too narrow there's a good chance that the deal flow will be narrow too. The second reason is that you may end up investing in companies that compete with each other, thus creating a conflict of interest within the incubator. That's why "a next generation anti-virus" can't be an investment theme, and why "picture taking apps" won't work either. When defining a theme, make sure you are not bedazzled by fashion and buzzwords—early stage technology investing has its share of fads. Don't go after a "special, flavor-of-the-month" theme since it will age rapidly and become irrelevant before you've made your first few investments. Choose a relevant, up-to-date, but perennial theme. Similarly, some themes are great (green packaging, for example) but may have too little deal flow to justify being the one and only theme for an incubator.

The theme should be defined broadly enough to allow for several companies to comfortably coexist within your incubator, yet be narrow enough so that the knowledge developed in the incubator can bring value to the companies. "Knowledge" here includes the art of creating a startup, hiring the right people, understanding the core technology, navigating through early product development phases, pricing the offering, developing a go-to-market strategy, partnering with the right strategic partners, and successfully bringing the company to a Series A round, among other things.

Take care in choosing your sector: it shouldn't be in the middle of a downturn or have little room for innovation. Choose a sector that is likely to undergo disruption, by which we mean it is ripe for innovations that "surprise" markets by taking product and market development into unexpected paths—by creating new consumers, lowering prices, changing distribution, or making long-held practices obsolete. Disruption can also happen when a technology becomes feasible and widespread, such as mobile telephony, battery-operated vehicles, etc. Eventually the disruption forms a market of its own and completely displaces preceding technologies, products, and markets.

When choosing themes, take evolution into account. Another way of saying this is that your investment theme should age well. Your incubator will run for several years and the market in your technology space will evolve. Over time, the products, competition, technologies, and strategies in the space will change. Embrace that. Just as incubator managers expect portfolio company CEOs to be sensitive to market changes and adapt quickly, they need to be adaptable and resilient themselves.

When defining your theme, you also must be aware of the amount of funding that it entails. For instance, the investment required to grow pharmaceutical companies is significant: you can't choose a "cure cancer" theme and expect companies to show significant progress with an investment of $1 to $1.5 million. That's why you don't see incubators that focus on pharmaceuticals or semiconductors, sectors that require large up-front investments. Yet, the definition of the incubator could change for these capital-intensive sectors, such as an incubator that will bring a semiconductor company to an earlier phase: a proof of concept rather than a chipset in production.

Themes shouldn't exist in a void. The incubator should tap into an existing ecosystem—for instance, an ecosystem of product managers, corporate players, marketers, designers, and technology people who are all focused on great mobile apps for consumers. However, in some countries, there is hardly any technology ecosystem for startups. That should not deter you, since incubators are excellent breeding grounds for ecosystems, as they bring many people and companies together who are all working on different variations of the same theme.

As one of the main investors in Cogent Communications, Erel Margalit and JVP joined forces with Dave Schaeffer, the founder and CEO, to take the internet by storm. As JVP continued to grow, Erel noted the dramatic increase in video traffic, recognizing the move to data and voice, to the world of visual. In 2007, JVP added the "media" theme to its JVP Media Lab incubator, joining the other themes of storage, big data, enterprise software, and business intelligence (BI). "Media" wasn't all the rage back then. The unifying theme of most Israeli investment vehicles was "enterprise" (i.e., offerings that serve the IT needs of companies). In fact, people weren't sure what JVP meant: Was it a video technology, mobile, or gaming technology theme?

No one else chose "media" as their investment theme in 2007. The rapid ascent of the smartphone was about to unleash a surge of new technology companies that catered to consumers rather than corporations. How did JVP define "media"? The idea was that individuals consume media in the broadest sense of the term. It can be many things—apps, content, even storage for the media consumer. It embraces new forms of advertising (web, mobile, digital signage), novel consumer applications, cloud storage, and transport and bandwidth optimization.

This ability to predict and leverage trends continued into 2013, when JVP expanded its technology focus to cover the pressing threat of cyber, among others, for its new incubator, JVP Cyber Labs.

Historically, Israel had been a huge innovator in IT security. Israel's CheckPoint Software pioneered the firewall.[1] But as technology evolved and more applications, services, and basic infrastructure became cloud connected, a new wave of technology disruption was unleashed. Cyber is about the changing paradigms of risks: the dangers entailed by people bringing their own devices to work, the vulnerability of big data to attack, and so on. Computer viruses are changing, and so are the ways to protect against them. As more systems that were previously self-contained become connected to the internet—things like power plants, highway systems, pipelines, and other large infrastructure projects—they become more vulnerable to attack.

Themes can also be related to the incubator's location: if, for example, it is near a university with a history of excellence in a certain field, or in an area with a substantial financial cluster, or where the government is investing heavily in certain projects, from cleantech to military infrastructure. Themes can also be chosen according to a desire to create spillover effects—for example, encouraging university graduates to stay in a locality and found companies there; or to encourage certain types of R&D or niche knowledge, such as software quality assurance.

And one last note about themes: passion matters most. The theme should be in a sector that you genuinely care and are passionate about and that entrepreneurs are excited to be in. Not only because you and the entrepreneurs are going to spend a lot of time together, but also, as we've discussed in Chapter 9, passion is a huge force behind any success, including the one of the incubator.

MAKING CHOICES: COMPANY STAGE

Most technology investors limit the scope of companies they invest in. As an incubator, you've already started narrowing your focus by choosing companies at a certain level of maturity—that is, the status ("stage") the company is in. Usually that will mean investing in pre-seed, seed, or post-seed/pre-A companies. Although you may have construed the use of the term "investment theme" earlier on to only apply to the company's business and technology, the stage of the company is also an important part of your investment strategy.

Each company stage presents a different degree of product definition, feasibility, and development. It also is different in terms of market testing or engagement, team maturity, and possible partnerships. While all these stages are excellent candidates for an incubator, choosing to focus on a certain stage has implications on how the incubator is funded and built.

Typically, the more mature the company is, the more funding it requires. It is likely to have more personnel and higher expenses. A more mature company is also likely to come at a higher valuation. Less mature companies will need more support from the incubator, even in core areas, such as marketing and business development.

- The funding requirement for **pre-seed** investments can be very modest: some mentorship to help the company crystalize its product and offering, and $50,000 to $150,000 to enable initial market testing, product proof of concept, and salaries to the entrepreneurs so they can spend all their time on the project. The pre-seed phase is relatively brief, usually no more than three to four months. Many accelerators follow this model.

- A **seed investment** can be in the range of $500,000 to $1.5 million and should last for twelve to eighteen months; the investor will get 20 to 40 percent of the company's equity in return, depending on variables that we will discuss later on. The investment should enable the company to complete its product and demonstrate some market traction, making it more likely to meet the requirements of A-round investors.

- A **post-seed** or **pre-A** investment will usually be in the area of $1.5 to $2.5 million. These are usually companies that already have a product that they have launched in the market, but still don't have enough traction to raise an A-round.

You can decide to focus on one of the stages, or on all three, but take into account the implications for the incubator's funding needs and investment capabilities.

INVESTMENT STRATEGY

An incubator needs to choose its investment strategy: What amount will be invested in each company? It needs to define its funding goal: To what stage will the funds bring the company? For instance, should the funds invested last long enough to bring the company all the way to a full A-round (approximately eighteen months), or just to a post-seed round?

As previously discussed, given the market circumstances (valuations, expenses, and more), getting a company to its A-round translates into funding rounds of between $500,000 and $1.5 million, depending on the geography, the investment theme, and the level of technology innovation, and R&D expected.

The underlying assumption is that the company consumes approximatly $40,000 per month during its early days at the incubator (or, to phrase it in VC jargon, its burn rate is $40K). This will grow to $80,000 to $100,000 per month when the company is in its final stages at the incubator. This assumes the company expends on average about $7,500 to $10,000 per employee per month, including all overhead expenses. (These rules of thumb apply to most startups in the West, but can differ per location.)

INVESTMENT, BUDGET, AND FOLLOW-ON INVESTMENTS

Choosing a theme and thinking about the sums required to bring companies to Series A are the first steps in defining the overall funding the incubator requires for its investment.

Next, the rate of investments made by the incubator comes into play. You must, at a minimum, assume a rate of investment of four to six companies per year—below that number, the operational effort to establish the incubator is not worth it. Some incubators are larger, investing in up to fifteen companies annually.

All this makes the answer to the question of "how much money?" pretty straightforward: the average investment in a company multiplied by the number of companies you expect to invest in each year, multiplied by the investment period of the incubator and including its operational expenses. If an incubator has a three-year investment period, and makes $500,000 to $1.5 million investments in four to six companies each year, its average annual investment budget is $5 million a year. In its three-year investing period, the incubator will require $15 million for the initial investment in the fifteen companies it invests in.

Another important decision to make is whether to leave funds for follow-on investments. A follow-on investment means that the incubator participates in later investment rounds in the company, after the incubation period is over. Follow-on investments are made according to the terms and valuation of the new round, and enable the incubator to keep its equity without being diluted, or only being diluted in a relatively minor way.

Follow-on investing isn't a must for all incubators or their companies. Yet they should be seriously considered if you believe in the future of the portfolio companies who are performing well. Assuming you will want to make follow-on investments of at least $1 million in one-half of all the companies you work with during your three-year investment period, you will need to add at least $8 million to your investment budget, and preferably more.

An incubator that doesn't participate in follow-on investments will see its holdings diluted as new money comes in and creates more shares; if the company raises several rounds of funding, the incubator's holdings may shrink to a low-single-digit number. These single-digit holdings may not generate enough return from an exit to cover other investments that may not have done well. This is why incubators should strive to make follow-on investments in its graduates who deserve them. Most investment vehicles will leave 40 to 50 percent of their funding for following investments.

In a way, follow-on investments are where the real returns are. If the initial investment was made before the company had a product, let alone product-market fit, then any subsequent investment is less risky. This is aptly summed up by entrepreneur David McClure, who was the CEO of the accelerator 500 Startups: "Invest *before* product/market fit, double-down *after*."[2]

FORMING THE INCUBATOR'S TEAM

The incubator's added-value to companies, entrepreneurs, the ecosystem, and its partners (from governments and universities to multinationals) is all derived from its core team. Choosing the right team and operating it well through the use of contacts, rigorous due diligence, an impactful advisory board, mentoring, and more, is a must.

The following are the minimal requirements for the incubator's staffing, based on the assumption that there is one investment theme, not several. It also assumes an incubator that makes a minimum of four to six seed investments a year.

- **Incubator Manager/Managing Partner**: First and foremost, the incubator needs an incubator manager. This person should have hands-on operational experience that has to do with the investment theme. The incubator manager should also have experience in investment management, since this is their primary role at the incubator and they should not lose sight of this fact.

   Some personal traits make incubator managers good at what they do. Integrity, professionalism, and people skills are important. Although passion about the theme is a prerequisite, the incubator manager should not go overboard with enthusiasm about ideas and companies—some distance needs to be kept before the investment is made and sometimes afterward too. Incubator managers should not fall hopelessly in love with an idea or company. We'll discuss methods of dealing with the infatuation some incubator managers have with companies later, when we discuss the role of the investment committee.

The incubator manager should be good at "reading" entrepreneurs to tell what drives them and whether they will be able to make their company "happen." This isn't just about assessing the intellectual capacities of the entrepreneur; it involves judgments about their genuine passion to build the company and their emotional and interpersonal makeup. The manager should be adept at idea validation, business plan understanding, technology management, market and product understanding, and also be able to find and understand any weak points a company has.

- **Analyst:** Another key incubator employee is the analyst (sometimes called an associate). The analyst's main role is to manage the incubator's deal flow and to prepare a thorough competitive analysis for investment candidates that are in the advanced stages of the screening process. Analysts should track and get to know all the companies that are relevant to the investment theme by keeping their fingers on the pulse of the industry and theme, being fully updated on any major developments, transactions, innovations in the space, and attending all relevant industry events and conferences. The main role of the analyst is to make the initial filtering and analysis work for the incubator manager. Analysts also work with the companies (we'll go into that in detail in a little while). Like the manager, the analyst should be highly involved in the local startup scene, attending get-togethers and innovation events. He or she should constantly scout for interesting companies and entrepreneurs early on, before the rest of the investment community.

- **Office manager/Community manager:** The incubator should also have an office manager, to take care of the facilities, produce the events the incubator will host, and much more. If the office manager has some HR background, that can be a great advantage as he or she can assist the portfolio companies in hiring the right personnel and building their teams. Many incubators and investors hire community managers as well—someone whose role is to make sure the network of sharing, events, and lectures from industry luminaries stays alive and benefits the companies in the space the incubator is operating in.

These three (or four) employees form the core incubator team. It's worth mentioning that if the early stage vehicle is a micro-VC or a VC, then there would be more investment professionals, and they will usually be general partners or partners in the fund.

Incubated companies can benefit from additional services provided by the incubator, but these services are not a must, and depend on the incubator's strategy and budget:

- **CFO services** can be offered to companies, either in-house or through outsourcing. An in-house CFO can be invaluable during the investment process by working with the companies to build and plan their budgets, and, later on, assisting company CEOs on an ongoing basis in budget and cash-flow management.
- **HR management services** can assist companies with the formidable recruiting challenges they face: startups are constantly hiring, good people are always difficult to find, and early hiring decisions have a profound impact on the company's performance and culture. This function can also be outsourced.
- **Marketing, branding, and PR services** can also be provided. Although these are functions that, in many cases, require market-specific expertise, there are many elements they can assist the companies with such as building their brand, creating the marketing plan, and identifying the right PR agency.
- **Legal and accounting services** can be offered as well, though these are more likely to be outsourced.

Services can be offered free of charge to companies, as part of the added-value given by the incubator, or for a fixed monthly fee. If the companies are also renting office space from the incubator, it can all be built into one financially attractive package.

All of the above—wages, rent, marketing, legal, finance, and HR services—make up the incubator's budget. The budget can be funded through management fees, for example 2 percent of the total funds to be invested; through a fixed annual budget; or a combination of the two. In any case, the budget for personnel, services, and space is typically between $400,000 and $750,000 annually.

As mentioned above, some of the expenses, such as rent, HR, and finance, can and should be paid for by the companies. It doesn't make sense, for instance, for the incubator to subsidize a company's rent. Yet, getting reimbursed by the companies is not a business model that should fund incubator operations or carry a profit. It should be a cost-basis service that the incubator provides to increase the chances for its companies to succeed.

INVESTMENT COMMITTEE

Like most investment bodies, an incubator needs an investment committee. Investment committees review the deal flow of potential investments, investment transactions, and company performance, and establish the policy and the strategy of the incubator. Most importantly, investments in companies cannot be done without the approval of the investment committee.

The committee's exact structure depends on the incubator's investors. The common practice is that it should be made of professionals—and not representatives of the limited partners who invested in the incubator. As with venture capital funds, the decisionmaking body doesn't consist of the investors in the fund but the fund's professional managers.

The committee will typically have between five to seven members, and it should include the incubator manager, other partners (if any), and the analyst. The committee should also include professionals with backgrounds that are relevant to the incubator's theme(s).

In one word, the role of the investment committee is to provide what the incubator manager may sometimes be missing: perspective. The incubator manager can fall in love with a deal, a team, or a vision, and may become less attuned to its flaws and potential pitfalls.

The committee should preferably meet every week, but no less than once a month—depending on the deal flow and investments that are in the pipeline. If a company comes in to present, it doesn't necessarily mean that an immediate decision must be made; the committee can certainly take some time to consider a deal. Prior to the investment committee's meeting, the analyst will have circulated a one-page "deal-alert" or "deal-memo" indicating the proposed deal terms (based on a preliminary negotiation with the company regarding equity, board composition, and valuation), as well as information about the team's background, its main proposition, its product and technology, its competition, and its fit with the incubator's theme and strategy.

When a company is brought to present to the investment committee for the explicit discussion of an investment, in many cases there is a go or no-go decision at the end of the discussion. Typically, the company's leadership (CEO, founders, and sometimes the active chairman) presents. Afterward, there is a general question-and-answer session. Once the company completes the presentation, it leaves and an internal discussion is conducted, leading to a decision.

The investment committee not only discusses new potential investments, but additionally gets reports on the progress of portfolio companies and various developments in them. When an incubator company has had a board meeting, its highlights will be reported to the team, and the investment committee will receive a report on the company's progress, any issues that may have arisen, and any other important topics that should be discussed. Naturally, when a portfolio company is reaching its next round of financing, the decision on a follow-on investment will also be made by the committee.

In some cases, when there's a "hot deal" or when there is fierce competition on the deal, the investment committee should have a high sense of urgency and be available and ready to make decisions in a relatively short time. The whole process should be condensed into a few days, with the team fully engaged in analyzing the deal and in preparing all the relevant documents.

ADVISORY BOARD

The advisory board has an important role to play in the incubator. It should consist of people that can assist the incubator companies—representatives of the limited partners (the incubator's investors), industry experts, experienced investors, and other highly connected individuals.

The advisory board helps the companies and the incubator itself. Its role isn't to deal with the daily operations or funding decisions. It should help open doors, introduce companies to potential partners that may be relevant for the incubator or its portfolio companies, and more.

In some cases, the advisory board members may be compensated by receiving a small equity in the incubator.

DAY-TO-DAY WORK

Assisting companies to take off and incubating them isn't an amorphous thing; it doesn't mean "we'll sit down with the CEOs every once in a while, and help them out a bit." It's structured around a management methodology that is designed to be maximally supportive of the companies in it, in every aspect of their operations. And "supportive" doesn't mean acting as a crutch for companies that are deeply lacking in some skill or knowledge. Supportive isn't even like "training wheels." It's about providing access to people and knowledge so that the company can make everything work by itself. It's about providing connections to the right people, ecosystems, and expertise.

Ideally, the incubator manager should divide his or her time between working with the incubated companies and searching for new companies to invest in. Another way to look at this is by using the "inbound/outbound" metaphor. Half of all work is outbound: meeting new companies, marketing the incubator, going to events, etc. The other half is inbound—working with the incubated companies, managing the relations with the incubator's limited partners/investors (LPs), meeting strategic investors in the fund, and working with the fund's personnel and investment committee.

The manager should stay close to all portfolio companies and meet with them at least once a week. The manager should not be the only incubator staff to be in touch with the company throughout the week. This is the role of the analyst, a member of the advisory board, and perhaps some of the supportive functions. In general, the analyst should also dedicate about one-third of their time to incubator companies—doing research for them and carrying out other supportive activities.

The incubator manager and analyst are there to help the companies through mentorship and they should not succumb to temptation to run the company's operations. This is the role of the CEO. In cases where the company requires additional leadership or managerial experience, they should consider having an active chairman. The incubator can be instrumental in selecting an active chairman, but it can't force one on a company, and should certainly not invest in a company that doesn't have a capable CEO. A company that is funded by the incubator should have the right management in place; the incubator's staff should not and cannot be its part-time managers.

15

LISTENING TO A HUNDRED SINGERS TO FIND YOUR NEXT STAR (OR, HOW TO BECOME THAT STAR IN YOUR INVESTOR'S EYES)

Talent is like electricity.
We don't understand electricity. We use it.
—MAYA ANGELOU

"**D**eal flow" is an expression that refers to the rate or flow of potential investments. It is important to venture capitalists and incubators, since it has a direct impact on the quantity and quality of deals they make. A deal flow is good if it contains quality companies, enabling the investing organization to function at its peak capacity in evaluating, choosing, and making investments. The quality of a company is subjective; depending on the strategy and focus of the investor, it may be rated quite differently. In general, it is one that fits well with the incubator's theme and expectations.

Early stage technology investors get deal flow from a variety of channels: referrals and contacts, through meetings at events or conferences, or from direct inquiries on their websites. A considerable amount of deal flow is generated by proactive activities on the investor's part.

Deal flow is one of the main reasons VCs and incubators should seriously market themselves. A VC or an incubator's goal is to be positioned and perceived in the market in a way that attracts quality companies that are relevant to it. Entrepreneurs should seek their investment early in their companies' lives, in the belief that the incubator has real value-add and the expertise that they need. Entrepreneurs should approach the incubator with the belief that obtaining funding from it, as opposed to getting funded by others, will materially increase their chances of success.

Once it is set up, an incubator should be able to see and filter dozens of companies in a relatively short time; otherwise, the incubator will find it difficult to begin operating at full speed and won't be able to meet its financial and operational goals.

DEAL FLOW MEANS OUTBOUND WORK, A LOT OF IT

The incubator's deal flow depends to a great degree on its ability to correctly market and position itself. This requires proactive and systematic outbound marketing work. The incubator should be present in the media, visible at events and conferences, and its team members should regularly contribute articles to blogs and media.

Organizing a conference is a great way for an incubator to kick off its marketing activity, make its investment focus known, and even plant the seeds of a startup ecosystem. A well-defined event (such as a talk by an industry visionary, a startup pitch contest, or even a theme-related movie night in the incubator) demonstrates to the entrepreneurial and investment community what the incubator's main theme is. You can invite a famous technology blogger in to meet companies that are in the incubator, making them aware of an overseas market they are targeting—and raising your profile when the blogger blogs and tweets about it. Events and conferences show passion and commitment. Instead of *telling* entrepreneurs about your added value as an incubator, your knowledge, and relevant connections to strategic players, an event *shows* them.

Make sure you publicize your core interests, your team, your strategic partners, and the ongoing successes of your portfolio companies (i.e., signing significant deals, attaining market traction). When there's an exit, make sure it gets good media coverage as this gives your team professional credibility. Exits, naturally, are one of the main things entrepreneurs are looking for when they consider pitching to an incubator. They are what potential investors look for when they are thinking about making an investment in the incubator.

Make sure people know you are there. Meet colleagues, investors, professors, graduate students, researchers, journalists, analysts, and anyone who is active in your theme. Explain what your subthemes are. Your ability to invest in the right companies will be greater if the market knows and understands what companies you're looking for.

GOOD DEAL FLOW
REQUIRES GOOD REPUTATIONS

One of the main goals of any incubator is to attract the best companies and entrepreneurs. Having the market become aware of your incubator is usually not enough. The main objective is to build the incubator's reputation.

The reputation of an incubator is a function of the team, its strategic partners, its portfolio, and its past exits. Reputation is also a function of the incubator's ongoing operational behavior. It reflects how quickly the incubator responds to a company approaching it, how readily it assists companies (both those it makes investments in and those it doesn't), how well it handles the investment negotiation, and how well it works with its portfolio companies.

Almost everyone in Israel's investment scene seems to know the importance of being responsive. According to a story that ran several years ago in one of Israel's financial papers, almost every Israeli VC that was approached by a no-name fake entrepreneur (who was actually the journalist) responded in less than twenty-four hours. The trick to being entrepreneur-friendly isn't to just respond quickly to the first approach, but also to provide a transparent and quick process throughout the entire engagement with a company.

The incubator's best ambassadors are the entrepreneurs it invested in. Treat every entrepreneur and company that you meet with dignity. Schedule enough time to hear their pitch, don't be late, and make sure you come back with thoughtful feedback, even when you've decided not to invest. When you give back to entrepreneurs, it also builds your reputation.

I often get asked whether an incubator should meet with just anyone who approaches it. The answer is a resounding "yes"—*if* that anyone is in the stage and spaces that the incubator is interested in. The incubator's initial filtering is mainly to sort out the companies that are not relevant to its theme and strategy. But once this initial filtering is done, the incubator should strive to meet as many entrepreneurs and companies as it can. Why?

You are probably familiar with those TV song contests in which the most improbable contestant takes the microphone, begins singing, and, to everyone's surprise, makes the judges cry with joy. This is why the incubator should meet almost everyone. Many people mistakenly believe that deal flow coming in through referrals is inherently better than an email communication through the incubator's site. That may be the case statistically, but you can't make assumptions about any individual instance. An incubator can't afford not to look at a presentation. You need to sit down and hear everyone sing. Surprises, good and bad, are bound to happen. Similarly, you should be able to meet and listen to anyone that comes to speak to you after a conference. You should hear every company pitch, even if your educated guess is that you will be better off just passing on it. The incubator and the people working for it should be approachable, and should be perceived as such by the entrepreneurial community. Asking for funding is not an easy task; getting repeat refusals is even worse. The incubator should never take anyone approaching it for granted. If an entrepreneur has decided to dedicate their life to their idea, you should be able to dedicate some time to listen to it, and to understand why they think it's a good venture.

ONE IN A HUNDRED

You will see many companies, hundreds if not thousands of them, and the odds are that you will invest in less than 2 percent of them (depending on the theme). The typical deal flow ratio is 1 to 100. You may not have physically met all one hundred; you may have chosen to meet with just fifty of the one hundred presentations you've received. It doesn't matter. Eventually, statistics show that you will make an investment in just one out of every one hundred companies that you see.[1] This is why, when choosing an investment theme, you need to make sure that there is enough deal flow to look at within this theme. For example, let's say that an incubator with a security theme has six hundred companies apply within a year. Let's assume the incubator met with half of them and invited a hundred of those for a second meeting. Due diligence was commenced on twenty-five companies. The incubator will probably end up investing in six of them.

In some subsectors—for example, water technologies—the amount of newly formed companies may be lower, and there the ratio will be higher. This can also be the case in certain geographies, where the startup scene is less active.

In either case, you should never compromise on a company because of insufficient deal flow. Compromising on the quality of the companies will have severe consequences on the incubator, its performance, its reputation, and its operations, standards, and personnel. You don't want to face them.

MEASURE OFTEN, MEASURE WELL

Deal flow is measurable and should be tracked and analyzed on an ongoing basis. Keep track of how many companies approach you and how many companies you've actually met. You should also track later events in the deal flow funnel: how many companies were invited for a second meeting, how many companies began the due diligence process, how many companies did you eventually make an investment in. The analysis is similar to a sales pipeline analysis except for one thing—you are the buyer and not the seller. You should also measure the percentage of companies in your theme that you've looked at. A good incubator should probably see no less than 85 percent of the relevant deal flow in its market.

The incubator should also keep track of the companies it chooses not to invest in. This is an important measure, as it allows the incubator to assess the quality of its decisionmaking. Have these companies raised capital? If they did, who was it from? How much did they raise? This activity is, in reality, a measure of quality control—someone else thought that a company you had passed on was interesting. That doesn't necessarily mean your decision was wrong, but it is worth taking a second look to see if and how these companies are developing.

Also, measure how many of the companies in the deal flow matched the theme and the subthemes you've defined. This will let you see whether you're able to attract enough companies within it. Don't forget that sometimes, when a great company shows up, you may want to invest outside of your theme's scope. However, if you discover that of a hundred companies you chose to meet fifty, and almost all of them were completely outside of your original investment theme, you might need to reevaluate your investment strategy.

MANAGING WHAT COMES AFTERWARD: SPEED MATTERS

During the initial process, the entrepreneur will meet the analyst, the incubator manager, and sometimes an industry expert that the incubator has brought in. The company will be discussed during the weekly deal flow meetings, and if all goes well, they will be invited to meet and present to the investment committee.

Make sure the entrepreneurs have a good experience with your team. Don't keep them waiting. The moment the incubator has a decision, good or bad, the company must be notified.

Anytime you meet a company, whether you're likely to invest in it or will never do so, try to provide them with value, connections, and advice. Don't be stingy.

You should set clear timelines on the flow of a company, from initial contact to signing a term sheet and completing definitive agreements. Ideally, if you think a company is good, you should be able to present it with a term sheet within three to four weeks of your first encounter. A really good company, sometimes a company that has additional investor suitors, should receive a term sheet within this time and receive the funds in its bank account right after the definitive agreement has been signed, within two to three weeks after the term sheet was signed. In this respect, an incubator has a faster process than a traditional VC, which may take three to six months to complete an investment.

Why is speed important? You should always take into account that if a company is looking for funding, it has also approached other potential investors. If you believe it's a good company to invest in, you should move fast, or someone will steal the deal.

Most term sheets contain a "no-shop" clause for a period of thirty to sixty days. What that means is that the company is barred from "shopping" itself, or soliciting other investment offers. This gives you more time to continue your due diligence and clear any concerns, should they arise.

Here are some general points:

- Each company that comes in should be documented. Keep a copy of the presentation they've sent in or presented. Should the company return after a few months, the presentation from the first encounter will help you assess the progress the company did or didn't make.

- Respond to any company that approaches you within less than twenty-four hours, even if it's just to confirm that you have received the presentation and will review it and get back to them soon. Remember that, for most entrepreneurs, this is one of the main events reflecting on the future of their venture—make sure you treat them with respect. If you find a company you want to meet, schedule a meeting within a week.

- If you're interested in a second meeting with the company, do that within a week, and begin investigating the company and its market. Make sure to set clear expectations in the second meeting, and indicate the specific topics that you would like them to cover, or specific materials or data that you would like them to present.

All of the above supposes a very quick turn of events; but that should be standard for incubators.

SCREENING AND CHOOSING

Once a company has sent in their presentation or other materials, the incubator should perform an initial screen: Does the company fit your investment theme? What is its status? Is it a pre-seed company or is it more advanced? Does it only have a demo or is its product working? Does it have any customers or any initial traction in the market?

When assessing a company, investors usually look at three things: its team, the market, and the product. The company must first pass through the team filter; the market and product come later.

The Team

When you meet the startup's team, make sure both your left brain and your right brain are active. You are evaluating two things: the team's professionalism, and how brightly their passion burns. Figuring out whether the company has a good team and the right talent can only be done in a face-to-face meeting. During the meeting, you should form an opinion about the team's background, its relevance to the company, their prior experience, and more. The deeper you dive in, the more you will learn. Sometimes it may take two or three meetings to form a solid opinion. Some of the things that give a good sense of the professionalism and experience of the team are the way they discuss the competition and the competitive landscape, how they describe the technology, their go-to-market plan, and their network in the space they operate in. Ask them to address all those issues. Listen well.

You should also find out how long they've been working together and try to get a sense of whether the founding team's personal chemistry is good. A team's passion is often underrated, but as we've previously discussed, passion is the only thing that will keep the company on track as it goes through its difficult journey. Their passion should be palpable. Passion is something that is very hard to fake, and if it's missing, you should consider whether you want to move forward with your investment.

Over time, the incubator's team develops a sixth sense and can tell when an entrepreneur comes to a meeting with low energy. If this is the case, make sure you understand why: Was the person under the weather with a slight cold or was their passion for the company petering out? This is important, because you don't want to invest in a team that lacks passion for the endeavor in which you just invested a million dollars.

The team should have the right amount of Chutzpah. They should be bold enough to present a real challenge to the conventional wisdom in their space. They should bring a new paradigm, demonstrate a hypothesis for a different future. If they are in the consumer space, they should have creative ideas about the changes in consumer behavior that their product can leverage. If they are in the enterprise software space, they should have a good hypothesis of how things will change in the next three to five years. This is true for any vertical a startup operates in.

One more thing you should be aware of is the chemistry you have with the team. You are going to spend a lot of time working with them. They should be able to listen to inputs and receive criticism, and your dialogue with them should be open and productive, because once you invest in them you become partners in the journey. You should try to spend some time with them before the investment, in which you can discuss the vision, operational plan, product milestones, go-to-market strategy, budget, and other topics. You want to be sure you share the same vision and approach to actual operational execution, and that the budget and funding match the objectives and targets of the company. Additionally, you can get a read on what it's like to work with the team. At the end of the day, you are creating something together, and even though the process is not easy, it should be fun.

The Market

Some investors qualify the market question by TAM—the total addressable market. In other words, is the company addressing a market whose potential size is $1 billion, $5 billion, or more?

Defining a market isn't always easy, especially if the company is creating a new category. However, in most cases, the company and investors should be able to define the market fairly easily. Here are some additional market-related elements the investor should consider.

First, on the macro level, an investor should have a good look at whether the market is growing, flat, or declining. Information, lots of it, is very accessible today, including analyst reports. All this can give you a good idea of what the trends and changes in the market are, plus some forecast numbers. This is important information, but it is not enough to make an investment decision. You should also remember that analyst forecasts are available to anyone in the market, and that some of them are wrong. Make sure you are aware of what analysts are saying, but don't stop there.

The second level is the subcategory. Every market can be defined on the macro level (the market for desserts) and at the subcategory level (the market for ice cream). For instance, the internet and mobile advertising market is huge and is growing annually. Yet some of its subcategories (certain types of online advertising) are on the decline, where others are growing rapidly (like video ads). Some will gain a significant share of the market and some are bound to remain a niche play. Each market has many subcategories. Make sure you know them well and that you place the company in the right one.

When looking at a subcategory, you should look for a few things. How crowded is it with active companies, how big are the companies you will compete with, how advanced are they from product and R&D perspectives, are any large strategic players active in the space, and is any one of them already a de-facto category leader? Another interesting element to explore is how companies in the category are funded—who funded them and with how much? A geographical analysis is sometimes relevant, as you may find out that there is fierce competition in one territory, whereas in others there's fairly little, even though the potential is high. Ask yourself whether the company can become the subcategory leader. Examine whether there is a lot of money in the market—for investments, for marketing efforts, of potential sales revenue.

As you make this analysis, you should also form an opinion about whether the company doesn't entirely belong to an existing subcategory, but is actually forming a new category of its own. The main advantage of this would be that it is easier to lead a category you have invented. CyberArc, for example, became a category leader of privilege identity management, a market it invented. Waze took the leadership of the social-driven traffic-navigation system, a category that didn't exist before they created it.

Looking at the market requires you to form a vision and an opinion as to where the market is going. The company together with the investors should form a hypothesis that attempts to forecast what the market will look like in three to five years' time, and what the company's role will be in it.

The company's vision about the market should be brave, bold, and disruptive. The company should attempt to make a significant change in the market, to draw a new paradigm, to challenge the existing products, propositions, and business models.

Market sizing should refer first to the entirety of the market, and then to the subcategory the company is in. The best way to look at this is to do both top-down and bottom-up calculations. Top-down means that you try to forecast the business potential and market traction based on the overall market size. When looking at the total available market, try to assess, as realistically as possible, what percentage of the market the company will be able to own (market share). A realistic approach will usually be in the low-to-mid single-digit range in the company's first years of operation. So, for example, if the overall relevant market is $10 billion, and the subcategory is $3 billion, then 1 percent of revenues from this market will be equal to $30 million. In this case, being able to grow to a few percentage points makes the company interesting in terms of its market potential. If, however, the market size of the subcategory is $100 million, than the potential of the company is relatively limited. Naturally, you should also look at the forecasts for the market growth or decline and not just refer to its existing size.

The bottom-up calculation answers questions such as how many salespeople the company will be able to employ based on its funding and operational budget, and how much revenue each salesperson can realistically generate. Compare the bottom-up calculation to the top-down and see whether they make sense together.

Another important question to ask is what the gross margins are in the market, and what gross margins the company can expect to make. Gross margins can range from 20 to 90 percent, depending on various factors. In some markets, the gross margin can drop beneath 20 percent. This creates a riskier financial foundation for a company and suggests that it might not be a good place for a young company to grow. This is why so few startups in the consumer electronics devices space get funded. If the gross margin is low, try to determine why: Are retail channels killing the margins or is the blame with intermediaries? Is the cost of goods high, bill of materials (BOM) high, or is the balance of power between sellers and buyers skewed?

Another factor is the common payment terms in the market. This should have a direct impact on the company's cash flow and must be taken into consideration when planning the company's budget and financial needs. If the company is already in a sales mode, there are indicators that would show how the market reacts to the company's proposition. Such indicators would be the company's current revenues, its growth over the last two to three years, its revenue forecast, the pipeline of potential customers, conversion rates, churn rates, and others.

The Product

The third element to look at when assessing a company is the product. Can the proposed product fulfill the company's vision? How is it different than anything else that is available?

In many cases, the product will contain technology-based innovation and differentiation. But technology alone doesn't make a product; there has to be a sound customer value proposition and a viable profit formula. On top of the technology, a product competitive advantage can be achieved by other means such as developing a unique user interface, an innovative user experience, a new kind of business model, or by having strategic relationships with major players and bundling the product with theirs.

You should expect to see different levels of product development in companies that are looking to raise money from an incubator. The level that is appropriate varies according to the sector the company is in. For instance, getting a consumer product "right" is absolutely key in the consumer space. It is advisable that a consumer product be in an advanced development stage and well into the UI and UX designs before an incubator invests. This is what is required to be able to launch a minimum viable product to the market within six months.

Ideally, the company will already have some initial market traction or usage analytics that will show the level of retention and engagement of its users when it makes its pitch.

In the enterprise software space, the product can be less mature, since other indicators can make the incubator comfortable that it can be launched within six months. Launching a good enterprise software company requires other competencies in terms of understanding the market, its needs, and the technology. Indicators of interest from potential enterprise customers will contribute significantly to the investment decision—an MOU (Memorandum of Understanding), LOI (Letter of Intent), acceptance for a POC (Proof of Concept), or any other indication that represents a real interest in the product.

MAKING CHOICES

Though it is important to filter team, market, and product, most companies will not have all these elements fully in place. If they did, they probably wouldn't be seed stage companies, which is what is most appropriate for an incubator investment. Usually the product will not yet be completed. The important thing here is to make sure that the definition of the minimum viable product is clear, and that a coherent product road map is in place.

If the team is missing a key person, such as a business or technology leader, a condition precedent to the investment may be recruiting this key person. (This is usually called "a condition for closing.") If the team is not experienced enough, you may want to consider bringing in an active chairman who knows the space well and can mentor the CEO and the team.

PART IV
ECOSYSTEM

16

FIRST, WE TAKE JERUSALEM; THEN, WE TAKE NEW YORK

A PRACTIONER'S GUIDE TO CHUTZPAH AND BUILDING AN INNOVATION ECOSYSTEM

Places that succeed in attracting and retaining creative class people prosper; those that fail don't. —RICHARD FLORIDA

Jerusalem, one of the oldest cities in the world, has about 800,000 inhabitants. With a poverty rate above Israel's average and a ranking of just four out of ten for the socioeconomic status of its inhabitants, it is an unlikely location for a high-technology hub. Tel Aviv, by comparison, is ranked eight out of ten in its socioeconomic status, and educated professionals ("the creative class") flock to live, work, and party in it. Yet, the story of Jerusalem Venture Partners (and of Israel's venture capital industry writ large) is tightly linked to Jerusalem's past and future. It turns on technology, of course, but also on the arts, social entrepreneurship, and community activism.

Dr. Erel Margalit, the founder and executive chairman of Jerusalem Venture Partners, as well as formerly a member of the Knesset (the Israeli Parliament), didn't start out as a technologist, nor as a businessman. In 1987, he moved to New York City so he could start studying toward a PhD in philosophy at Columbia University, while working at Moishe's Movers to finance his education.

While in the US, he discovered the work of Michael Porter, a professor at the Harvard Business School. "I was really impressed by his lectures on clustering as a source of competitive advantage," Margalit says.[1] Those lectures culminated in Porter's 1990 book, *The Competitive Advantage of Nations,* which radically changed our understanding of the drivers behind prosperity and sustained success in a modern global economy.[2] On returning to Israel, Margalit would take those principles and apply them to Jerusalem, changing our understanding of creating ecosystems, eventually impacting Israel's venture capital economy as a whole.

One of the book's main ideas was the concept of "clusters":

> Today's economic map of the world is characterized by "clusters." A cluster is a geographic concentration of related companies, organizations, and institutions in a particular field that can be present in a region, state, or nation. Clusters arise because they raise a company's productivity, which is influenced by local assets and the presence of like firms, institutions, and infrastructure that surround it.[3]

Clustering occurs when companies that operate in the same industry (shoemaking, cybersecurity, or anything in between) are located in close proximity to one another. While the instinctive reaction to clustering may be that it doesn't make sense to have many firms in the same place, all vying for the same customers, it actually does. Clusters bring smaller companies considerable economies of scale. There is a deep pool of expertise and talent, easy access to suppliers, and more.

Drawing on the examples of the flower industry in the Netherlands and the technology cluster in Silicon Valley, among many others, Porter argued that clusters:

- Increase productivity and operational efficiency

- Stimulate and enable innovation
- Facilitate commercialization and new business formation

One may argue, as Thomas Friedman did in *The World Is Flat,* that when globalization and internet-enabled communications become the standard, location shouldn't matter as much.[4] Yet both Silicon Valley as well as Israel's rise as a startup nation prove otherwise. It is ironic: while high-tech makes it possible for far-flung technology companies in India and Israel to have a global impact, clusters prove that geographical proximity still matters a lot. As this chapter moves from Jerusalem to Be'er Sheva, you'll see how general and more specialized clusters (such as Be'er Sheva's cyber cluster) come into existence and then thrive.

"Coming back to Israel, in 1990, I began to think about clusters that can apply here," says Margalit. Initially he had thought about the northern part of Israel, but then turned his sights to Jerusalem, the city where he had spent most of his childhood. He met Jerusalem's legendary mayor Teddy Kollek, and decided to join a government body, the Jerusalem Development Authority, whose goal was to promote economic development in the ancient city. "At first, Kollek was very skeptical about my ideas of bringing technology companies to the city," Margalit says. "He told me Jerusalem was a city of scholars, less of workers, and that you can't come out of nowhere and suddenly engage the city in technology productivity. We were sitting together in his office. At the time, the Mormons had just set up the Brigham Young University Jerusalem Center. I told Kollek that we should take an example from the Mormons, with their approach to enterprise software and biotechnology in Salt Lake City. If the Mormons can build centers of expertise in Salt Lake City, then we can build a technology cluster in the center of Jerusalem. He became less skeptical."[5] Kollek and Margalit even traveled to Salt Lake City to understand what drives its economy, and began to develop a blueprint for bringing technology companies to Jerusalem.

After Kollek was on board, legislation to encourage high-tech investments in Jerusalem was enacted. "We aggressively marketed plots of land in Jerusalem's industrial Har Hotzvim area, which was slated for high-tech, traveling abroad and looking for companies interested in relocating a branch to Israel. When we were in the US, we brought with us Kollek and prominent Israeli industrialists who were on the Development Authority's board, to give the most impact to our visits." In three years, Margalit led dozens of companies to open their centers in Jerusalem's Har Hotzvim location, including IBM and Digital.[6]

But selling all the plots in the Har Hotzvim zone wasn't enough for Margalit—real estate for technology was just the beginning. Now, employment and investment needed to be created.

"In 1991, I heard about venture capital for the first time. I immediately began to look at how the VC industry was built in the US and how that could foster an even greater growth in the high-tech sector in Israel. At the Jerusalem Development Authority, we asked for a program that would bring venture investment to Jerusalem. The Yozma program was born in 1993."[7]

Yozma was an initiative of the Israeli government to seed venture capital funds (the word *Yozma* is Hebrew for "initiative" and also "entrepreneurship"). Venture capital funds that were formed under Yozma still dominate Israel's venture capital space today; they are one of the initial core drivers behind the startup nation. The Yozma program attracted foreign investment into local startups by offering significant tax incentives as well as government dollar-for-dollar matching investments.[8]

In 1993, Margalit left the Jerusalem Development Authority, having decided to set up one of the first Yozma funds by himself. It raised $12 million from investors, which the Israeli government then complemented with a further $8 million. "I told investors that Israel was a hotbed of innovation in communications, that there is a lot of military research, and that the only missing piece is startup money. It took me eight months to raise the fund. At the time, I thought that eight months was too long, that it wasn't going well, but now I understand how quickly the process went. I went over my Rolodex, flew to meet potential investors, and raised money in increments of $250,000.

One of my investors kept pointing to the Persian Gulf on a map to explain to their management what they were investing in."[9]

"In 1995," Margalit continues, "I began investing in earnest. Within five years, the fund returned more than nine dollars on the dollar. I was actively involved with some of the portfolio companies, prompting people to found them and working on their initial business development."

By 2001, Jerusalem Venture Partners had established offices in New York, London, and China.[10] "We were doing exceptionally well with investments in non-Israeli companies, such as Qliktech, and were chosen by *Forbes* magazine as one of world's leading international venture capital funds," Margalit says.[11] He moved to New York, heading JVP's office there.

In 2002, as the US was coming to grips with 9/11 and Israel was reeling from the second intifada (a Palestinian uprising in the West Bank and Gaza) and an unprecedented wave of suicide bombings, Margalit decided to spend more time in Israel, ultimately moving back with his family in 2004. "I could easily have grown the fund even more by staying in New York. But my love for my country and specifically for Jerusalem didn't let me do that," he says.

Jerusalem is a city with large pockets of poverty, and Margalit returned to the social and community work that got him started with venture capital in the first place. "You can't return from New York to Jerusalem without wanting to change reality. During my years in New York, I was taken by how art can change a city—like De Niro's Tribeca film festival, which helped bring the neighborhood back to life after 9/11. So at the height of the intifada, my wife, Debbie, and I founded 'Bakehila' [Hebrew for *in the community*] to enter the poorest areas in a city that is rife with poverty." Bakehila has since impacted over 33,000 children in schools in impoverished neighborhoods in Jerusalem and is currently expanding operations into neighborhoods in the Arab and Ultra-Orthodox sections of Jerusalem, where it is developing new programs to foster the next generation of social leaders in Israel.[12] Furthermore, Bakehila has successfully performed several "social exits" from communities, who now run their own long-term program operations in a self-sustainable and independent fashion.[13]

Margalit also founded a theater called The Lab—"Hama'abada"—which opened its doors in 2003 in a renovated train station warehouse dating back to the Ottoman Empire. It has hosted thousands of in-house and external performances.

Bakehila and The Lab were just the beginning. Margalit also wanted to connect urban renewal in Jerusalem to the fund. So, in 2006, JVP began renovating the historic national Mint building, which is located next to The Lab Theater. Built at the time of the British Mandate in 1937, it was abandoned by the Israeli government in the 1980s. After extensive preservation and renovation efforts, JVP's venture capital fund offices, the JVP Media Labs incubator, and a few of JVP's leading portfolio companies moved in. The entire complex was called "The JVP Media Quarter," and it has become a destination for technology, culture, art, and business.

"When creating The Media Quarter to house the JVP fund, I didn't want to take people to a remote technology park located outside the city but rather to use technology to revive an area which was abandoned and misused," Margalit explains. "The point here is to show change by building a presence, not by talking about it. This is concrete change people can see and understand. New media was very new to venture capital investing at the time and it was a perfect fit with the art and community activity and high-tech activity we wanted to have in the JVP Media Quarter."[14]

Adding media to the existing categories as an investment theme also marked a change. "Instead of saying that Israeli companies can't do new media and consumer-related stuff, that it only belongs in New York, we set up the new media fund in JVP in 2008."

Having raised close to $1.4 billion across nine funds, JVP specializes in technology that is transforming key industries, from communications in the 1990s, to enterprise software and storage in the early 2000s, and on to cybersecurity, big data, and media in the following decade. Today, JVP focuses on the intersections of technology and target markets, with the addition of major themes such as artificial intelligence, computer vision, mobility, and more. As noted earlier, the fund has led thirty-five successful exits, twelve of which were IPOs on the NASDAQ, with a total exit transaction value of over $20 billion.[15] In 2005, *Forbes* magazine selected Margalit as the top-ranking non-American venture capitalist on its "Midas List."[16]

The tech ecosystem in Jerusalem grew dramatically in a matter of a few years' time. From fifty to over five hundred startups and over six hundred tech companies and from zero to fifteen accelerators and coworking spaces, Jerusalem has been dubbed one of the five fastest emerging tech hubs by *Time* magazine.[17] As a member of the Knesset, Margalit argued that Israel's periphery was in a grave crisis, unable to benefit from the fruits of the startup nation.[18] Of the thirty-six countries that form the OECD, Israel is one of the "leading countries" in income inequality.[19] Margalit's vision is to turn Israel's periphery into seven regions of high-tech excellence that will attract innovation and international investments. The idea is to create an ecosystem around a chosen theme and turn it into a region of innovation. The Eastern Gallilee would become a center for agri-tech and food-tech; Haifa, which is in the west-north part of Israel, would become the center of excellence for digital health; and so on.

BE'ER SHEVA

Following the transformation of Jerusalem in 2011, Erel was visiting students in the distant southern desert capital of Be'er Sheva, home to the Ben Gurion University of the Negev. With one of the world's first graduate programs in cyber studies, the university's visionary president, Professor Rivka Karmi, had ideas to create a biotech park adjacent to the university. Taking a deeper look into the planned demographics of the region, the university's clear expertise in cyber studies, and the nation's plans to move a large number of its leading tech units to the south, Margalit convinced the president to contemplate turning the park into a cyber park, leveraging the strengths of the various potential players. This gained further support from the city's municipality and the idea was born. Cyberspark remains to this day Israel's cyber capital and one of the main international cyber centers of the world. In 2014, at the Sixth Negev Conference, Israel's prime minister, Benyamin Netanyahu, declared that "Beersheba will not only be the cyber capital of Israel but one of the most important places in the cybersecurity field in the world."[20] Just a few years before, no one would have thought that the southern city would develop any technology expertise, let alone be globally recognized for it. No one except Margalit and the JVP team.

"Establishing the JVP Cyber Labs [JVP's Cyber Incubator, in partnership with the State of Israel's Incubator Program, and Ben Gurion University] in Be'er Sheva was an act of Chutzpah," says Yoav Tzruya, a JVP general partner who previously headed the JVP Cyber Labs in Be'er Sheva.[21] On one of the walls at JVP Cyber Labs there's a photograph that embodies his thoughts. The photo was taken a few years back while visiting the future location of Be'er Sheva's Advanced Technologies Park, where JVP Cyber Labs is located today. In it, you can see camels crossing a dusty road, against a backdrop of the desert and a modern steel-and-glass office building that is under construction.[22]

Be'er Sheva is a less privileged city in Israel's southern periphery, where the Mediterranean climate gives in to the desert, and where Bedouins and camels aren't a rare sight. Yet it is also home to a renowned cyber center whose investments have done remarkably well. "Look at these camels in the picture," says Tzruya. "At the time it seems like an irrational vision and almost a crazy dream to create at this location a technology high-tech hub. Today it is one of the fastest developing and one of the more specialized and professional acclaimed hubs in the country . . . and we have hundreds of international delegations coming every year to Be'er Sheva, where the JVP Cyber Labs is one of the 'must' locations to visit. They come here to learn from the Israeli experience of how to create a local ecosystem, how to leverage venture capital investment, how to create a productive public-private partnership, how to engage with the local university and municipality, how to turn small startups to scale-up companies, how to raise foreign capital for a future tech innovator, as well as how to attract leading multinationals to open their activity as part of the mix. Basically, to create something out of nothing. Many of them want to build ecosystems and open incubators in their own countries and are eager to learn what we have done that have made it so successful."[23]

Tzruya explains the almost perfect storm that made Be'er Sheva into a cyber capital. "What's so special about Be'er Sheva? I think the secret lies in the concurrence of many factors: a highly focused investment theme, a healthy and growing ecosystem, and the geography. We knew that a regional competitive advantage for Be'er Sheva was truly emerging. We envisioned a perfrect storm coming to the desert. We hoped to be able to leverage Israel's investment in state-of-the-art cyber professionals, to tap public-private partnerships to create the bedrock of a thriving ecosystem, to be able to access core research performed in the universities in Israel, and to invite multinational companies and start-ups to take part in this ecosystem. In 2012, we could already see this starting to bud. EMC and Deutsche Telekom already had centers there. We knew the army was planning to move its cyber units to the south, giving the city access to great talent. The military generates between three and four thousand trained, state-of-the-art engineers that know everything about cybersecurity, each and every year."[24]

In a move to rejuvenate the IDF's aging infrastructure and to make available wide swaths of real estate in Tel Aviv and central Israel that are now needed for urban growth, the IDF decided to build a "city" near Be'er Sheva in the Negev desert that would consolidate many of its activities. The Negev accounts for nearly two-thirds of Israel's land, but less than 10 percent of its population lives there. The mega-base, one of the biggest infrastructure projects in Israel's history, is slated for completion by 2020 and is expected to bring jobs and investments to the south.

"It's important not to forget the talent question," Tzruya says, "as it is closely tied to the entrepreneurship question. Ben-Gurion University is a center of excellence in cybersecurity, cryptography, computer science, and mathematics, and it has a unique graduate studies program in cybersecurity. We also knew that Israel has successful cybersecurity companies—such as CyberArk and Checkpoint—and that this talent pool will also be available to our investment theme.

Be'er Sheva isn't the only cyber talent pool in the world. The Washington, DC, area has a huge cyber talent pool coming from the NSA. But something is missing there, and the spillover effect, where people transition from governmental organizations to civilian industry, that we saw happen almost immediately in Be'er Sheva, didn't happen in Washington, DC. In the DC area, cyber innovation happens in the government sector for the most part, not in the entrepreneurial sector. People join the NSA in their late twenties and work there for the rest of their lives. The personal qualities of people in Be'er Sheva strike me as the opposite of that. The people I meet here are hungry for success. If one of your friends was part of Fraud Sciences [one of the first companies to have a successful exit in the cyber space], Checkpoint [the inventor of the firewall], or another cybersecurity startup with people you were in the army with, you, too, would feel compelled to found a company. A startup is a basic expectation here.

"What's more important is that we were following the market, and there were signs that the need for cyberprotection was at an inflection point. Previously, most enterprises thought about cybersecurity as a necessary expenditure for doing business. Suddenly we saw enterprises, which are the entities that buy the products that our cyber startups sell, thinking about cybersecurity as a must beyond the need for business continuity in case of a cyberattack. They began to think about cyber capabilities as a new source of revenue, a differentiator whose value spills over into the product. Suddenly enterprises wanted companies to tell them which cybersecurity measures they'd taken. These were signs that we were choosing the right investment theme at the right time.

"And yet Be'er Sheva still required a leap of faith," Tzruya adds. "Most startups in Israel are located in central Tel Aviv or in Herzeliya, a city that's a twenty-minute drive from Tel Aviv. There were many engineers and entrepreneurs there. But we couldn't create an ecosystem for cyber in Israel's center. We felt the cyber theme would drown in the noise of other investment themes and there would be too much competition for talent. We began thinking that focusing solely on cybersecurity in a new place is a better option. Instead of making incremental changes—adding something new to the innovation in the center of Israel—we could dedicate a special type of activity to the south of the country. We would be there first, but that means we had to do the heavy lifting to create the ecosystem. With municipal support, we established a footprint—a high-tech park—that was close to both the university and the army base. The fact that all of Be'er Sheva's commercial cyber activity—EMC, Deutsche Telekom, PayPal, and the JVP Cyber Labs incubator—reside in the same two buildings is important—it ensures the cross-pollination of ideas. Every day, startups can easily partake in projects with both the multinationals that have a presence in Be'er Sheva and the university. This is a big factor in creating critical mass. The proximity of the buildings is really important. No driving to important meetings. When I have visitors, we spend three hours in the buildings, and people are very impressed with what they see. There are many joint projects between the three types of players in the ecosystem and they all make an effort to sustain these ties."

For example, JVP invests in its ties with the university by sponsoring an entrepreneurship project. It helps the university attract students. "We grant scholarships—it's a small thing but the students understand that there are startups here," Tzruya explains. "We invested in getting the local government—the municipality—on board. The local municipality wants to see a spillover effect, justifiably so. We work with local businesses; we want the local population to see the incubator as a meaningful player in their environment. We did not want the Cyber Park to become a disconnected place. When we opened, no one knew there was a cyber cluster in Be'er Sheva and we wanted to tell the world that we were open for business. So we organized a big cyber conference. We offered a $1 million prize—and we invited our ecosystem partners to act as judges. All the prize finalists had to come to a large security trade show in the US and make presentations. We wanted to make sure our message was presented on a global level."[25]

"In many respects our greatest Chutzpah was going to Be'er Sheva," says Liran Tancman of CyActive, JVP Cyber Labs' first exit. "Many thought our going to Be'er Sheva was a dumb idea, or a crazy bet.

Well, it wasn't a dumb idea. Look around you in Tel Aviv. A hundred and fifty cyber startups are struggling to recruit anyone that knows anything about cyber. Shlomi, my partner in CyActive, taught a course at Ben Gurion University; everyone came to listen to him. He could choose the best people. Not to mention the fact that the Ben Gurion University has Israel's only evolutionary algorithm research lab. We controlled the hiring pipeline and it worked well for us."[26]

To create critical mass, JVP started Cyberspark, a nonprofit organization designed to be the central coordinating body for joint cyber industry activities in Be'er Sheva. The initiative is promoting the region and the city of Be'er Sheva as a global cyber center, encouraging joint academia-industry partnerships, and supporting the articulation of plans to recruit and develop human resources in the field, as well as incentive plans to draw additional companies, both international and Israeli, to establish projects or base themselves in the region.

"We joined forces to ensure that the momentum behind Be'er Sheva is growing," Tzruya explains. "Each company in Cyberspark may compete with the others for the same resources. But we still work together to bring more multinationals to Be'er Sheva, to create an explosion effect and prevent potential implosion. It also creates solidarity and closer relationships between the companies that make up the Be'er Sheva cluster. In a way, this body cools the competitive forces between the different players, by moderating the way they work together, creating some central points of agreement, and managing the flow of information between them."[27]

SHIMRIT TZUR-DAVID, COFOUNDER and CTO of Secret Double Octopus, tells her story of working with JVP Cyber Labs. She had a PhD in Information Security, and had just finished her post-doctorate at the Hebrew University of Jerusalem. "For me, each academic paper I published was a startup, since I described an operational system. I loved doing this work. I loved inventing these ideas."[28]

Tzur-David was always passionate about computers: "As a twelve-year-old I already had this passion for computers. My brother studied computer science in high school, and my parents bought our first PC. I grew up in a small community—a Moshav—and most people didn't have one. I went through my brother's books, began to copy code and write it on the computer, just to see what it does. It was so much fun! You write something and it happens! To study computer science, you have to be thrilled by the process of coding and seeing what happens. If you don't have that, you won't succeed. Studying computer science isn't easy, and that's why you need the passion and the thrill."

In 2014, Prof Shlomi Dolev of Ben Gurion University (today a cofounder and CSO at Secret Double Octopus) posted an opening for a post-doc researcher. Tzur-David applied. "Initially I thought I shouldn't go there, Be'er Sheva is too remote, but I decided to check it out anyway. I went to Be'er Sheva and the first idea that came up when I was chatting with Prof Dolev was the idea behind Secret Double Octopus. I remember the moment. I told him that everyone today takes a key and encrypts their data. I said, why don't we do this in another way, with the secret sharing scheme?"

Secret sharing is about splitting a secret and giving its parts to many different people, so in order to discover the secret you need the parts from all (or enough of) these people. "I took the idea of secret sharing but instead used the internet to create different paths for each part of the secret from point to point. We could split the secret not between a few people but between a few paths, so it is as proven as secret sharing and can't be decrypted no matter what the computing power is."[29]

"You can throw away the keys, throw away the dependence on a third party, and that's it—let's go write a paper about this, I said. I thought it was a great idea academically. I wasn't interested in a career in industry, I wanted to pursue an academic career, but Prof Dolev immediately understood it was a great idea that can have great applications. I remember him giving me a very intense look and saying that he thought we should go meet JVP Cyber Labs. He also said we have to write a patent really quickly."

In 2018, Tzur David won the Geektime Award for The Best Technology R&D Manager in Israel.[30]

THEN WE TAKE NEW YORK

In October 2018, JVP launched its newest hub in SOHO, New York's first international cybersecurity investment hub, with the goal of growing cyber startups into major businesses.[31] The initiative forms part of the New York City Economic Development (NYCEDC) Cyber NYC program, which aims to make New York City a global leader in cybersecurity, producing ten thousand jobs within five years.[32] It is also a collaboration with a few of New York's academic institutions, including Columbia University, New York University, Cornell Tech, and the City University of New York.[33] "If the West Coast is the US technology hub, New York can become an international technology hub in close partnership with Israel and the international community to build the next generation of cybersecurity companies to counter the new threats," said Margalit.[34] Nicholas Lalla, Assistant Vice President for Urban Innovation at NYCEDC and project lead for Cyber NYC, notes that "it is one of the biggest and boldest and most multifaceted cybersecurity initiatives in the world. Siting it in New York signals the criticality of cybersecurity. We're saying that cybersecurity will be a permanent fixture in the world economy and in our lives."[35]

Yoav Tzruya adds: "The value of this work will trickle down to organizations everywhere. Cyber challenges, primarily as they relate to underserved markets such as the small-medium-business sector, are universal, and the effort to find technological solutions for them can only benefit from international collaboration. We also hope the collaboration will have a positive impact on awareness, information exchange, standardization, legislation, incident response, and best practices, which are all much needed."[36]

17

THE SIX PILLARS OF A SUCCESSFUL ECOSYSTEM

You don't start communities. Communities already exist.
The question to ask is how you can help them do it better?
—MARK ZUCKERBERG

erusalem and Be'er Sheva might have seemed like unlikely locations for startups, but as has been proven, they both had attributes that could be developed into genuine ecosystems for high-tech entrepreneurship. Can an ecosystem for startups be created from scratch? What do we tell the delegations from China, Europe, the US, South America, South East Asia, Australia, and Africa who come to us for advice on how they can duplicate this success in their own countries and regions?

The answer to the first question is yes and no. Technology clusters and startup ecosystems *can* be nurtured and developed, but even with the best of intentions and all the money in the world, they can't simply be willed into being. They must be planted in fertile soil. This chapter is my attempt to answer the second question.

When analyzing the Israeli ecosystem, or any other successful ecosystem around the world, one can point to six main pillars that they were built on. This kind of analysis can help stakeholders in their efforts to build new ecosystems, allowing them to focus on what is missing or needs further development. And it can be invaluable to entrepreneurs who are looking for the ideal place to locate their venture.

PILLAR NO. 1: TALENT

Talent, Talent, Talent! This is probably the most important DNA of any ecosystem. Without talented people, you cannot build an ecosystem! It is as simple as that.

Sometimes people think that talent just means computer science engineers, mathematics PhDs, scientists, algorithmicists, and so on. These people are obviously very important assets for the talent pool, but they are not enough. When we talk about talent, we are also talking about talented entrepreneurs, people who want to change reality, to challenge the status quo. People with true passion, who have a real sense of urgency to build companies that can transform whole categories. Entrepreneurs don't just come out of STEM programs (Science, Technology, Engineering, and Mathematics). They can come from business, marketing, content, security, or in the case of Erel Margalit, from philosophy and literature.

The nice thing about talented people is that they attract other talented people. *Talent attracts talent!* If you built your ecosystem well enough to attract the right kinds of people, more will follow, until you have a positive growing spiral of talent. On top of that, talent is what many of the other players in the ecosystem, such as investors, multinationals, and academia, are looking for. So, the first and most important thing to do when planning and building a high-tech ecosystem would be to nurture, grow, and develop local talent, as well as to attract talent from other locations. Developing talent is a process that may take a few years, and should start as early as primary school. Ideally, governments are making sure that they are creating the right programs and incentives for kids to pursue their mathematical, scientific, and entrepreneurial talents.

If you want to retain that talent, they need to have affordable places to live, to have cultural activities, a variety of entertainment, good schools to send their kids to, and amenities to keep their lives outside of work interesting.

PILLAR NO. 2: CROSS STAGE FUNDING

A healthy ecosystem has a variety of investment vehicles, from Angel investors and incubators through early stage and mid-stage VCs, all the way to late stage and growth funds. Multi-stage funding enables startups to invest the time and capital they need to develop and commercialize their innovative products and grow them at the right pace. It doesn't mean that these startups should not acquire clients, users, and build effective sales teams and channels. They should definitely do all those things! They should also drive for revenues, in order to prove that they have a good product-market fit, and that they have found a successful and repeatable business model. However, when the funding environment is a healthy one, the startups can afford to not be profitable in their first few years, but rather focus on market share and growth. Naturally, any company should strive to be a highly profitable one, but this is not necessarily the most important KPI in the first years of a startup.

When the funding environment is limited to a certain stage, such as early stage funding only, when there are no follow-up investors to take startups to the next level, they will be forced to reach breakeven or profitability before they are ready, and the chances that they will be able to become a global category leader become that much slimmer.

Governments can do much to attract investors, by providing them with tax incentives and, as Israel did with its Yozma program, matching grants.

PILLAR NO. 3:
PRESENCE OF LARGE CORPORATES
AND MULTINATIONAL ENTERPRISES

Multinationals play a very important role within the global high-tech industry but also within local ecosystems. More than three hundred different multinationals have a presence in Israel: Apple, Intel, Google, Microsoft, SAP, Huawei, Barclays, and Deutsche Telekom, just to name a few.

Each of these multinationals has a different kind of presence. Some have an R&D center; some a local accelerator; others invest in local VCs and have scouting teams on the ground that are constantly looking for relevant startups. Each develops a local presence that suits its needs. But the common denominator is that they all want to be close to the latest innovations, and the talent.

Physical presence is only half of the story when it comes to multinationals. The other half is how involved in the local high-tech community they are. They create and participate in almost every event and they are in ongoing dialogues with startups, Angel investors, VCs, and other multinationals. Apart from their interest, they bring a lot of value to the ecosystem in various ways. First, they can say what it is that they are looking for, what it is that the market is looking for, what their pains are, what kind of technologies they are interested in today, and what technologies they will need in the future, given their forecasts and strategies. This is highly valuable both for entrepreneurs and investors. Another advantage of their presence is that they are highly accessible. Investors can consult them during the due diligence process with a potential company, they can share deal flow that they see, and in some cases they can invite the multinationals to co-invest as a strategic investor in a company. Many of them have an inorganic growth strategy and thus they are also potential buyers of startups.

One trend that is interesting to mention is that only a few years ago, these multinational corporations would only look at companies that had already finalized their product development, and that had proven market traction and revenues to show—companies that were in at least their A-round, and preferably their B- or even C-round. But today the situation is different. Corporations have acknowledged that in order to be on the cutting edge of innovation they must engage with the ecosystem and the startups at a much earlier phase—sometimes as early as seed round companies, with no product yet, but that may have a strong team with a bold and ambitious vision or a unique intellectual property. They have opened dozens of accelerators in Israel so they can be in touch with early stage startups on an everyday basis.

PILLAR NO. 4: GOVERNMENT SUPPORT

The role that governments can play in building and supporting high-tech ecosystems is often underestimated. Since high tech is a high-risk business, some of this risk should be absorbed and budgeted for by the government. This kind of support should not only come from the federal government, but also from local regions and municipalities.

The main test for any government commitment is the budget that they allocate for this purpose. The larger the budget that is allocated for high tech, the higher the commitment is. But that is only the first step. Industry-friendly mechanisms are needed that enable startups to receive funding without too much bureaucracy, according to clear and well-defined criteria, and via a variety of programs that support various company stages, from very early seed stage to late stage companies that still need to invest heavily in R&D.

In Israel, the government sets aside hundreds of millions of dollars a year to support startups. The programs are managed by the Israeli Innovation Authority, which is a part of the Ministry of Economy.[1] On top of that, municipalities also support local ecosystems. Various programs target the main three players: entrepreneurs, investors, and corporates. To mention a few, a risk-free loan of $500,000 is available to seed-stage companies that join one of the nineteen government licensed incubators; there are significant capital gains tax incentives and many incentive programs for entrepreneurs, investors, academia, and corporations.[2] These kinds of supports not only enable the creation of more technology jobs, but have spillover effects. Research shows that for every technology job, on average, four more jobs are created in the service sector.[3] An interesting data point is that the economic effects (in terms of incremental GDP) of the government's investment in R&D are, at a minimum, more than five times the amount of money invested by the government.[4] This investment is also paid back to the country in other forms, such as taxes coming from high-tech export and large exits, higher employment figures, peripheral development, and so on.[5]

PILLAR NO. 5: ACADEMIA

Many countries have very strong universities and research centers. But relatively few of these institutions are connected to the local high-tech ecosystems. There are various ways in which research institutions and academia can engage with high-tech industry. The most common is by forming tech-transfer companies, fully owned by the institutions, whose main role is to commercialize the intellectual property (IP) that they create, register, and patent. This can come in various shapes and forms, all the way from starting and building a new company based on such IP, to licensing the IP to large multinational corporates. The main advantage of starting a company based on an existing IP is that in most cases the technology research is already complete. The main task of the new startup is to productize the technology and optimize a go-to-market strategy. Productizing an existing strong technology is usually a much faster process than actually developing it; the company saves a lot of time and preferably has a significant technological edge on its competitors. The largest exit through M&A that ever came out of Israel, the $15 billion sale of MobileEye to Intel, was based on academic research done by Hebrew University's Professor Amnon Sha'ashua.[6]

Another important role that universities play within high-tech ecosystems is turning out new generations of computer engineers, mathematicians, business management professionals, designers, and others who join startups. Many of these institutions offer practical courses on entrepreneurship. Some have formed their own internal accelerators to support students who are interested in starting a company while they are still enrolled at the university.

PILLAR NO. 6: THE ENTREPRENEURIAL CULTURE AND THE CHUTZPAH FACTOR

As we've discussed throughout this book, this pillar in some cases is the make-or-break factor of a high-tech ecosystem. Chutzpah, audacity, risk-taking, skepticism of authority, a burning sense of urgency, a global vision, an ability to turn failure into a learning experience, and other entrepreneurial cultural factors are what define successful ecosystems and drive entrepreneurship. You don't need to be born with all of these elements; many of them can be taught or trained.

But the passion for creating a new venture that will challenge the status quo and disrupt it in a significant way, that will change an industry and the world—that passion cannot be taught. It is easy enough to snuff it out, and many cultures do. But when it is recognized, nurtured, and enabled, it can create miracles.

BUILDING A CENTER OF EXCELLENCE

A large and mature ecosystem can contain a variety of verticals and players from various kinds of disciplines. Places like Silicon Valley, Israel, London, and a few others have grown to be a home for many high-tech startups and corporations, serving a vast range of different ventures.

However, new and emerging ecosystems would probably succeed more if they could be more focused, and brand themselves as centers of excellence in a specific field. In Chapter 14, we discussed the theme that an investment vehicle should have, and we've talked about verticals and horizontals. Just as an early stage investment vehicle chooses a certain theme to focus on, so should an emerging ecosystem, in order to create competitive advantages that will attract talent, capital, and businesses to that ecosystem.

Preferably, the theme chosen should be based on existing cornerstones that are already in the market. For example, if there is a strong financial system, a few local startups, an international financial institution, and initial activity around fintech, it is good soil to grow a fintech ecosystem. Similarily, one can think of a potential ecosystem where there are many hospitals, health-related research centers, and a few healthcare IT startups as a good starting point for a healthcare, wellness, and medical device focus. The focus could also be on a horizontal topic such as artificial intelligence, computer vision, robotics, IoT, and so on. The vertical or the horizontal should be focused and well defined, but also wide to grow into a significant ecosystem that can be positioned as a world-class center of excellence. Such an ecosystem can have more than one theme, but it should probably grow in a linear way, starting with one, and then expand to the second theme, and so on.

The reason it is important to focus is that by doing so all six pillars of the ecosystem can be targeted at this vertical. So there will be a special focus on education and training in this theme, investors who are focused on the theme would be interested in having a presence and scouting the startups operating there, the corporations and the multinationals who are active in this theme would be interested in the technologies and the innovations that are emerging from there, the government and the municipalities will know what kind of targeted incentives to give to the relevant startups, investors and corporations that are active in the space, and finally academic and other research centers could have a special focus on the conduct and the commercialization of IP in this space.

Anyone who is in charge of a high-tech ecosystem, or planning on launching one, can use these six pillars in order to make an analysis of their ecosystem, and prioritize the actions to take in order to strengthen the ecosystem wherever needed. This should be based on a thorough collection of quantitative and qualitative data, so the outcome will be as accurate as possible. This data should include, for example, the capital invested and the breakdown of investments in the last three years; the breakdown of various verticals in which the investments were made; the number of active startups and the breakdown of the stages they are in; the number of accelerators, incubators, and VCs and their sizes; the number of exits that came out of the ecosystem; the density of engineers and computer scientists per capita; the main differentiators and competitive edges of the local industries and local enterprises; the presence of multinationals in the market and the acquisitions they have made; the government programs that support the high-tech industry, such as tax incentives, preferred tax areas, special early stage programs, foreign capital investment laws, and incentives for multinational operations; and the leading academic institutions and their strongest departments and research domains.

Once this data is collected and analyzed, it can also be presented in a user-friendly visual diagram. If one presents these pillars as a hexagonal (see below), one can create a diagram based on the ecosystem

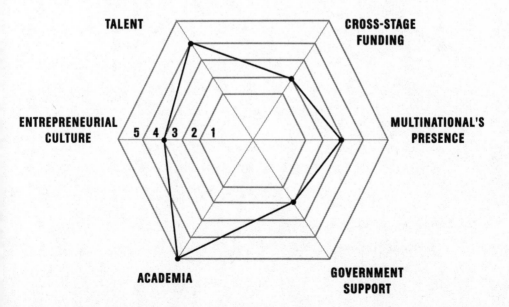

data, which will graphically demonstrate the strengths and weaknesses of the ecosystem. It could be on a scale of 1 to 5, where 1 is the lowest rank and 5 is the highest.

Once such an exercise is made, it can assist the leaders of the ecosystem with their decisionmaking and guide their prioritization. For example, what actions need to be taken in order to strengthen the multinational presence? What government programs and incentives should be initiated in order to attract private capital for investing in this ecosystem? What actions should be done to bring the academia closer to the industry? And so on.

This exercise is also relevant when looking for the right strategic theme to focus on. When collecting and analyzing the data, one should examine if there is a potential theme emerging from the numbers. If there are a few cornerstones that support a certain theme (i.e., healthcare, aviation, agriculture), even small ones, this can be very relevant for the strategic planning phase and the decisionmaking regarding the vertical to focus on. There are preparations to be made beforehand, such as collecting relevant data for each of the pillars, analyzing this data, and giving the right weight to each of the data points, so the diagram will indeed reflect the reality of the ecosystem.

EPILOGUE

I n the introduction of this book, I told how the trigger for writing it came from a question (or perhaps I should call it a challenge) posed by a member of the audience during a talk I was giving at an international high-tech conference: Could I summarize my fifty-minute talk about Israel's high-tech success in a single 280-character tweet. My answer, you may recall, was that "it is all about Chutzpah."

Many questions I field in such venues relate to the initial decision-making process of building or investing in new ventures: "What should I focus on when building my next startup?" or "What companies should I look at when considering my next investment?" The answer I give, based on my personal observations and my many conversations with entrepreneurs, is that people are driven by different motivations, which means that their decisionmaking is propelled by a variety of vectors. I've tried to categorize the variations and have come up with a list of ten drivers for decisionmaking. Naturally, many decisions are driven by more than one of them, but in most cases, there is one main driver, followed by others.

1. VERTICAL DRIVEN

Some entrepreneurs and investors choose specific verticals, such as healthcare, fintech, agri-tech, medical devices, travel-tech, water-tech, renewable energy, or cybersecurity.

The main advantage of this approach is that one becomes an expert in a specific industry. Given today's fierce competitive landscape and the rapid pace of technological developments, you need to be on top of everything that is going on in your space—the new innovations that are constantly being developed, the research at academic and other institutions, the patents that have been registered, the activity of the various players in the vertical, and so on. The more you know about a certain domain, the better your chances of creating or investing in a company that will introduce a real innovation to the market and have high potential to dominate it.

The main challenge of this approach is that many of the boundaries between the traditional verticals are blurring; what we used to call a clear vertical is harder to define nowadays. Many domains are becoming multi-verticalized. For example, fintech companies have elements of cybersecurity; there are many common denominators between agri-tech and food-tech, and quite a few of them also relate to healthcare in some form. This does not mean that the vertical approach is no longer relevant, but the definitions need to be reexamined and in many cases rewritten.

2. HORIZONTAL DRIVEN

Other entrepreneurs and investors choose a specific horizontal, such as artificial intelligence, blockchain, computer vision, robotics, big data, sensors, materials, and so on.

Like the vertical approach, the main advantage here is that one becomes an expert in a specific domain. But since this approach is more technology-driven than market-driven, the main disadvantage is that your expertise may be too broad to leverage commercially. For example, "materials" can range from construction materials to new fabrics. "Robotics" can range all the way from an industrial robot to a home appliance robot. Moreover, isolating a certain technological horizontal may limit the broader picture that should be examined. Many of the developments today, and probably even more in the future, will use a mix of technologies to come up with the best product. A new fabric may have a sensor embedded in it, or a robot will use a computer vision technology and natural language processing (NLP) capabilities.

In order to overcome these challenges, an entrepreneur or investor who is focusing on a certain horizontal will seek advice from market experts who can assist with the business aspects, as well as experts who know the other technologies that are needed to complete the full picture.

3. NEED/PAIN DRIVEN

Some entrepreneurs and investors identify an existing pain in the market that does not have a good enough solution, or forecast a future need that will emerge and focus on solving it. Whether a user is an individual, a small business, a corporation, a city, a government, or anyone else, new needs are constantly emerging—for example, the need to be connected, the need for information in real time, the need to be able to manage tasks on the go, or the need to protect privacy or to analyze large amounts of data in real time. Industrial plants need to predict machine breakdowns before they occur, financial institutions need to protect their computing systems, cities need new kinds of transportation solutions, and much more. The means for meeting these needs are constantly changing, and are one of the main forces behind innovation. Forecasting future needs is not trivial at all, and most people who adopt this approach base their assumptions on their analyses of data, trends, technological breakthroughs, and forecasts of leaders in certain fields, whether they are individuals or corporate structures. However, as history has proven more than once, these leaders' predictions are often wrong, so one should approach them more as opinions than absolute truth.

The main advantage of this approach is that it is market-driven. One must be very close to the market and know it extremely well in order to understand where it is going, and what new needs will emerge. For example, when the IoT market began to develop, the need to protect the billions of devices that could be hacked and compromised (smart-cars, smart-homes, smart-medical-devices, smart-infrastructures, and so on) emerged with it.

The main disadvantage of this approach is that if the need already exists, it is likely that numerous teams around the world are already working on finding a solution for it. There may be various approaches to the solution, but from day one a fierce race is underway. When forecasting a need, there is the risk of timing and scale—when will this need occur and will it be significant enough that the solution will scale accordingly? There are numerous examples of companies that were either too early or too late to the market, or the market they forecast turned out to be much smaller than they originally anticipated.

4. TEAM/TALENT DRIVEN

This approach is based on the simple fact that behind almost any successful company, there is a great team with talented individuals and strong leadership. There are many examples of successful companies that started with a team that at first didn't know exactly what they wanted to do, but knew that whatever they decided on, they would do it together. There are also examples of investors who invested in a strong team before they knew what it was that they wanted to build. The assumption behind this approach is that smart and talented people will come up with breakthrough ideas, and will know how to execute them in the best way.

The main advantage with this approach is that, in a constantly changing environment, the only constant variable that has a significant impact on a company's performance is the founding team. Naturally, the larger team of the company is dynamic, growing, and changing, but the founding team is like its DNA. Many people use the metaphor of a marriage between founding members of a new venture or between an investor and the team. You want to make sure you are "marrying" the right people, and only then can you decide what you want to do together.

The main disadvantage of this approach is that the team may take more time than expected to come up with a winning idea. Some entrepreneurs spend a year or two just researching and investigating markets before they align on their next venture.

5. FUNDING/CO-INVESTORS DRIVEN

The main idea behind this approach is that since it takes capital to build a company, startups should be appealing to the investors who can provide it. An entrepreneur may focus on what is considered a "hot space" or build a strong and "fundable" team. By doing so, the chances of funding their venture will increase.

From an investor perspective, this approach turns on the presence of co-investors. Many investors, whether they are Angels or late stage investors, would never commit money if they are the only ones at the table.

The main advantage of this approach from the entrepreneur's angle is that from day one the main thought is on how to build a fundable company. This mindset increases the chances for funding and thus for the company to actually happen. From the investor's perspective, sharing the financial support of the company with other investors lowers costs, and having other experts' due diligence mitigates risks.

The main disadvantage is that in some cases a negative "club investment" dynamic may lead to a wrong decision. As one large and successful investor once told me, "The heaviest losses I have had and the most painful company write-offs I've done were done together with the biggest names and the best investors." That doesn't mean that co-investing is not a positive thing: in many cases it works very well, but one should be cautious when relying only on other investors' decisionmaking.

6. TECHNOLOGY/IP DRIVEN

The rationale behind this approach is that in today's cluttered and competitive market, a company must have a real technological advantage, preferably with a unique and distinctive IP. Many market breakthroughs and large technology-related M&As happen thanks to a core-technology innovation. Some large companies were built based on strong IP, which was either developed internally or at academic and other research institutions. Many universities have their own dedicated fund to invest in startups that are built based on IP that they helped develop.

The main advantage of this approach is that the startup has a competitive advantage out of the gate. Moreover, sometimes the IP is based on years of costly research, which the company doesn't have to pay for or develop, but only productize and commercialize it.

The main disadvantage is that it's a technology-first approach, and the technology comes before the definition of the market, the product, the go-to-market strategy, the distribution strategy, the business model, and other market-business topics that should be considered early on. This approach sometimes leads to companies "looking for their market" or "searching for the need," i.e., they have an amazing technology but don't really know what to do with it, who will use it, who will pay for it, and so on. There's a real risk that the market for the technology will turn out to be small, or in some cases, nonexistent.

7. BUSINESS MODEL DRIVEN

This approach is premised on the idea that if there's no strong and proven business model, there is no justification for the company to exist. It doesn't mean that the company needs to be profitable—it may decide to invest in topline growth and expansion—but having revenues is crucial. Some entrepreneurs adopt this model due to a lack of funding in their market. Since they cannot rely on external investments, they must think from day one how their company will fund itself through its own sales. There are also quite a few investors who see the proven business model as the only real indicator for market traction, i.e., if someone is willing to pay for a product or offering, then it means that there is value in it. Of course, there are more questions that must be asked before following a business model approach, such as how much are consumers willing to pay, is it a recurring or non-recurring revenue model, are there opportunities for an up-sell to increase the revenues, and so on.

The main advantage of this approach is that the product-market fit is not a theoretical question but is being put to the ultimate business test of sales from the very beginning; the company knows how the market views its offering and what it is worth. For investors, there is less risk, as the company has already proven that it has a real value to the market and is self-sustaining.

The main disadvantage of this approach is that in many cases the disruption is not only in the product but also in the business model, and since the business model is new it sometimes takes time to refine it and prove that it actually works.

In cases where the business model approach is a necessity due to lack of funding, the disadvantage is that the rate of growth may be relatively slow, and a better-funded competitor may overtake the startup and win the market. Fast scaling is key in the race to become a category leader, and external funding is often what fuels a company's engine to run faster.

8. NEW CATEGORY/DISRUPTION DRIVEN

This approach focuses on companies and innovations that are game changers, either because they invent a new category (like Twitter, for example), or because they will disrupt the market in a way that changes everything that was known before (as Uber and Airbnb disrupted the transportation and hospitality markets).

The main advantage of this approach is that companies that manage to either create their own category or significantly disrupt an existing one have the highest chance to become the category leader. In many cases, they become synonymous with the category, and so even if a competitor emerges (which in most instances will be the case), they will still be perceived as the market leader and the others as me-too products. Naturally, the rewards for the entrepreneurs and the investors in terms of valuations and multiples are very high.

The main disadvantage with this approach is that it usually is a very big bet. If entrepreneurs and investors truly believe that their idea will conquer the market, their confidence is likely to translate to large investments, not only in research and development but in business development and marketing as well. And there is always the possibility that they are wrong.

9. IMPACT DRIVEN

In recent years, more and more entrepreneurs and investors are looking to build or invest in companies that have impact, companies with "double bottom lines." The term double bottom line (DBL) means that, alongside the traditional bottom line that measures financial profit or loss, a second bottom line measures a company's performance in terms of its positive social impact. The definition of social impact is very wide and can include a range of criteria, from cultural to environmental. When I asked a self-described impact investor how he defines it, his definition was very simple and wide. "Anything that does good," he replied.[1]

The main advantage of this approach is that the company has an additional purpose, another reason for being, on top of the traditional financial one. Management and employees can identify with a higher cause, which gives them a much stronger sense of solidarity with the company.

The main challenge with this approach is to actually create that second bottom line, i.e., to measure the impact that it has by defining clear and quantitative impact KPIs. There are various ways to do this, but in many cases, it is complicated, and in some cases almost impossible. Some impact investors will condition their investment based on the company's ability to measure its second bottom line, and will invest only in startups that can prove that they are able to do it. Organizations such as B Corporations are addressing this issue by assessing the company's overall positive impact on its workers, customers, community, and environment.[2] The combination of third-party validation, public transparency, and legal accountability helps the companies they've certified build trust and value.

10. PASSION DRIVEN

The last approach is much more intuitive and emotional than any of the others, and less driven by data or facts. It is more of a "gut-feeling" approach than an analytical one. However, as described earlier in this book, passion is one of the most important and powerful assets that a new venture can have. Passion is what drives any good entrepreneur, giving them the energy they need to overcome the many obstacles that any startup runs into. The passion of the entrepreneur should be for that thing that they are building. It doesn't matter what vertical or horizontal it is, whether it is considered to be in a hot space or not, or whether it has a proven business model or a groundbreaking technology. Naturally, this approach will also be relevant for investors. The passion could be for a certain vertical or for a certain horizontal. It could be for a certain team, or it could be for a product that they've fallen in love with.

The main advantage of this approach is also its main disadvantage—it's purely emotional. The positive aspect is that it is powerful, contagious, and real. The negative side is that in some cases the passion is so strong that the decisionmaking process is not based on any data, market research, or competitor analysis.

OBVIOUSLY, WHEN STARTING a new venture or considering investing in one, more than one approach can be adopted simultaneously. But there will always be the main drive and its satellites. There is nothing wrong with that; on the contrary, once you are conscious of the main drive behind your decisionmaking, you can address your challenges in a better and more coherent manner.

At the end of the day, the force of innovation is unstoppable, just as any startup should be.

ACKNOWLEDGMENTS

Due to the fast pace of life, the demands of our careers, and myriad other distractions, we don't get too many opportunities to stop, take a deep breath, and thank the people that are such important parts of our journeys. I want to take full advantage of this opportunity to do so.

First and foremost, I want to thank my beautiful, loving, and amazing wife of seventeen years, Michal Adoni Kroyanker. She has been my biggest supporter in every endeavor I have undertaken, including this book. She has been a true partner throughout the process of writing it; without her, it could not have happened.

My mother, Professor Hanna Adoni, always encouraged me to do the things I like, even if some of them—like scuba diving, backpacking in third-world countries, trips in the desert, and joining a combat unit at the IDF—made her worry a bit. From my childhood until today, she has believed in me and made me believe in myself. Thank you for always being there for me, for always telling me what you think, and for making me learn the difference between mediocre, good, and excellent, and to always strive to get there.

I want to thank my sister, Judge Michal Agmon Gonen, for being the best older sister I could ask for, and for sharing my passion for innovation and technology.

My wonderful parents-in-law, Leorah and David Kroyanker, loving grandmother and grandfather to my kids, are always there to assist

whenever needed. As my work requires frequent business trips overseas, their presence always gives me peace of mind.

I would like to thank the founder and executive chairman of Jerusalem Venture Partners, Dr. Erel Margalit, who believed in me and
recruited me to JVP. Erel has been a true mentor and an amazing
guide to the world of venture capital. He also taught me that a busi-
nessperson should be involved in social impact, in culture, in urban
development, and that in many cases these things have a direct positive effect on each other.

Yoav Tzruya is a dear friend, a true partner, and one of the smartest
and best venture capitalists I know, and he was one of the first people
I consulted with when the idea for this book came to me. He assisted
me throughout the writing process, generously sharing his experience,
wisdom, and advice. So thank you, Yoav, for your friendship and all
that you do.

My dear friend, partner, and colleague Fiona Darmon is one of
those rare people who with one sentence can open a whole new perspective for you. Thank you, Fiona, for your endless positive energy,
for your smart comments, for finding the time in your extremely busy
schedule to go over the text and give all those detailed and professional inputs.

I would also like to thank my other partners and colleagues, past
and present, at Jerusalem Venture Partners—Kobi Rozengarten, Gadi
Tirosh, Rafi Kesten, Haim Kopans, Michal Drayman, Pnina Ben
Ami, Nimrod Kozlovski, Tali Rabin, and Gadi Porat—for being such
team players, for being so professional, and at the same time, for being
my second family. There's a saying: "If you are the smartest person in
the room, you are probably in the wrong room." I am happy to say
that in all my years at JVP I was never in the wrong room.

To Chemi Peres, Imad Telhami, and Itzik Frid, my fellow board
members and founders at Takwin Labs, the Impact fund that invests
in Israeli-Arab entrepreneurs, thank you for the privilege of being
part of a team that has made such a real and significant impact! By
building this unique bridge between Jewish and Arab high-tech entrepreneurs, Takwin is not only developing entrepreneurship in the

Arab community, but strengthening the Israeli high-tech community as a whole.

To Wendy Singer from Startup Nation Central for supporting this book from day one, and for being such a great partner in buiding and developing the ecosystem in Jerusalem. To Saul Singer, the cowriter of *Startup Nation*, for sharing his experience and giving great advice along the way.

I would also like to thank the founders and the board of Siftech, the first accelerator in Jerusalem that has been such a key player in growing the Jerusalemite ecosystem. Also, thank you to my fellow board members at Shamayim, the not-for-profit organization that fosters leadership and active citizenship among at-risk youth by developing a sense of efficacy and self-empowerment.

To all the entrepreneurs I invested in, thank you for letting me be part of your journey, for being such great team players, and for letting me contribute wherever I could. To all the board members I have served with, thank you for sharing your experience, your enthusiasm, and your knowledge to help the companies succeed.

A special thank-you goes to Roni Floman, who has been my right hand throughout this project. She assisted me across the board, from the chats we've had about conceptualizing the structure of the book, to joining me in many of the interviews, and all the way to the writing and editing of the book. Her professionalism and commitment is second to none, and her friendship and support means the world to me.

To my colleague and friend Adi Soffer Teeni, thank you for writing an amazing Foreword, and for being such a team player throughout the years.

A *huge* thank-you to all my interviewees, who took the time to share their stories, experience, and points of view. Since the whole concept of the book was based on demonstrating cases, telling personal anecdotes, and sharing stories from behind the scenes, this book could not have been written without your collaboration. It was fascinating for me to listen to each and every one of you and learn about your journeys, the hurdles and challenges you've faced, and how your perseverance, commitment, and passion ultimately prevailed. So in alphabetical order, to Gil Ben Artzy, Kfir Damari, Yinnon Dolev, Mark Gazit, Eyal Gura, Guy Horowitz, Dr. Eyal Inbar, Shahar Kaminitz, Uri Levine, Erel Margalit, Udi Mokady, N. from the IDF, Daphna Nissenbaum, Adi Pundak Mintz, Kobi Rozengarten, Liran Tancman, Yoav Tzurya, Shimrit Tzur-David, Eran Wagner, Tzahi (Zack) Weisfeld, and Ido Yablonka, *thank you*!

I want to thank Danny Gold, the team leader and inventor of the Iron Dome system, for not giving up when everyone said it was impossible to do. For his leadership in developing this amazing technology that has saved many Israeli lives from the thousands of rockets that were launched at Israel in the last decade.

To Moishe Mana and the Mana Group team, thank you for letting me be a part of your inspiring vision of building first-of-their-kind high-tech communities as part of a unique and innovative urban development model, starting with Miami and soon to be expanded to other cities.

I also want to thank my colleague and friend Ayelet Gurman for her amazing energy, her ability to make things happen, and for always being 100 percent honest and genuine.

To my dear close friend Roni Dunevitch, author, copywriter, graphic designer, photographer, and overall one of the most creative, talented, and smart people I know. Thank you for sharing your experience as a writer, for your ongoing creative inputs, for your help with the title of the book and its cover, and for many years of true friendship.

To Amir Seraya, my friend of over thirty-five years, for being such a true friend, for his smart inputs and clever insights at the times needed, and the best partner for our 4x4 trips to the desert.

I'd like to thank my friend Jake Cohen from MIT, for initiating and running The Israel Lab at MIT, and exposing Israel's high-tech to his students. Thank you for supporting the book and for your valuable inputs.

To my dear friend and colleague Mauro Muratorio Not, thank you for opening my eyes to the growing high-tech ecosystem in Brazil and LATAM, and for sharing our passion for technology and innovation. Osvaldo Barbosa de Oliveira and Ricardo Coelho Duarte, thank you both for organizing the highly efficient trips and for the introductions to your networks in Brazil.

I owe a huge thank-you to my agent, James Levine, who liked the idea of the book from the very first time he heard about it, and for representing me with such professionalism, commitment, and belief. James's inputs were highly valuable, and the end result is much to his credit.

Thank you to my smart, professional, detailed editor, Arthur Goldwag, for improving the book dramatically by rearranging its structure, and for deleting all the sentences and paragraphs that needed to be deleted.

Thank you to my legal counsel, Mr. Tony Greenman, for his professional guidance and ongoing assistance throughout the process.

Thank you to Tim Burgard from HarperCollins Leadership, who believed in the book's uniqueness, and for his highly professional and also very friendly guidance throughout the whole publication process. He is the one who made this book happen. Thank you also to Becky Powell from HarperCollins Leadership for her commitment and contribution to the marketing of the book. To Jeff Farr and Beth Metrick from Neuwirth & Associates, thank you for being so professional, for looking at every single detail in the book, and for your extremely valuable guidance and input.

Thank you to the team at Smith Publicity, Corinne Moulder, Mike Onorato, and Emma Boyer for their highly professional guidance and execution. To Kait LeDonne, Pamela Lewerenz, and Helen Fickes from Ledonne Brands, thank you for your smart and valuable professional inputs, for getting into the details, and for being fully involved with the overall marketing strategy. Thanks to Brent Bamberger from Brandish Studio for his fruitful ideas and for building, designing, and running my website.

Last but far from least, I would like to thank Lia and Daniel, my beloved kids, for giving meaning to everything that I do, and for being the best kids I could ever wish for.

ENDNOTES

Introduction

1. Leo Rosten, *The Joys of Yiddish* (McGraw-Hill, 1968).
2. Guy Kawasaki, quoted in Tzvi Freeman, "What Is Chutzpah? And Is It Good or Bad?" Chabad.org, https://www.chabad.org/library/article_cdo/aid/1586271/jewish/Chutzpah.htm.
3. Personal interview with Dr. Eyal Inbar. The article is called "Israel's secret is its Chutzpah: The Role of Chutzpah in Israel's entrepreneurship and innovation Scene—An Interpretive Essay", and was accepted to be published in the International Journal of Business and Globalization.
4. Nickolas Ashford and Valerie Simpson, "Ain't No Mountain High Enough" (Tamla, 1966), first recorded by Marvin Gaye and Tammi Terrell in 1967.
5. Gil Avnimelech, "VC Policy: Yozma Program 15-Years Perspective," SSRN Electronic Journal, 2009, 10.2139/ssrn.2758195, https://www.researchgate.net/publication/228921726_VC_Policy_Yozma_Program_15-Years_perspective.
6. Yaniv Avital, "The Big Winners of Geek Awards 2016 Are..." Geektime, January 31, 2016, https://www.geektime.co.il/geekawards-2016-winners/; "Israeli VC JVP Named One of Top Consistently Performing VC Firms in the World by Preqin," JVP, press release, January 16, 2018, https://www.jvpvc.com/press-releases/israeli-vc-jvp-named-one-top-consistently-performing-vc-firms-world-preqin/; "Our Story," JVP, https://www.jvpvc.com/story/; "IVC Report: Most Active Venture Capital Funds in Israel - 2014," IVC Research Center, press release, February 10, 2015, https://www.ivc-online.com/Portals/0/RC/FundPRs/Most%20Active%20VC%20Funds%202014%20Report%20PR_Final.pdf.
7. "Our Story," JVP.
8. Eytan Halon, "City of New York and Jerusalem Venture Partners Launch 'Cybersecurity Moonshot Challenge' to Protect Small Businesses from

Cyberattacks," *Jerusalem Post*, September 26, 2019, https://www.jpost.com
/Jpost-Tech/JVP-celebrates-25-years-of-investments-exits-and-returns
-602932; "City Of New York and Jerusalem Venture Partners Launch
'Cybersecurity Moonshot Challenge' to Protect Small Businesses from
Cyberattacks," JVP, press release, https://www.jvpvc.com/press-releases
/city-of-new-york-and-jerusalem-venture-partners-launch-cybersecurity
-moonshot-challenge-to-protect-small-businesses-from-cyberattacks/.

9. Beth Snyder Bulik, "Inside the 'Inside Intel' Campaign," *Business Insider*,
September 21, 2009, https://www.businessinsider.com/inside-the-inside
-intel-campaign-2009-9; Gary Shapiro, "The Marketing Backstory of
How Intel Became a Household Name," Fast Company, January 8, 2013,
https://www.fastcompany.com/3004135/marketing-backstory-how
-intel-became-household-name.

Chapter 1

1. Dave Mosher, "Elon Musk says SpaceX Is on Track to Launch People to
Mars Within 6 Years—Here's the Full Timeline of His Plans to Popu-
late the Red Planet," *Business Insider*, November 2, 2018, https://www
.businessinsider.com/elon-musk-spacex-mars-plan-timeline-2018-10;
"Reality Distortion Field," Wikipedia, https://en.wikipedia.org/wiki
/Reality_distortion_field.
2. Personal interview with Liran Tancman.
3. Interview with Dr. Eyal Inbar.
4. Geert Hofstede, *Culture's Consequences: International Differences in
Work-Related Values*, 2nd ed. (Beverly Hills, CA: SAGE Publications,
1984).
5. Personal interview with Kobi Rozengarten.
6. Geert Hofstede, *Culture's Consequences*. See also Hofstede's website for
updates to the theory, http://www.geerthofstede.nl/.
7. Interview with Kobi Rozengarten.
8. Interview with Dr. Eyal Inbar.
9. Interview with Dr. Eyal Inbar.
10. Interview with Kobi Rozengarten.
11. Interview with Liran Tancman.
12. Interview with Liran Tancman. Details of the plan Tancman refers to
cannot be specified as it remains confidential.
13. Interview with Liran Tancman.
14. Tzvi Freeman, "What Is Chutzpah? And Is It Good or Bad?"
15. Interview with Kobi Rozengarten.
16. "Startup," Dictionary.com, https://www.dictionary.com/browse/start--up.
17. For startup founders quoted in *Forbes*, see https://www.forbes.com
/pictures/ghjl45fl/ariel-garten-cofounder-a/#28c18c081648, https://

www.forbes.com/pictures/ghjl45fl/daniel-roubichaud-founde
/#69c3aadd5e67, https://www.forbes.com/pictures/gdfd45fede/iqram
-magdon-ismail-left-cofounder-of-venmo-2/#2798e884735b,
https://www.forbes.com/sites/natalierobehmed/2013/12/16/what-is-a
-startup/#4b7014f54044, and https:/www.forbes.com/pictures/gdfd45
fede/dave-gilboa-left-and-neil-blumenthal-right-cofounders-of-warby
-parker-2/#40d9c534132c; see also Alyson Shontell, "This Is the Definitive Definition of a Startup," *Business Insider*, December 31, 2014, https://
www.businessinsider.com/what-is-a-startup-definition-2014-12.

18. Alex Wilhelm, "What the Hell Is a Startup Anyway?" Tech Crunch, December 30, 2014, https://techcrunch.com/2014/12/30/what-the-hell-is
-a-startup-anyway/.

19. Steve Blank, "What's A Startup? First Principles," Steve Blank blog, January 25, 2010, https://steveblank.com/2010/01/25/whats-a-startup-first
-principles/; Andy Aretio, "What Is a Startup and How Is It Different
from Other Companies (New and Old)?" Medium, December 13, 2018,
https://medium.com/theventurecity/what-is-a-startup-and-how-is-it
-different-from-other-companies-new-and-old-428875c27c29; Kevin
Ready, "A Startup Conversation with Steve Blank," *Forbes*, August 28,
2012, https://www.forbes.com/sites/kevinready/2012/08/28/a-startup
-conversation-with-steve-blank/#b1e1d79f0dba.

20. Eric Ries, "The Lean Startup: Methodology," http://theleanstartup.com
/principles.

21. Eric Ries, "The Lean Startup."

Chapter 2

1. All Danny Gold quotes are from an open talk that he gave a few years
ago in Be'er Sheva. The consensus was that such a system would be extremely expensive at best, and most thought that from a technological
perspective it was impossible to do.

2. "Qassam rocket," Military Wikia, https://military.wikia.org/wiki/Qassam
_rocket.

3. Danny Gold open talk in Be'er Sheva.

4. Danny Gold open talk in Be'er Sheva.

5. See, for instance, Michael Martinez, "Iron Dome: Missile Defense System a Game Changer, Israelis Say," CNN, November 20, 2012, https://
www.cnn.com/2012/11/17/world/meast/iron-dome-israel-gaza
-conflict/index.html or Aron Heller, "Iron Dome Game-Changer in
Latest Round of Fighting," *The Times of Israel*, July 10, 2014, https://
www.timesofisrael.com/iron-dome-game-changer-in-latest-round-of
-fighting/.

6. Danny Gold open talk in Be'er Sheva.

7. Danny Gold open talk in Be'er Sheva.
8. For instance, you can see a "before" video at https://www.youtube.com /watch?v=mKpFOgBkJ1Q, and an "after" video at https://www.youtube .com/watch?v=uwswiIBZ4jg.
9. You can view this YouTube video at https://www.youtube.com/watch?v =8kAyqbKwd1o.
10. Danny Gold open talk in Be'er Sheva.
11. Danny Gold open talk in Be'er Sheva.
12. Danny Gold open talk in Be'er Sheva.
13. Danny Gold open talk in Be'er Sheva.
14. Danny Gold open talk in Be'er Sheva.
15. Charles Levinson and Adam Entous, "Israel's Iron Dome Defense Battled to Get Off the Ground," *Wall Street Journal*, November 26, 2012, https://www.wsj.com/articles/SB10001424127887324712504578136 931078468210.
16. Danny Gold open talk in Be'er Sheva.
17. Charles Levinson and Adam Entous, "Israel's Iron Dome Defense Battled to Get Off the Ground."
18. Danny Gold open talk in Be'er Sheva.
19. "Obama Gets Lawmakers' Okay on Boosting Israel against Rockets," *Haaretz*, May 29, 2010, https://www.haaretz.com/1.5126504.
20. "Brig. Gen. (Res.) Dr. Daniel Gold," Ministry of Public Security page, https://www.gov.il/en/Departments/general/ihsf_gold.
21. Daniel Boffey, "EU Declares War on Plastic Use," *The Guardian*, January 16, 2018, https://www.theguardian.com/environment/2018/jan/16 /eu-declares-war-on-plastic-waste-2030.
22. For more on TIPA®, see https://tipa-corp.com/.
23. Personal interview with Daphna Nissenbaum.
24. Interview with Daphna Nissenbaum.
25. Interview with Daphna Nissenbaum.
26. Interview with Daphna Nissenbaum.
27. Interview with Daphna Nissenbaum.
28. Interview with Daphna Nissenbaum.
29. "HFN Sponsors Cleantech Startup Competition," Herzog, Fox & Neeman, press release, March 4, 2012, https://www.hfn.co.il/hfn-sponsors -cleantech-startup-competition.
30. For the 2013 funding round mentioned, see "Biodegradable Packaging Co Tipa Raises $1.5m," Globes, May 27, 2013, https://en.globes.co.il /en/article-1000847317; for a more recent article after their last funding round, see Hagar Ravet, "Compostable Packaging Company TIPA Raises $25 Million," CTECH by Calcalist, October 9, 2019, https:// www.calcalistech.com/ctech/articles/0,7340,L-3770029,00.html.
31. Interview with Daphna Nissenbaum.

32. Interview with Daphna Nissenbaum.
33. Interview with Daphna Nissenbaum.
34. Lauren Stine, "Packaging Tech TIPA Raises $25m to Fuel European, Australian, US Growth," AFN, September 9, 2019, TIPA availability, https://agfundernews.com/packaging-tech-tipa-raises-25m-to-fuel-european-australian-and-us-market-growth.html. See also "Davos: The Compostable Bags Trying to Replace Plastic," BBC News, January 22, 2020, https://www.bbc.com/news/av/business-51205524/davos-the-compostable-bags-trying-to-replace-plastic; and Waqas Qureshi, "TIPA CEO to Talk at Davos 2020," Packaging News, January 17, 2020, https://www.packagingnews.co.uk/news/environment/recycling/tipa-ceo-talk-davos-2020-17-01-2020.

Chapter 3

1. Frank Buytendijk, Howard J. Dresner, Bill Hostmann, and Alan H. Tiedrich, "Hype Cycle for Business Intelligence, 2003," Gartner, June 6, 2003, https://www.bus.umich.edu/kresgepublic/journals/gartner/research/115400/115425/115425.html.
2. For details on the Qlik IPO, see https://www.crunchbase.com/ipo/qlik-technologies-ipo--749c00fb.
3. A home run in the venture capital industry refers to an investment whose proceeds return the entire value of the fund that invested in it. This is highly sought after but rarely achieved. While there are a few definitions for a home run that differ based on the size of the funds, in $200 million to $500 million funds this definition is probably the right one.
4. Interview with Kobi Rozengarten.
5. For more on Siemans, see https://new.siemens.com/global/en/company/about.html.
6. Interview with Kobi Rozengarten.

Chapter 4

1. Fahmida Y. Rashid, "Salesforce.com Acquires SaaS Encryption Provider Navajo Systems," eWeek, August 26, 2011, https://www.eweek.com/security/salesforce.com-acquires-saas-encryption-provider-navajo-systems.
2. "Cloud Security Market 2019 Global Industry Size, Share, Regional Trends, Development Strategy Competitor Analysis, Complete Study of Current Trends and Forecast 2023," MarketWatch, press release, April 2, 2019, https://www.marketwatch.com/press-release/cloud-security-market-2019-global-industry-size-share-regional-trends-development-strategy-competitor-analysis-complete-study-of-current-trends-and-forecast-2023-2019-04-02.

3. For more on ThetaRay, see https://thetaray.com/.
4. "Mark Gazit," https://en.wikipedia.org/wiki/Mark_Gazit.
5. "Nice Cyber," https://en.wikipedia.org/wiki/NICE_Ltd.
6. Personal interview with Mark Gazit.
7. For more about Averbuch, see https://thetaray.com/management-board/.
8. For more about Coifman, see https://cpsc.yale.edu/people/ronald -coifman.
9. "Ronald Coifman," https://en.wikipedia.org/wiki/Ronald_Coifman.
10. Interview with Mark Gazit.
11. "What Is Stuxnet?" McAfee, https://www.mcafee.com/enterprise/en-us /security-awareness/ransomware/what-is-stuxnet.html.
12. Mark Clayton, "Stuxnet Worm Mystery: What's the Cyber Weapon After?" *Christian Science Monitor*, September 24, 2010, https://www .csmonitor.com/USA/2010/0924/Stuxnet-worm-mystery-What-s-the -cyber-weapon-after.
13. Interview with Mark Gazit.
14. "ThetaRay Announces New Funding," Cision PR Newswire, August 5, 2013, https://www.prnewswire.com/news-releases/thetaray-announces -new-funding-218352921.html.

Chapter 5

1. "Eyal Gura," World Economic Forum, https://www.weforum.org/people /eyal-gura.
2. See, for instance, https://www.aitimejournal.com/news/zebra-medical -vision-secures-a-fourth-fda-clearance-for-ai-for-medical-imaging.
3. "Transforming Patient Care with the Power of AI," Zebra Medical Im- aging, https://www.zebra-med.com/.
4. "India: Apollo Hospitals Group and Zebra Medical Vision (Ze- bra-Med) Collaborate to Validate and Deploy AI (Artificial Intelligence) Based Screening Tools Across India," MarketWatch, March 19, 2019, https://www.marketwatch.com/press-release/india-apollo-hospitals -group-and-zebra-medical-vision-zebra-med-collaborate-to-validate -and-deploy-ai-artificial-intelligence-based-screening-tools-across-india -2019-03-19.
5. Personal interview with Eyal Gura.
6. Interview with Eyal Gura.
7. Interview with Eyal Gura.
8. Interview with Eyal Gura.
9. "Getty Images Acquires PicScout," Getty Images, press release, April 28, 2011, http://press.gettyimages.com/getty-images-acquires-picscout/.
10. Clayton Christensen, *The Innovator's Dilemma: The Revolutionary Book That Will Change the Way You Do Business* (HarperBusiness, 1997. Re- print edition 2011).

11. Amir Mizroch, "530 Multinationals from 35 Countries Innovating in Israel," *Forbes*, May 27, 2019, https://www.forbes.com/sites/startup nationcentral/2019/05/27/530-multinationals-from-35-countries -innovating-in-israel/.

12. "Acquisitions," Corporate Strategy Office News, Cisco, https://www.cisco .com/c/en/us/about/corporate-strategy-office/acquisitions.html; Hilton Romanski, "Cisco's 200th Acquisition—a Tradition of Advancement, Disruption, and Growth," Cisco Blogs, October 19, 2017, https://blogs.cisco.com/news/ciscos-200th-acquisition-a-tradition-of -advancement-disruption-and-growth.

13. Marco Antonio Cavallo, "The FinTech Effect and the Disruption of Financial Services," CIO, December 13, 2016, https://www.cio.com /article/3148756/the-fintech-effect-and-the-disruption-of-financial -services.html; Dennis Gada, "Five Ways Fintech Is Disrupting the Financial Services Industry," FinExtra, March 5, 2018, https://www .finextra.com/blogposting/15105/five-ways-fintech-is-disrupting -the-financial-services-industry.

14. For Prosper (previously Billguard), see https://www.prosper.com/; for Behalf (previously Zazma), see https://www.behalf.com/; for Credit-Karma, see https://www.creditkarma.com/?ckt=navClickL1.

15. "Groupon Clones Are Still a Thing . . . Outside the US," CBInsights, June 4, 2015, https://www.cbinsights.com/research/grou-pon-clones-meituan-active-globally/.

16. Suzaan Hughes and Chantal Breytenbach, "Groupon's Growth and Globalization Strategy: Structural and Technological Implications of International Markets," *International Business & Economics Research Journal* (IBER), 12 (12) (2013), pp. 1589–1604, https://doi.org/10.19030/iber.v12i12 .8252; for a list of Groupon acquisitions, see https://www.crunchbase.com /search/acquisitions/field/organizations/num_acquisitions/groupon.

Chapter 6

1. "Infographic: Google's Biggest Acquisitions," CBInsights, November 1, 2019, https://www.cbinsights.com/research/google-biggest-acquisitions -infographic/.

2. Noam Bardin, "A Unicorn? In Israel?" LinkedIn, April 3, 2014, https:// www.linkedin.com/pulse/20140403204459-174756-a-unicorn-in-israel/.

3. Noam Bardin, "A Unicorn? In Israel?"; "Israeli-Founded Unicorns," Techaviv, https://www.techaviv.com/unicorns.

4. Aileen Lee, "Welcome to the Unicorn Club: Learning from Billion-Dollar Startups," Techcrunch, November 2, 2013, https://techcrunch.com /2013/11/02/welcome-to-the-unicorn-club/.

5. "Your Startup Has a 1.28% Chance of Becoming a Unicorn," CBInsights, May 25, 2015, https://www.cbinsights.com/research/unicorn

-conversion-rate/; "Unicorn Probability of VC Startups at About 1%: Study," EJI Insight, September 11, 2018, http://www.ejinsight.com /20180911-unicorn-probability-of-vc-startups-at-about-1-study -suggests/.

6. Personal interview with Uri Levine.
7. Darin M. Klemchuk, "Breach of License Agreement or License Infringe- ment?" Klemchuk LLP, December 28, 2015, https://www.klemchuk.com /ip-law-trends/breach-of-license-or-intellectual-property-infringement.
8. Interview with Uri Levine.
9. Interview with Uri Levine.
10. Phone interview with Udi Mokady.
11. Gadi Tirosh was one of JVP's representatives on the board, following the company's former chairman, Margalit's, move to the Israeli Parlia- ment (Knesset). The bankers included Morgan Stanley and Christina Morgan, who had worked with JVP before, accompanying the Qliktech IPO.
12. Interview with Udi Mokady.
13. "Google Lunar X Prize: The New Space Race," https://lunar.xprize.org /prizes/google-lunar.
14. "Google Lunar X Prize: The New Space Race."
15. Personal interview with Kfir Damari.
16. Interview with Kfir Damari.
17. Interview with Kfir Damari.
18. For more on the costs for SpaceIL, see https://en.wikipedia.org/wiki /SpaceIL.
19. Interview with Kfir Damari.
20. Lauren Grush, "SpaceX Launched a Trio of Spacecraft, Including a Lander Bound for the Moon," The Verge, February 21, 2019, https:// www.theverge.com/2019/2/21/18233768/spacex-falcon-9-rocket -launch-spaceil-beresheet-moon-spaceflight-nusantara-satu.
21. Mike Wall, "Why It'll Take Israel's Lunar Lander 8 Weeks to Get to the Moon," Space.com, February 22, 2019, https://www.space.com/israel -lunar-lander-long-trip-moon.html.
22. See, for instance, http://www.spaceil.com/education/education-page/ and http://www.spaceil.com/general/spaceil-shows-the-youth-their-way -to-academic-future/.
23. Interview with Kfir Damari.
24. Interview with Kfir Damari.
25. Interview with Kfir Damari.
26. Mike Wall, "Israel's Beresheet Spacecraft Crashes into Moon During Landing Attempt," Space.com, April 11, 2019, https://www.space.com /israeli-beresheet-moon-landing-attempt-fails.html.
27. Mike Wall, "Israeli Moon Lander Snaps Epic Space Selfie with a Full Earth," Space.com, March 5, 2019, https://www.space.com/israel-moon

-lander-earth-selfie.html; Yafit Ovadia, "Selfie from 20,000 Miles Away: Israeli Beresheet Snaps First Space Shot," *Jerusalem Post*, March 7, 2019, https://www.jpost.com/Israel-News/Israeli-spacecraft-Beresheet-takes -first-selfie-in-space-582512.

28. Rebecca Morelle, "Beresheet Spacecrft: 'Technical Glitch' Led to Moon Crash," BBC News, April 12, 2019, https://www.bbc.com/news/science -environment-47914100.

29. "Morris Kahn," SpaceIL Team Members, http://www.spaceil.com /team-member/%D7%9E%D7%95%D7%A8%D7%99%D7%A1 -%D7%A7%D7%90%D7%94%D7%9F/attachment/morris-kahn/.

30. "XPrize Foundation Awards $1 Million 'Moonshot Award' to SpaceIL," XPrize.org, press release, https://www.xprize.org/articles/xprize-awards -1m-moonshot-award-to-spaceil.

Chapter 7

1. Interview with Mark Gazit.
2. Interview with Daphna Nissenbaum.

Chapter 8

1. For IDF service details, see, for instance, https://en.wikipedia.org/wiki /Israel_Defense_Forces#Military_service_routes.
2. See, for instance, https://en.wikipedia.org/wiki/Mission_command.
3. Personal interview with N. Due to his position, I can't reveal his name.
4. Interview with N.
5. Personal interview with Uri Levine.
6. Interview with Uri Levine.
7. Brandon Gaille, "43 Incredible Ben Horowitz Quotes," Brandon Gaille Small Business and Marketing Page, May 29, 2017, https://brandongaille .com/43-incredible-ben-horowitz-quotes/.
8. Interview with Uri Levine.
9. Interview with N.

Chapter 9

1. Deborah Gage, "The Venture Capital Secret: 3 Ourt of 4 Start-Ups Fail," *Wall Street Journal*, September 20, 2012, https://www.hbs.edu /news/Pages/item.aspx?num=487.
2. Andrew Chen, "Why Startups Are Hard—The Math of Venture Capital Returns Tells the Story," Andrew Chen newsletter, https://andrewchen .co/venture-capital-returns/.
3. "The Top 20 Reasons Startups Fail,"CB Insights, November 6, 2019, https://www.cbinsights.com/research/startup-failure-reasons-top/.

4. Interview with Uri Levine.
5. Interview with Daphna Nissenbaum.
6. For TIPA products, see https://tipa-corp.com/wp-content/uploads/TIPA-A5-catalog-01-2020-screen.pdf.
7. Interview with Daphna Nissenbaum.
8. Robert Schuller, *You Can Become the Person You Want to Be* (New York: Penguin, 1973).
9. Interview with Kfir Damari.
10. Interview with Uri Levine.
11. Leon C. Megginson, "Lessons from Europe for American Business: Presidential Address Delivered at the Southwestern Social Science Association Convention in San Antonio, Texas, April 12, 1963," *Southwestern Social Science Quarterly*, Volume 44, Number 1 (June 1963).
12. Interview with Uri Levine.
13. For instance, see Allison Schrager, "Failed Entrepreneurs Find More Success the Second Time," Bloomberg, July 29, 2014, https://www.bloomberg.com/news/articles/2014-07-28/study-failed-entrepreneurs-find-success-the-second-time-around.

Chapter 10

1. See http://upwest.vc/.
2. Personal interview with Gil Ben-Artzy.
3. See https://www.honeybook.com/.
4. Interview with Gil Ben-Artzy.
5. Interview with Gil Ben-Artzy.
6. Interview with Eyal Gura.
7. Lisa Sibley, "EBay Acquires the Gifts Project," Silicon Valley Business Journal, Spetember 8, 2011, https://www.bizjournals.com/sanjose/news/2011/09/08/ebay-acquires-the-gifts-project.html.
8. Katie Roof, "Intuit Buys Check App for $360 Million," Fox Business, May 27, 2014, https://www.foxbusiness.com/features/intuit-buys-check-app-for-360-million.
9. Interview with Gil Ben-Artzy.
10. Interview with Gil Ben-Artzy.
11. Interview with Udi Mokady.
12. Interview with Udi Mokady.
13. For details on CyberArk move and A round, see https://www.crunchbase.com/organization/cyber-ark-software.
14. Interview with Udi Mokady.
15. For details on CyberArk B round, see https://www.crunchbase.com/organization/cyber-ark-software/funding_rounds/funding_rounds_list.
16. Interview with Udi Mokady.

17. Interview with Udi Mokady.

18. Bryan Burrough, Sarah Ellison, and Suzanna Andrews, "The Snowden Saga: A Shadowland of Secrets and Light," *Vanity Fair*, May 2014, https://www.vanityfair.com/news/politics/2014/05/edward-snowden -politics-interview.

19. Interview with Udi Mokady.

20. For details on Intucell series A round, see https://www.crunchbase .com/organization/intucell; Josh Constine, "Cisco to Buy Israeli Mobile Startup Intucell for $475 Million Cash, and Bessemer Will Get Nearly Half," Tech Crunch, January 23, 2013, https://techcrunch. com/2013/01/23/cisco-buys-israeli-mobile-startup-intucell-for-475 -million-cash-and-bessemer-gets-nearly-half/.

21. "Cisco to AT&T: Thank You for Intucell," Seeking Alpha, January 26, 2013, https://seekingalpha.com/article/1135151-cisco-to-at-and-t-thank -you-for-intucell.

22. Personal interview with Adi Pundak Mintz.

23. Interview with Adi Pundak Mintz.

24. Interview with Adi Pundak Mintz.

25. Interview with Udi Mokady.

26. "IBM Completes Acquisition of Worklight," IBM, press release, February 27, 2012, https://www-03.ibm.com/press/us/en/pressrelease/36919 .wss.

27. Amir Mizroch, "530 Multinationals from 35 Countries Innovating in Israel."

28. Personal interview with Eran Wagner.

29. Noam Bardin, "A Unicorn? In Israel?"

30. Thomas Friedman, *The World Is Flat 3.0: A Brief History of the Twenty-first Century* (Picador, 3rd edition, 2007).

31. Noam Bardin, "A Unicorn? In Israel?"

32. Noam Bardin, "A Unicorn? In Israel?"

33. Interview with Gil Ben-Artzy.

34. Interview with Gil Ben-Artzy.

35. Interview with Uri Levine.

36. "Carmagadon: 64-mile L.A. Traffic Jam?" CBS News, July 14, 2011, https://www.cbsnews.com/news/carmageddon-64-mile-la-traffic-jam/.

37. Interview with Uri Levine.

38. Jennifer Valentino-DeVries, "Traffic App Waze, ABC Team Up to Fight 'Carmageddon' in L.A.," *Wall Street Journal*, July 5, 2011, https://blogs .wsj.com/digits/2011/07/05/traffic-app-waze-abc-team-up-to-fight -carmageddon-in-l-a/.

39. Interview with Uri Levine.

40. Interview with Uri Levine.

41. Noam Bardin, "A Unicorn? In Israel?"

42. Noam Bardin, "A Unicorn? In Israel?"
43. Noam Bardin, "A Unicorn? In Israel?"

Chapter 11

1. "About Intel Israel," Intel, https://www.intel.com/content/www/us/en/corporate-responsibility/intel-in-israel.html.
2. "Defining Intel: 25 Years/25 Events," Intel, https://www.intel.com/Assets/PDF/General/25yrs.pdf.
3. "Intel in Israel," Intel, https://www.intel.la/content/www/xl/es/corporate-responsibility/intel-in-israel.html.
4. "Dov Frohman," https://en.wikipedia.org/wiki/Dov_Frohman.
5. Dov Frohman, "Leadership Under Fire," *Harvard Business Review*, December 2006, https://hbr.org/2006/12/leadership-under-fire.
6. Niv Elis, "Microsoft's Nadella in Israel to Mark 25-Year Cooperation," *Jerusalem Post*, February 25, 2016, https://www.jpost.com/Business-and-Innovation/Tech/Microsofts-Nadella-in-Israel-to-mark-25-year-cooperation-446062.
7. David Shamah, "Microsoft Employs More Workers per Capita in Israel Than Anywhere Else on Earth, Says Ballmer," *Times of Israel*, November 5, 2012. Acccessed at https://www.timesofisrael.com/microsoft-ceo-ballmer-israels-high-tech-remarkable/.
8. Sylvie Barak, "Microsoft Opens New R&D Facility in Israel," *The Inquirer*, May 21, 2008, https://www.theinquirer.net/inquirer/news/1023955/microsoft-r-amp-d-facility-israel via Wayback Machine.
9. "Microsoft Accelerator," Gan Accelerators, https://www.gan.co/engage/accelerator/microsoft-accelerator/.
10. Tzahi Weisfeld, articles on Microsoft and startups, https://www.linkedin.com/in/tweisfeld/?originalSubdomain=il.
11. For more on Microsoft for Startups, see https://startups.microsoft.com/en-us/benefits/.
12. Telephone interview with Tzahi Weisfeld.
13. Interview with Tzahi Weisfeld. Microsoft has not published numbers more recent than 2015. The numbers cited here were given by Tzahi recently.
14. Interview with Tzahi Weisfeld.
15. Personal interview with Guy Horowitz.
16. Interview with Guy Horowitz.
17. For more on Sompo Digital Labs, see http://sompo.io/en/.
18. Personal interview with Yinnon Dolev.
19. Interview with Yinnon Dolev.
20. Interview with Yinnon Dolev.
21. Interview with Mark Gazit.

22. Interview with Mark Gazit.
23. Interview with Mark Gazit.

Chapter 12

1. Interview with Adi Pundak Mintz.
2. Interview with Adi Pundak Mintz.
3. Interview with Adi Pundak Mintz.
4. Interview with Udi Mokady.
5. Interview with Adi Pundak Mintz.
6. Jason Rowley, "Here's How Likely Your Startup Is to Get Acquired at Any Stage," Tech Crunch, May 17, 2017, https://techcrunch.com /2017/05/17/heres-how-likely-your-startup-is-to-get-acquired-at-any -stage/.
7. Interview with Adi Pundak Mintz.
8. Interview with Liran Tancman.
9. "Formlabs Announces the Completion of Its Kickstarter Campaign," Formlabs, press release, December 3, 2013, https://formlabs.com/uk /company/press/formlabs-kickstarter-completion-announcement/.
10. "Formlabs Announces $19 Million Series A Round to Disrupt 3D Printing," Formlabs, press release, October 24, 2013, https://formlabs .com/company/press/formlabs-series-a-funding-announcement/; for later rounds see https://www.crunchbase.com/organization/formlabs.
11. Interview with Adi Pundak Mintz.
12. Interview with Guy Horowitz.
13. Interview with Liran Tancman.
14. "Ideation (Tnufa) Incentive Program," Innovation Israel, https:// innovationisrael.org.il/en/program/ideation-tnufa-incentive-program.
15. Ingrid Lunden, "PayPal Doubles Down on Israel: Confirms CyActive Acquisition, New Security Hub," Tech Crunch, March 10, 2015, https://techcrunch.com/2015/03/10/paypal-confirms-acquisition -of-cyactive-plans-to-open-new-security-hub-in-israel/; John Nai, "PayPal Makes Acquisition of CyActive Official," PayPal, press release, April 9, 2015, https://www.paypal.com/stories/us/paypal-makes-acquisition -of-cyactive-official.
16. Interview with Liran Tancman.

Chapter 13

1. "WTF Is a Minimal Viable Product," Techstars, June 7, 2015, https:// www.techstars.com/content/community/wtf-minimal-viable-product/.
2. Ash Maurya, *Running Lean: Iterate from Plan A to a Plan That Works* (Lean Series) (O'Reilly Media; 2nd ed., 2012).

3. Steve Blank, "An MVP Is Not a Cheaper Product, It's Abbout Smart Learning," Steve Blank blog, July 22, 2013, https://steveblank.com/2013/07/22/an-mvp-is-not-a-cheaper-product-its-about-smart-learning/.
4. Eric Ries, *The Lean Startup: How Today's Entrepreneurs Use Continuous Innovation to Create Radically Successful Businesses* (Currency, 2011).
5. You can view the DropBox video at https://www.youtube.com/watch?v=7QmCUDHpNzE.
6. "How Dropbox Got Their First Users," Benchhacks, http://benchhacks.com/growthstudies/dropbox-growth-hacks.htm.
7. Eric Ries, *The Lean Startup*. See also http://theleanstartup.com/principles.
8. Personal interview with Ido Yablonka.
9. Interview with Ido Yablonka.
10. Personal interview with Shahar Kaminitz.
11. Interview with Shahar Kaminitz.
12. Interview with Ido Yablonka.
13. Interview with Ido Yablonka.
14. Personal interview with Shimrit Tzur David.
15. Interview with Shimrit Tzur David.
16. Interview with Shahar Kaminitz.
17. "IBM Advances Mobile Capabilities with Acquisition of Worklight," IBM, press release, January 31, 2012, https://www-03.ibm.com/press/us/en/pressrelease/36660.wss.
18. Interview with Shahar Kaminitz.

Chapter 14

1. "Check Point History," CheckPoint, https://www.checkpoint.com/about-us/check-point-history/.
2. David McClure, "MoneyBall for Startups," Master of 500 Hats, July 30, 2010, https://500hats.typepad.com/500blogs/2010/07/moneyball-for-startups.html.

Chapter 15

1. Satya Patel, "Homebrew's 1%: The VC Metrics Behind Investing in One of Every 100 Companies We Meet," Venture Generated Content, January 9, 2014, https://venturegeneratedcontent.com/2014/01/09/homebrews-1-the-vc-metrics-behind-investing-in-one-of-every-100-companies-we-meet/.

Chapter 16

1. Personal interview with Erel Margalit.
2. Michael E. Porter, *The Competitive Advantage of Nations* (New York: Free Press, 1998).
3. Porter, *The Competitive Advantage of Nations*. For more on clusters, see also https://www.isc.hbs.edu/competitiveness-economic-development /frameworks-and-key-concepts/Pages/clusters.aspx.
4. Thomas Friedman, *The World is Flat 3.0.*
5. Interview with Erel Margalit.
6. For more on companies opening in Har Hotzvim, see, for instance, https://en.wikipedia.org/wiki/Har_Hotzvim and https://en.wikipedia .org/wiki/IBM_Israel.
7. Interview with Erel Margalit.
8. For more on the Yozma program, see http://www.yozma.com/overview /default.asp.
9. Interview with Erel Margalit.
10. Interview with Erel Margalit.
11. Interview with Erel Margalit.
12. For more on Bakehila, see https://bakehila.wixsite.com/english.
13. For more on Bakehila's social exits, see https://bakehila.wixsite.com /english/story.
14. Interview with Erel Margalit.
15. Eytan Halon, "JVP Celebrates 25 years of Investments, Exits and Returns," *Jerusalem Post*, September 26, 2019, https://www.jpost.com /Jpost-Tech/JVP-celebrates-25-years-of-investments-exits-and-returns -602932.
16. "Erel Margalit, VC," The Midas List, *Forbes* award, https://www.forbes .com/lists/2006/99/BLMA.html.
17. "Jerusalem Tech Tours," Made in JLM, https://www.madeinjlm.org/tech -tours; Daniel K. Eisenbud, "Catching Up to Tel Aviv, Jerusalem Rising in World's Rankings of Start-Up Hubs," *Jerusalem Post*, March 17, 2017, https://www.jpost.com/Israel-News/Jerusalem-rising-in-worlds-rankings -of-start-up-hubs-484442.
18. Tom Teicholz, "Erel Margalit: Bringing 'Start-Up Nation' to Israeli Politics," *Forbes*, July 21, 2015, https://www.forbes.com/sites/tomteicholz /2015/07/21/erel-margalit-bringing-start-up-nation-to-israeli-politics/.
19. "Income Inequality," OECD Data, https://data.oecd.org/inequality /income-inequality.htm.
20. Niv Elis, "Netanyahu Declares Beersheba Cyber Security Hub," *Jerusalem Post*, January 27, 2014, https://www.jpost.com/Business/Business-News /Netanyahu-declares-Beersheba-Cyber-Security-hub-339539.
21. "Yoav Tzruya," JVP, https://www.jvpvc.com/person/yoav-tzruya/.

22. "Israel's Cyber Sector Blooms in the Desert," i24 News, January 30, 2016, https://www.i24news.tv/en/news/israel/society/101128-160130 -israel-s-cyber-sector-blooms-in-the-desert.
23. Personal interview with Yoav Tzruya.
24. Interview with Yoav Tzruya.
25. Interview with Yoav Tzruya.
26. Interview with Liran Tancman.
27. Interview with Yoav Tzruya.
28. Interview with Shimrit Tzur David.
29. Interview with Shimrit Tzur David.
30. "These Are the Big Winners of the GeekAwards 2018 Awards," GeekTime, January 17, 2018, https://translate.google.com/translate?hl=en&sl=iw &u=https://www.geektime.co.il/geekawards-2018-winners/&prev =search.
31. Matthew Flamm, "City Kicks Off Massive Cybersecurity Venture," *Crain's New York Business*, October 2, 2018, https://www.crainsnewyork .com/real-estate/city-kicks-massive-cybersecurity-venture.
32. "NYCEDC Unveils Global Cyber Center, Innovation Hub, and New Talent Pipelines to Secure NYC's Future," NYC EDC, press release, October 2, 2018, https://edc.nyc/press-release/nycedc-unveils-global-cyber -center-innovation-hub-and-new-talent-pipelines-secure-nyc.
33. "NYCEDC Unveils Global Cyber Center, Innovation Hub, and New Talent Pipelines to Secure NYC's Future."
34. City Launches $100m Effort to Make New York Cyber Security Capital of World," *Real Estate Week*, https://rew-online.com/2018/10/city -launches-100m-effort-to-make-new-york-cyber-security-capital-of -world/.
35. Mary K. Pratt, "Cyber NYC Initiative Strives to Make New York a Cybersecurity Hub," SearchSecurity, February 2019, https://searchsecurity .techtarget.com/feature/Cyber-NYC-initiative-strives-to-make-New -York-a-cybersecurity-hub.
36. "City of New York and Jerusalem Venture Partners Launch 'Cybersecurity Moonshot Challenge' to Protect Small Businesses from Cyberattacks," JVP, press release, https://www.jvpvc.com/press-releases /city-of-new-york-and-jerusalem-venture-partners-launch-cybersecurity -moonshot-challenge-to-protect-small-businesses-from-cyberattacks/.

Chapter 17

1. For more on the Israeli Innovation Authority, see https://innovationisrael .org.il/en/.
2. Some incentive programs are outlined, for instance, at https://innovation israel.org.il/en/Booklet_2018.pdf and https://innovationisrael.org.il/en /page/programs?persona=9.

3. "New Study: For Every New High-Tech Job, Four More Created," Bay Area Council, December 10, 2012, https://www.bayareacouncil .org/community_engagement/new-study-for-every-new-high-tech-job -four-more-created/.

4. Gil Press, "How Startup Nation's Innovation Catalyst Masters the Art of Public-Private Partnership," *Forbes*, July 20, 2015, https://www.forbes .com/sites/gilpress/2015/07/20/how-startup-nations-innovation-catalyst -masters-the-art-of-public-private-partnership/#3e08fc9c6226.

5. Nick Ismail, "Israel's Tech Start-Up Scene: The Heartbeat of the Economy," Information Age, February 19, 2019, https://www.information -age.com/israels-tech-start-up-scene-123479255/.

6 . Ingrid Lunden, "Intel Buys MobileEye in $15.3B Deal, Moves Its Automotive Unit to Israel," Tech Crunch, March 13, 2017, https:// techcrunch.com/2017/03/13/reports-intel-buying-mobileye-for-up -to-16b-to-expand-in-self-driving-tech/; John Reed and Madhumita Murgia, "Intel Buys Mobileye in $15.3bn Deal," *Financial Times*, March 13, 2017, https://www.ft.com/content/9acd9644-ea54-30b9 -99a8-2a8b8f2d174f.

Epilogue

1. Dustin Clendenon, "How to Invest in Companies That Pay Employees Well, Clean Up the Environment, and Care about the Future," *Business Insider*, October 18, 2019, https://www.businessinsider.com /what-is-impact-investing-how-to-get-started.

2. See https://bcorporation.net/ or https://bcorporation.eu/.

INDEX

ABOUT THE AUTHOR

URI ADONI has more than twenty years of experience in high tech and more than twelve years of being a partner at Jerusalem Venture Partners Media Labs (www.jvpvc.com). JVP has listed twelve companies on NASDAQ and sold numerous others to leading tech companies such as Cisco, Microsoft, EMC, PayPal, Sony, Broadcom, AUO, Alcatel, and many more. Adoni served on the board of several JVP companies, early- and late-stage ones, and is also on the board of SifTech, one of Israel's leading accelerators, and Takwin, an impact venture capital firm that focuses on investing in Israeli-Arab entrepreneurs. Prior to joining JVP, Uri was the CEO of MSN Israel (Microsoft Networks) and was one of Israel's new media pioneers. In his military service at the IDF (regular and reserve), he was an officer (major) and served as a commander of a combat unit.

Uri recently departed from JVP in order to join a US-based real estate entrepreneur that is developing a new and innovative approach for building local high-tech ecosystems and communities across the US.